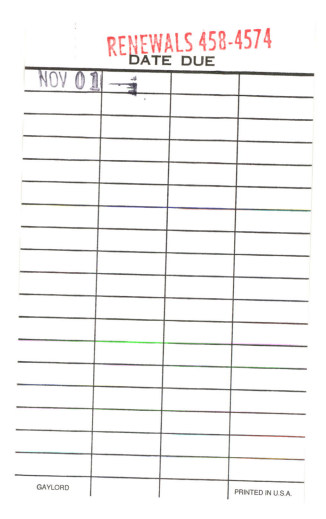

RENEWALS 458-4574

DATE DUE

NOV 0 1			
GAYLORD			PRINTED IN U.S.A.

Purchasing and Financial Management of Information Technology

Purchasing and Financial Management of Information Technology

Frank Bannister

Department of Statistics, Trinity College Dublin

ELSEVIER
BUTTERWORTH
HEINEMANN

AMSTERDAM BOSTON HEIDELBERG LONDON NEW YORK OXFORD
PARIS SAN DIEGO SAN FRANCISCO SINGAPORE SYDNEY TOKYO

Elsevier Butterworth-Heinemann
Linacre House, Jordan Hill, Oxford OX2 8DP
200 Wheeler Road, Burlington, MA 01803

First published 2004

British Library Cataloguing in Publication Data
A catalogue record for this book is available from the British Library

ISBN 0 7506 5854 1

For information on all Butterworth-Heinemann publications visit our website at: www.bh.com

Composition by Genesis Typesetting Limited, Rochester, Kent
Printed and bound in Great Britain

Contents

Contents

Computer Weekly Professional Series

There are few professions which require as much continuous updating as that of the IT executive. Not only does the hardware and software scene change relentlessly, but also ideas about the actual management of the IT function are being continuously modified, updated and changed. Thus keeping abreast of what is going on is really a major task.

The Butterworth-Heinemann – *Computer Weekly* Professional Series has been created to assist IT executives keep up to date with the management ideas and issues of which they need to be aware.

One of the key objectives of the series is to reduce the time it takes for leading edge management ideas to move from the academic and consulting environments into the hands of the IT practitioner. Thus this series employs appropriate technology to speed up the publishing process. Where appropriate some books are supported by CD-ROM or by additional information or templates located on the Web.

This series provides IT professionals with an opportunity to build up a bookcase of easily accessible, but detailed information on the important issues that they need to be aware of to successfully perform their jobs.

Aspiring or already established authors are invited to get in touch with me directly if they would like to be published in this series.

Dr Dan Remenyi
Series Editor
dan.remenyi@mcil.co.uk

Other titles in the Series

'Have you ever met a computer salesman?'

It was November 1978. I was a young, wet behind the ears, consultant in Price Waterhouse about to embark on his first ever computer selection assignment sales presentation. The question was posed by a Senior Consultant to whom I had been assigned as bag carrier and who seemed to me, at that point, to be almost godlike in his command of this type of engagement. As it happened, I had met computer salesmen before, but in circumstances where I was a long, long way down the chain of command. This would be the first time I had to confront one in real sales mode. I decided on a safe answer.

'No.'

'Well, let me explain how it works. We have six suppliers bidding and six presentations to sit through. If the salesmen are any good, you will leave each presentation wondering why you would ever consider anybody else's product. Just bear that in mind before you rush to any conclusions.'

And some of them were good. And Michael was quite right, I did come out thinking, yes, let's go, where do we sign?

Twenty-five years and many hundreds of sales presentations later, I am less easily impressed; too much hype has flowed under the bridge. In later years, I often found myself on the other side of the table, mastering the sometimes black art of selling to the as yet unconvinced.

Purchasing and financial management of IT, on the other hand, is not a black art. There are rules, do's and don'ts, good procedures, good practices and sound methodologies for getting things right. It is true that there are certain aspects of the job, negotiating contracts being a good example, where there is no substitute for learning from observation and experience. Nevertheless, even here there are tricks to know about, both ones the buyer can use and ones that the buyer needs to watch out for. Forewarned is forearmed.

World-wide expenditure on IT today is measured in trillions of dollars per annum. If we are to believe the research, a goodly proportion of this expenditure continues to be wasted. While good purchasing and financial management cannot eliminate all of this wastage, it can reduce it dramatically. The objective of this book is to provide the reader with a set of practical tools to achieve this. While there is some theory, most of what is in this book is based on long experience, observation and occasionally learning the hard way. Many lessons are encapsulated in what I have called 'case histories'. Though, in many instances, details have been changed to protect the identity of the organizations or individuals concerned, each of these stories is true, incredible though some of them may seem. It cannot be said that IT purchasing and financial management is without its lighter or more bizarre moments. Most of the case histories I have observed first hand; in a few cases they are war stories I have heard from some of the many IT consultants or IT managers I have met over the years.

Much, then, of what follows is organized common sense though I hope some of the material may come as new, even to experienced IT and financial managers. A veteran IT manager and long-standing friend of mine, now retired, used to stand in the middle of his computer room, surveying the machinery and numerous staff around him and declare, 'There is nothing common about sense'. Alas, that is sometimes all too true.

Looking back on hundreds of IT purchases, big and small over the years, I can remember decisions that might have been better, but none that was actually bad and most that were right. This is how it was done.

Frank Bannister
2003

1   IT acquisition policy

1.1 Introduction

In a typical organization, the percentage of total expenditure accounted for by IT spend varies between 3% and 7%. In many companies, particularly those that are highly dependent on technology, this figure can rise to 20% and IT outlay can be the second largest operating cost after the payroll.

IT expenditure is a peculiar beast. Accounting for most business expenditure is straightforward. For example, notwithstanding the occasional accounting scandal, it is usually clear what is capital and what is current expenditure. The life and value of assets is generally well understood. Assets are clearly visible and there is a market against which one can measure their current value. This is not always so with IT. For example, is the purchase of a PC capital or current expenditure? How much is the customer database worth? How does one account for the disruption costs incurred in IT projects? The answers to these and many other questions are not clear.

This book addresses these and many other questions. It is intended to be a comprehensive guide to all aspects of planning, managing and controlling IT purchasing and finance. This opening chapter contains an overview of the subject as well as specific guidelines for purchasing policy. Later chapters cover these subjects and other topics in more depth.

In addition to good management skills, good IT purchasing requires skills in:

- technology
- purchasing
- finance.

Many managers possess one or even two of these skill sets. Only a small number of managers can claim to be reasonably proficient in all three. This book is intended to provide the material for specialists in any one of these areas to understand the key features of the other two.

1.2 The objectives of purchasing

If primary schooling is sometimes said to be about the 'three Rs', purchasing is sometimes said to be about the 'five Rs', i.e. to obtain:

- The right goods
- at the right time
- in the right quantity
- from the right source
- at the right price.

This definition is neat and works well for most purchasing. It is particularly suited to routine purchasing of goods such as raw materials, energy or office supplies. However, as a definition of the objectives of purchasing policy for non-routine items, in particular for investment or project-based purchasing, it has a number of shortcomings. These shortcomings are all applicable in IT purchasing which has several special and unusual features that distinguish it from many other types of purchasing. These features include:

- A substantial amount of IT expenditure is one-off. Often, one-off purchases, while small in number, represent the bulk of the financial outlay. Consequently, many routine purchasing procedures do not work well when applied to IT.
- Much IT purchasing is essentially capital in nature, but gives rise to continuing costs. While IT expenditure can be classified into current/expense (i.e. routine or continuing) purchasing and capital (or project) purchasing, the latter tends to give rise to yet more purchasing and the point at which capital becomes current is not always clear.
- The costs of changing suppliers can be high. While open systems have greatly reduced the problem of supplier lock-in, where an organization can become a virtual captive of its IT supplier, changing IT supplier can still be painful.
- IT purchasing decisions are rarely isolated. Unlike some other capital purchases, a decision to acquire a particular piece of hardware or software may have complex knock-on effects and lead to unforeseen consequential costs.

- Value is complex to assess and rarely simply a question of price. A core theme of good IT purchasing is the importance of value. In IT, best value frequently does not equate to lowest price (see Case history 1.2).
- Central to the concept of value is quality, which in the case of IT can be difficult to assess. Quality includes factors such as reliability, flexibility and ease of maintenance which can be difficult to measure, particularly at the point of purchase.

Case history 1.1 describes a common dilemma which illustrates the problems of short term thinking.

Case history 1.1: The cost of short term thinking?

The following (true) story illustrates a common dilemma in IT decision making.

A small company had a large customized software system written in a leading fourth generation language and database management system. The supplier of the language and database announced a new release of the software which required that existing systems be substantively modified in order to upgrade. Despite the fact that over £500 000 was already invested in the software, the £100 000 cost of the upgrade was difficult for the company to swallow. The new version of the software would do nothing that the current version could not do, so the money would produce no immediate business benefits. The argument that the upgrade would have to be done sometime and the sooner the better was not convincing to a management team focused on short-term performance.

As a result, the decision was deferred for four years until eventually the software supplier announced withdrawal of support for the old version. By this time two things had happened. The number of lines of code in the Company's system had almost doubled and the software package had gone through several further releases. The result was that when the upgrade became a matter of no choice, the cost had risen to nearly £250 000. Short term thinking had cost the company £150 000.

Or had it? Was this a good or a bad decision?

> Interestingly, in a discussion of this case, an argument was put forward that the potential return on £100 000 over the four years of the delay might have been greater than £150 000. To do so would, however, have required an annual return on investment of the order of 26% or better (and assumed absolutely no other benefits from the new version of the software). In fact the company was not realizing anything like this level of return on its capital at the time so deferral was not the correct decision.

Within any organization, IT can be considered as a living system which needs day-to-day maintenance, continual improvement/replacement and continuing (or at least occasional) enhancement and expansion. No other aspect of most organizations' operations exhibits all of these features and, as a consequence, requires such a complex mix of purchasing procedures.

1.2.1 Secondary objectives of IT purchasing

IT purchasing policy has a number of supplementary objectives. These are:

- Ensuring that all purchases conform to IS strategy and IT policy. There is a close linkage between IS strategy and IT purchasing. For public sector bodies, this may include government guidelines or regulations.
- Assisting management to monitor and control IT expenditure. Monitoring and control has several components of which purchasing policy is one.
- Ensuring that the purchasing process itself is efficient. Purchasing procedures should be efficient and easy to work with. Unduly cumbersome procedures can be self-defeating.
- Achieving the optimum balance between local/user and central /IT management control. This has become an increasingly complex issue with the widespread use of distributed computing technologies.
- Control of IT inventory. Many organizations do not know exactly what the state of their IT inventory is. The best point to trap information is at the point of purchase.
- Being as flexible as is compatible with meeting the preceding objectives. It is important that purchasing policy not be unduly rigid. Even where an organization is operating in a

stable business environment, rapid changes in IT can present management with unexpected decisions at short notice.

Taken together with the primary objectives, these present a considerable management challenge to define and implement.

1.3 What makes IT purchasing different?

While IT purchasing shares much in common with other types of purchasing, there are important differences. In order to develop and implement good IT purchasing policies, it is important to understand these differences. One reflection of the different nature of IT acquisition can been seen in many organizations where responsibility for IT purchasing is not vested in the Purchasing Department. In some organizations the Purchasing Department may have little or no role at all in IT acquisition. This may not be desirable from a management viewpoint. Nevertheless, the fact that it is so is indicative of several features of IT acquisition which make it different. These differences are:

- Linkage. In a sense, IT is like a never ending capital construction project. In modern systems, particularly with the evolution of distributed processing and the complexities that this entails, few decisions can be made in isolation.
- The range of technical skills involved in purchasing decisions. As IT has become progressively more integrated, both into the organization's operations and with other technologies such as telecommunications, the range of skills necessary to control and manage IT systems has increased. As a result, IT acquisition requires not only management of a widening group of internal technical specialists, but also of outside advisors and suppliers.
- The speed at which the technology changes. There is a rule of thumb in the IT industry that the half-life of IT knowledge is about 3 years, i.e. of all the things people know about the technology at the moment, half will be out of date within three years' time. The pace of change presents enormous challenges both in keeping abreast of developments and, more specifically, in determining replacement strategies and system life spans.
- The difficulties in costing IT accurately. There are several problems in trying to compute exact costs for IT. Traditional costing methods are often inadequate and new techniques such as value chain analysis and activity based costing are

often needed to obtain an accurate view of costs. There are also complicated accounting rules as to how IT expenditure should be treated in financial reporting.

- Obsolescence and turnover. A modern passenger aircraft will give between 20 and 30 years of normal service. Properly maintained, a modern car will give at least 10 to 15 years' service. Modern PCs have a practical life (as opposed to a physical life) of under four years in a 'normal' organization and less than two years in organizations where leading edge IT is an integral part of the product or service. Organizations are continually faced with pressure for upgrading systems.

- Difficulties in assessing the benefits derived from IT expenditure. Because IT is integral to the day-to-day operations of most organizations, it can be difficult to assess its precise impact. The view in some quarters that IT has proved a poor investment over the past ten years arises in large part from the failure of conventional accounting and economics to measure the real impact of IT. Most managers are confused as to what the value of IT is. The IT and Finance managers need to be able to assess whether an investment is justified.

- Difficulties in controlling expenditure. Most capital expenditure projects are directly under the control of a manager or a small group of managers. IT, by its nature, is used in every aspect of the business. Because the individual components of IT are both numerous and relatively inexpensive, it is easy for individual users and managers to circumvent purchasing controls. This gives rise to a variety of problems and special management techniques and structures are needed to control them.

- Lack of completeness and/or precision in stating requirements. Many users are unable or unwilling to state their IT requirements precisely. Users may also be unsure of what they require or unaware of what the technology can do for them. The result is often a gap between what the system provides and what users expect. This can be aggravated by changes in perception as knowledge, and expectations based on that knowledge, grow.

- Long-term effects. A particular feature of IT purchasing is the long-term and subtle impact of not just major decisions, but also of seemingly minor decisions. This impact can be a large multiple of the original expenditure. It is critical to good purchasing policy that such long-term implications be foreseen and that the dynamics of IT costs be fully understood.

- Risk. Purchasing policy has to consider risk. In some larger purchases, particularly of new and/or untried technology, there may be a substantial element of risk.

From the above it is evident that IT purchasing is *qualitatively* different from many other types of business purchasing. This difference requires special purchasing policies which need to be carefully thought out.

In certain organizations, and in particular in service organizations, IT purchasing may also be *quantitatively* different from other types of purchasing.

Many modern organizations are IT- and people-intensive. They may have little by way of traditional capital equipment such as plant and machinery or even buildings. Examples include banks, professional services firms and retail outlets. It is not unusual in such organizations to find that IT is the second largest element of capital expenditure after property. Where offices are rented or leased, IT will often be the largest single item of capital expenditure[1]. In some organizations, where staff work from home or from their car and do not have an assigned office desk, this is already the case. In such organizations, IT will be the dominant form of capital expenditure and may even be the second largest item of expenditure after the payroll.

1.4 IT strategy and purchasing

There is a close relationship between IS strategy and IT purchasing. To understand this relationship, it is useful to look briefly at the components and outputs of IS strategy.

IS strategy is concerned with the medium to long-term application and deployment of IT in the organization. Over the past 25 years there has been an evolution of thinking in the role and function of IT from systems that were designed simply to *automate*, through systems that were designed to *inform* to systems that, today, are designed to *transform* the business. This change in thinking is driven in part by improvements in technology but also by a need to justify the high and growing levels of IT expenditure.

Development of IS strategy is a top-down process which starts from corporate strategy and objectives and makes use of tools such as critical success factors and gap analysis to identify ways

---

[1] An extreme example of this was the arbitrage firm Long Term Capital Management whose collapse nearly brought down the US banking system in 1998. LCTM had close to a trillion dollars in financial assets (such as loans), but employed only 200 people. Its only significant physical assets were its computer systems.

in which IT can transform the business, giving it competitive advantage by means of product or service differentiation and/or by reducing its cost base.

These latter may be achieved by a wide variety of means. The IS strategy determines, *inter alia*:

- the systems and technologies needed
- the overall system architecture
- the scale of the investment needed
- the priorities for investment
- the infrastructure (human, hardware, software, telecommunications, etc.) needed.

These will be consolidated into an IT plan. The time horizon of an IT strategy is typically five years, but it may be more or less depending on the industry or the organization's inherent stability. This plan will specify:

- new systems required (i.e. which have no current equivalent)
- new systems to be developed/built
- new systems where packaged solutions are appropriate
- which existing systems are to be replaced
- which existing systems are to be retained
- which existing systems are to be upgraded
- resources needed.

Ultimately these will translate into purchasing requirements. Prior to this, the overall IT plan will be translated into a series of specific sub-projects designed to meet the strategic goals. It is the function of IT management to prepare a detailed plan for what will then become a series of projects. For example these might include:

- replacement of the current general ledger system
- moving the present centralized custom database to client server system
- moving all PCs from Windows 98 to Windows XP
- linking the cash registers to the stock system
- installing a smart card clock-card system

and so on.

Each project in turn generates hardware, software, telecommunications and other resource requirements. It is at this point that IT purchasing policy comes into the picture.

IS strategy will impact on IT purchasing and acquisition in a number of ways. First, for major acquisitions/investment, formal statements of requirement must be prepared. These may be put out to tender. Second, the strategy may lead to global decisions on products or product ranges. For example, a company may standardize on one word processing package or have a minimum specification for any PC purchased. Third, it may result in more generic strategies such as 'best of breed' acquisition which can, in turn, give rise to specific issues in purchasing policy. Finally, a good strategy will specify the benefits that the organization expects to realize from its IT investment programme (although these will often be stated in fairly broad terms). It is a part of the whole process of managing the finances of IT to specify these benefits precisely and to set up mechanisms for measuring them. All of these have implications for purchasing policies and procedures as well as for finance.

The sequence is shown in Figure 1.1.

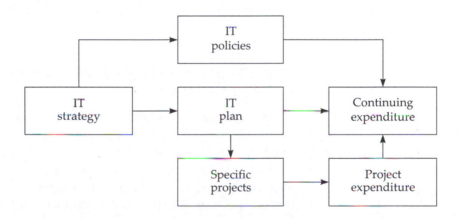

Figure 1.1

One of the problems with IS strategy is that it is rarely fixed for long. The best intentions of 'freezing' strategy tend to melt quickly in the heat of unforeseen business pressures. Most organizations will have a process of continuing review as the business changes and new technology emerges. Strategy may also have to be adapted to handle changes in regulations or new government policies.

In summary, strategy lays down broad criteria within which purchasing policy can be formulated. However, even in the absence of a strategy, a good purchasing policy can still provide considerable benefits, save time and avoid certain problems that might otherwise occur. Formulation of purchasing policy is described in more detail below.

1.5 IT value

The interest in IT value is fuelled by a widespread perception that much of the IT expenditure in the last 20 years has brought little or no measurable benefits. While this perception may, in many cases, be misguided, the interest in IT value is healthy and indicative of management awareness of and attention to IT. Value can be defined, somewhat pompously, as 'the receipt of benefits which are commensurate with the expenditure involved'. For most IT expenditure, value for money should be measured in the medium to long-term. Decisions based on short-term considerations can prove to be expensive in the longer term. Case history 1.2 shows, on a small scale, the type of problem that arises during periods of technology transition when the temptation to go for a quick and dirty (and usually inexpensive) solution can get an organization into trouble in the longer term.

Case history 1.2: Lowest price is not always best value

Many years ago, a company needed to replace a number of ageing 386 PCs. Two options were considered: to use 486 machines or the then relatively new and more expensive Pentium. When pressed, the users had to admit that the 486s could do the work, however they wanted the better performance and expansion capabilities of the Pentiums. Management disagreed and purchased 486s.

A few months later, there was a new release of their key operational software. This would only run on the recently acquired 486s if substantial memory were added, and then only slowly. As a result, the company was forced to replace all the 486s with Pentiums. Although the Pentiums had by that time dropped in price, the net outlay was still significantly higher and, of course, there were all the additional costs from the disruption of two change-overs rather than one – not to mention a number of very annoyed users.

Case history 1.2 illustrates the principle that in IT, the best value for money does not usually equate to lowest price. It is not unusual for price to rank between 5th and 8th place in importance when selection criteria are ranked. For more on this, see Chapter 9.

1.5.1 Measuring IT value

The definition of IT value implies that assessing value requires both accurate estimation and recording of the expenditure and clear definition and measurement of the expected benefits. Any assessment of value is of little use unless it can be quantified. Likewise benefits, monetary or otherwise, must be computable and measurable. A summary of these benefits is given below. Value can be measured for all IT expenditure, but it is more critical in discretionary expenditure. Differentiating out this is important.

IT expenditure may be mandatory or discretionary. If it is mandatory, the benefits of the expenditure are by definition self-evident. The following are common mandatory reasons for IT expenditure.

- It is driven by external events. For example, a decision by the Government to change the income tax system will mean changes in every payroll in the country. The Y2K problem was a large-scale example of this.
- The business could not be run otherwise. It is impossible to imagine a modern bank or airport operating without its IT systems. These systems must be maintained and developed.
- It is a cost of staying in business. Much IT expenditure is driven by the need to stay competitive. If one's competitors use IT in a particular area, then a company may have no choice but to follow – even in circumstances where the actual financial benefit in other terms may not justify the expenditure.

With discretionary expenditure, benefits need to be identified. In this case, IT may be competing with other projects for scarce resources. There are many benefits of IT, both hard and soft. Some of the most important business benefits delivered by IT are listed below. IT may:

- Reduce costs. IT can reduce costs in many ways, for example by reducing staffing, by reducing the required stock holding levels and by reducing the volume of paper flow.

- Restructure costs. This is a subtle effect and of major significance in many organizations. Costs can be restructured by shifting costs from labour to capital, altering the balance of production costs and changing the allocation of overhead costs.
- Improve efficiency. IT can improve efficiency in a number of ways including eliminating or replacing unproductive work, improving ease of communication between staff and reducing or eliminating paper. An increase in efficiency may or may not reduce costs.
- Improve effectiveness. IT can enable staff to carry out many tasks more effectively, for example by improving accuracy or designing products better.
- Improve existing service to customers. Examples of improved services to customers include reduced ordering times, faster response to enquiries, reduced paperwork, better after sales service and better communication.
- Provide new products or services to customers. Examples of the type of improved services include providing on-line purchasing, quotations and price lists, 24 hour delivery, direct monitoring of stock levels with automatic re-ordering, provision of product or market information, on-line access to accounts and so on.
- Gain competitive advantage by differentiation. Much of the justification for IT today is in terms of better competitiveness, for example yielding shorter delivery times, adding value to the product at minimal cost, giving customers on-line access to product information and using IT to form mutually beneficial alliances.
- Lead to better decision making. This might be done by identifying most profitable products/customers, use of various tools such as on-line analytical processing, expert systems and decision modelling.
- Improve staff morale and thus productivity. Staff morale and productivity may be improved in a variety of ways including by making processing local, providing better information, providing more information, a better and more rewarding work environment and by eliminating boring and repetitive tasks.
- Help to attract and retain better staff. Good IT systems can also help attract a higher calibre of staff by providing attractive working conditions, attracting creative and innovative staff who want to use their skills.
- Improve the organization's image. For example, by higher public visibility (e.g. automatic point of sales machines),

personalized letters, use of loyalty and other card technology.

- Give better insight into performance and operations. Falling costs have enabled many smaller organizations to undertake business modelling and analyses that were hitherto impractical or only available to organizations with very large computers. Benefits here include faster reporting, powerful analytics, access to external information and simulation modelling.

- Improve quality in the products. IT can add value to products in a variety of ways by use of computer-aided design, automated quality control systems, more accurate measuring systems and so on.

- Improved communications. The scope and scale of business today is supported by IT communications which provides an enormous breadth, speed and depth of communication possibilities.

It is not sufficient that benefits be identified. They must also be measurable in some way if IT value is to be meaningfully assessed. This is one of the most difficult areas in IT/Finance. This issue is discussed in more detail in Chapter 3.

1.6 Foundations of IT purchasing policy

Good management practice requires clear purchasing policies. The need for good purchasing policy is driven by the need for short-term controls and the implicit long-term costs of many IT purchasing decisions. Purchasing also needs to be efficient, and the procedure and controls need to be commensurate with the importance of the purchase being made. IT purchasing policy and procedures should be based on:

- the IS strategy
- the scale of the explicit expenditure involved
- the scale of the implicit expenditure involved
- the potential business impact of the purchase
- normal company purchasing policy and procedures.

Most organizations have established purchasing procedures. While these can be a source of good principles as well as useful guidance and information, they are rarely ideally suited to IT purchasing. For this reason, development of separate IT purchasing policies and procedures are quite common.

1.6.1 Policy components

IT purchasing policy consists of the following components.

- Approved products. These are products and services which have been vetted and passed for purchasing. Approval may be at a number of levels.
- Purchasing procedures. These are the steps by which goods are requisitioned, approved, acquired and paid for.
- Approved suppliers. It is generally advisable to have a controlled list of approved suppliers. There are many reasons for this, which are covered in Chapter 2.
- Monitoring and control procedures. These state the way that purchasing is monitored and expenditure is controlled, and are described in detail in Chapter 5.
- Review and audit. There should be a periodic audit on routine expenditure and a specific audit on major expenditures. This audit will check not only the level of expenditure but that the anticipated benefits have been realized.

IT purchases can vary from a few pounds for a box of CDs to a major application development costing hundreds of millions of pounds. Purchasing procedures and controls need to be appropriate to the level of expenditure. There are many examples of major expenditures where lack of controls have led to disaster. Equally, purchasing procedures which are too heavy handed can lead to user resentment and delays in decision making.

In order to decide the appropriate level of control, it is necessary to understand not just the costs of a purchase, but its potential longer term consequences, financial and otherwise.

1.6.2 Significant purchase decisions

A purchase is *significant* if it has, or has the potential to have, a major impact on the organization. A significant purchase need not involve major expenditure. What starts out as a small purchase, can rapidly grow. The following is an example.

Case history 1.3: Small decisions can lead to big costs

Department C is part of a large public sector organization. The organization as a whole used a text screen version of a popular word processing package. This was run on a large number of stand-alone PCs within the Department.

In 1994, the package supplier brought out a new GUI-based version of his product which had a number of attractive features that the earlier version lacked. A trial copy was obtained and put on one of the largest PCs in the Department. It was noted in passing that the new version took up a great deal more disk space on the PC than the previous version, but in the enthusiasm this was forgotten. The supplier offered the Department a one-off upgrade licence which worked out at under £50 a copy for each PC in the Department, and the Department accepted.

Unfortunately when the support team went to install the software they ran into a number of problems with the capacities of their current PC population, Most needed additional memory to run the system and several needed additional hard disk drives. The cost of the additional hardware alone was a multiple of the software upgrade cost. The Department were then faced with having to train all their staff in the new software. Working in a 'what you see is what you get' (WYSIWYG) environment is quite different and, to maximize its potential, it was decided that all staff should undergo a two-day training course. The Department also discovered that its standard font, while fine on the text-based screen, was unreadable on the WYSIWYG screen. Changing the standard font was simple, but all existing documents had to be converted and in some cases re-formatted. This took several work-weeks.

Finally, the Department found that while documents prepared under the old version were readily convertible to the new version, the converse was not true! Consequently the exchange of documents with the rest of the organization became a further hassle as it required continual conversion back to the old format.

When all the bills were added up, the initial cost on the software licence turned out to be a very small fraction indeed of the final cost.

IT management faces two common expenditure control problems:

1 Where non-technical users (and on occasion even technical users) purchase equipment, or more commonly software, without either any analysis or understanding of the knock-on

effect or the longer term cost implications of the acquisition (as in the above example).

2 Users or managers deliberately using 'salami' tactics, to make what is, in effect, a large purchase under the guise of many smaller purchases. This needs to be spotted and stopped at an early stage.

Organizations are sometimes stunned when they undertake an *ex post* inventory of IT expenditure at just how much they have spent. An objective of good purchasing is to avoid such unpleasant surprises.

1.6.3 Approved products

A simple and effective way of controlling a large proportion of IT expenditure is to have an approved products list. Approved products can be:

- hardware
- software
- services
- consumables.

Approved products may be specific or generic.

1 Specific. These state the product, the supplier/manufacture and the model(s) or version number(s) approved. For example:

- Operating systems on all PCs must be . . .
- The following PCs have been approved . . .

and so on.

2 Generic. These are products for which the IT department provides a general technical specification, but where the brand or model is not mandated. It generally only applies to hardware. For example, a policy might be:

> 'All laser printers must be at 600 dpi with Postscript 3 and PCL compatibility and a minimum speed of 16 pages per minute.'

A procedure for vetting hardware, software, services and/or consumables is central to good purchasing. All such products must have been evaluated and approved by IT management and be in line with the organization's IS strategy.

A useful classification is as follows. Products may be:

- Generally approved. These are products which can be purchased by anyone with the requisite authorization without prior reference to IT management. Generally these are minor items such as blank DVDs or small items of personal software and hardware.
- Controlled. This is the most important category. Controlled items are those which meet the organization's technical requirements, but because of possible knock-on cost or enterprise level implications, must be monitored. There may, for example, be licence fee issues or other implications. There needs to be a procedure in place for reviewing such products from time to time.
- Unapproved. By default, this applies to all products which do not come under the other two headings. Such products may carry corporate risks (e.g. virus infection, compatibility problems, etc.). Some organizations apply severe disciplinary measures to staff who install unapproved products.

All users should be familiar with the approved products list. In particular, the list should be circulated to all managers with IT purchase authorization authority.

1.6.4 Selecting approved products

There are some common-sense criteria for selecting an approved product. An approved product should:

- Conform with the company's IS strategy and policy. IS strategy may or may not specify products (specific or generic). If it does not, or if there is no IS strategy, then IT management should devise such a policy.
- Be suitable for the purpose for which it is required. It is an important role for IT management to ensure that users are using the right software. It is quite common for users with limited knowledge to attempt to use one piece of software (usually a spreadsheet) for every conceivable application.
- Be reliable. This is particularly applicable to software. An often cited maxim in IT is that one should never buy version 1.0 of anything. It is, unfortunately, not unknown for even packaged software from reputable suppliers to be unstable (e.g. early versions of DBase IV and Microsoft Word).

- Be well supported either internally and/or externally. The importance of this will depend on the nature of the product and its role in the organization. Either a product should have good external (supplier or third party) support (via network or modem, for example) or proper internal support structures should be in place.
- Be from a reputable and financially sound supplier. Where a key supplier goes out of business a whole variety of problems can ensue. Further development of the product may stop. Support and/or spare parts (or in the case of software, people who can fix bugs) may become hard or impossible to find. In extreme cases, the viability of the user organization can be threatened.
- Be in the industry mainstream. Standard approved products should not be high risk or unduly innovative. Innovative developments need to be carefully controlled and the risk associated with them properly managed. Purchase of approved products should not require IT management to carry out continual risk assessments.
- Represent value for money. As noted above, this is not the same as lowest price. Factors that should be taken into account when assessing value for money include:
  - product quality
  - performance
  - supplier policies on future product development
  - support
  - site licensing arrangements and options
  - discounts
  - product warranty.
- Comply with industry standards. Industry standards, while by no means universal, are now widespread. In general, it is a good policy to stick to industry standards (*de facto* or *de jure*) unless there is a good reason not to do so.

Approved product lists should be kept under constant review. New products and new versions of existing products appear all the time. There needs to be a mechanism in place for both monitoring the announcement/release of new products and tracking industry standards and any implications these may have for the current systems or architecture. This type of control may also include moves from one version of (approved) software to another. This is particularly important when a new release of widely used software is likely to create a need to upgrade a large number of PCs, printers or other hardware or software.

1.7 Purchasing procedures

All purchases, apart from the trivial, must be requisitioned, approved, placed, (sometimes) chased, received and checked. There should be a simple, tight and easy to follow set of procedures for this. For the purpose of purchasing procedures, IT expenditure can be classified as:

1 Expense or routine expenditure. This may include operations, maintenance, consumables, insurance, security, back-up, etc.
2 Capital expenditure. This is investment in new systems. This may include replacement of current hardware or software, acquisition of new hardware, or communications, development of new systems, and so on.

The lines between these are not always clear and sometimes judgment needs to be exercised. A traditional problem in IT budgeting has been to regard IT as an overhead. This is wrong and can lead to poor decisions. A full understanding of the nature of IT expenditure is therefore important. The following section gives an overview of this. A more detailed description is contained in Chapter 3.

Ideally all purchasing should be based on agreed budgets. In reality, purchasing procedures need to be able to deal with four different situations:

- budgeted expense expenditure
- budgeted capital expenditure
- unbudgeted expense expenditure
- unbudgeted capital expenditure.

Each of these are considered in the following paragraphs.

The best way to have simple and efficient IT purchasing procedures is to have good planning and budgeting. Purchasing procedures which attempt to compensate for weaknesses in IT budgeting and planning are a symptom of poor management.

1.7.1 Budgeted expenditure

Where there is an agreed budget and the proposed expenditure is within the agreed budget, purchase procedures, be they for capital or expense items, should be as simple as is compatible with proper control. The following is a simple and sensible procedure for such expenditure.

- The required item(s) is(are) costed. This is best done by the IT department or the Purchasing department, although user departments sometimes present proposals with costs attached. In certain circumstances, it may be appropriate for the user to obtain a quotation, but this should always be double-checked by IT or Purchasing management. For standard items there may be internal price lists with discounts and/or bulk purchase arrangements.
- The purchase is approved by user department management. It is a central principle of good budgeting that users are responsible for their own expenditure.
- The user completes a purchase requisition form. Figure 1.2 shows a sample form. The requisition should show:
  - Who is making the request. This may be the user or the person with purchase authority.
  - Confirmation that this is both planned and budgeted expenditure. If budgets are large and complex, the appropriate budget code heading should be shown. It may be appropriate to show the amount budgeted on the form.

Acme Enterprises IT Purchase Requisition Form		
Description of purchase	Financial Information	
	Cost (excl. VAT)	
	Budgeted cost	
	Cumulative cost to date	
	Cumulative budget	
	Deviation from budget	
Budget code	Comment	

Supplementary information for unbudgeted requests only

Reason for request/change
Benefits/justification
Alternatives considered

Requested by	Approved by	Date

Please attach supporting documentation

Figure 1.2
Sample requisition form

- If the expenditure is only part of a budgeted heading, the amount that will remain in the budget after purchase is made. Certain public sector and some private organizations use the concept of commitment accounting. This shows some or all of the following for each budget heading or code:
  - The budgeted amount;
  - Expenditure to date;
  - Amount of budget not yet spent (or overspent) to date;
  - Committed expenditure;
  - Orders actually placed;
  - Amount of budget remaining (overspent) after commitments.

  Example 1.1 shows how this works.
- Whether there is any deviation from budget. It is common to set a level of budget tolerance for over-spending. Typically this is of the order of 5%. All deviations from budget should be shown.

Example 1.1: Commitment accounting

Company Legal Department
Project : Document Image Archive
Position as at 31 July 200x
All figures in £

	Budget	Actual	Committed to date	On order	Amount remaining
CD servers	40 000	23 000	11 000	6000	6000
Main server	10 000	10 500	0	0	(500)
Scanners	8000	4000	4000	4000	0
Workstations	35 000	12 500	14 500	14 500	8000
Cabling, etc.	4500	5200	0	0	(700)
Software	7500	7500	0	0	0
Development	50 000	25 000	27 000	n/a	(2000)
Implement	6000	0	6000	0	0
Data uptake	20 000	0	20 000	0	0
Project total	181 000	87 700	82 500	24 500	10 800

- If there is a major deviation from budget in either direction, an explanation why this is so. Deviations from budget may arise from:
  - a change in price
  - a change in the specification of the item(s) being purchased
  - a change in the volume of items being purchased.

  Where a deviation is material, supplementary information will normally be required before permission to make the acquisition is given.
- The signature of the person making the request.
- The signature of the person authorizing the expenditure if different from the person making the request.

- The IT department should purchase all goods on behalf of the user. This is desirable for a number of reasons including efficient and effective management of suppliers.
- All items should be delivered to the IT department and not to the user. There is a number of good reasons for this.
  - The IT department can check that the correct goods have been delivered. Often the IT Department will be in a better position to do this than the user.
  - Where appropriate, the goods can be checked and, if necessary, tested and set up. This may involve several steps. Typical activities include setting up software, creating a network address and adding virus protection.
  - All items can be logged at point of receipt and entered into the IT inventory. This is the surest way of keeping track of equipment and software.
  - For software, licences can be checked, quantity or corporate discounts confirmed and any necessary registration or site licence agreement compliance procedures carried out.
- Finally the IT and/or Purchasing department can check the invoice. This is to ensure that it is correct and that all appropriate discounts have been given. It can then be passed to Accounts for payment with a copy to the user department for information.

This procedure ensures that:

- all acquisitions have been budgeted
- all acquisitions comply with IT purchasing policy
- costs are in line with (or under) budget or, if not, that approval is given at the appropriate level to exceed the budget
- all hardware and software is logged and that inventories are up-to-date and accurate
- all licence terms and other legal requirements are met.

Speed and simplicity are important. Cumbersome procedures can lead to user frustration and, in the worst case, attempts to bypass the procurement system.

The above procedure can be used for budgeted capital project expenditure with the following modifications:

- with each item of expenditure, the total project expenditure must be monitored
- the requisition form should also be signed by the project manager.

1.7.2 Unbudgeted/unplanned expense expenditure

Purchasing procedures should prevent unauthorized expenditure occurring, but provide a mechanism for handling necessary but unplanned/unbudgeted expenditure. Unplanned expenditure can arise for two reasons: either a cost overrun on budgeted expenditure and/or a requirement for new expenditure. There are two approaches to handling such unplanned expenditure. One can either force the user to go through the normal budgetary procedure or an exceptional expenditure procedure can be used. The following is a simple exceptional expenditure procedure.

By definition, exceptional expenditure is outside of normal budgeted procedures. In such circumstances, the case for exceptional treatment must be clear, concise and contain all the necessary facts for management to make a decision. It should therefore include:

- what is being purchased
- who is making the request
- the reason for the request
- why these items/services required were not budgeted
- why they are now needed
- the amount of expenditure (including immediate expenditure and consequential expenditure)
- the net cost (if appropriate)
- the benefits that will be derived
- the implications of not proceeding (if appropriate)
- risk analysis (including risk management steps being taken)
- a comment on consistency with the IT plan.

It should be emphasized that this is essentially an emergency procedure and should not be regarded as normal. Except in exceptional circumstances, users should be told that they must comply with the normal capital expenditure approval procedures. Example 1.2 shows such an unplanned expenditure request.

Example 1.2: Emergency capital expenditure request

To: Head of Finance

From: Head of Marketing

Re: Upgrade of PCs in Marketing Department.

The Marketing Department seeks approval to upgrade its current laptop population to the latest models.

The total expenditure involved for 20 PCs will be £34 000 (plus VAT).

Reasons for Request

The new machines are needed to run the latest version of the marketing analysis software. This software is vital to the day-to-day operation of the department in product pricing. We are currently two releases of the software behind due to the inability of our current hardware to give adequate performance with later versions. It was anticipated that this software would be upgraded next year, however the suppliers have just informed us that they are withdrawing support from our version with effect from the end of next quarter. This will leave the Marketing Department and the Company exposed should any problems with the software subsequently develop. While the current software is relatively stable, it has a number of known problems which have been fixed in the later releases. These will not now be fixed in the current version.

Alternatives Considered

We have considered the option of upgrading the existing machines by adding more memory. While this will enable the new software to be run, the speed would be unacceptably slow. This is likely to lead to a loss in productivity and to overtime costs necessary to complete the work which already has the department at full stretch.

As noted above, the current machines are slow. Replacing them with modern machines will increase productivity and enable us to save approximately £5000 p.a. on what will otherwise be incurred as overtime.

Cost Analysis

The total cost will be £34 000 made up as follows:

Net capital outlay on hardware of £30 000 (£40 000 list price of machines less £10 000 from sale of existing machines (for which there is still a market) and company discount). Upgrade of the software is £50 per machine and training and overtime incurred as a result of the consequent disruption will cost £3000. Additional hardware maintenance charges will be £500 per annum.

The annualized cost (depreciating the new machines over three years) will be as follows:

	This year	**Year + 1**	**Year + 2**
Depreciation	£10 000	£10 000	£10 000
Software upgrade (£50×20)	£1000	–	–
Additional maintenance	£500	£500	£500
Training	£3000	–	–
Less:			
Savings on overtime	–	(£5000)	(£5000)
Net annual cost	£14 500	£5500	£5500

We would like permission to proceed with this expenditure.

1.7.3 Authorization levels

For IT expenditure, as elsewhere, it is usually appropriate to have different authorization levels. As a general rule, managers should be responsible for their own expenditure (i.e. hold their own budgets – see Chapter 5). It may also be appropriate to segregate authorization by category. For example, department managers may approve all hardware purchases for non-infrastructural items or software may only be authorized by IT management. (An example of where this might apply would be if the organization had a site licence with a limited number of users.)

Finally all IT expenditure and systems should be subject to regular audit to ensure that purchases are being put to the use for which they were acquired and to assess to what extent the expected benefits have been realized. Review and audit of expenditure, including assessing to what extent anticipated benefits are being realized, is covered in Chapter 5.

2   Dealing with suppliers

2.1 Introduction

Effective management of suppliers is a key part of good IT financial management. Organizations should aim for good and mutually beneficial long-term relationships with their suppliers, even if life does not always work out this way. This is particularly true in IT where an organization can be critically dependent on one or more of its IT suppliers, even without any significant outsourcing in the conventional sense (see below). The more mission-critical and complex the system, the more important the role of the supplier is likely to be and the more important the relationship with the supplier will be.

This chapter addresses the following questions:

- what qualities should be expected in a good supplier?
- what makes for a good supplier relationship?
- what are the various supplier management strategies?
- what is outsourcing?
- when should outsourcing be used?

along with many other subsidiary questions as well as providing guidelines on how to manage suppliers effectively.

2.2 Good supplier relationships

Good supplier relationships have a number of characteristics:

- They are built on trust and respect. In a good relationship both sides will trust the other implicitly. From the purchaser's viewpoint, trust includes basics (such as that the supplier is honest) and business trust, i.e. the supplier will deliver what is wanted, on time, to the required quality and so on.

- They are mutually profitable over the long term. This means that one partner should not continually exploit the other. It is generally not in the purchaser's long term interest to be an unprofitable customer. Suppliers have to make a profit if they are to continue to invest and develop their products, their services and their staff.
- There is regular two-way communication. A good supplier maintains contact with its customer whether or not there is an immediate sale in prospect. It is important that communication is two-way. For example, when there is a clash of views, the purchaser should always at least listen to the supplier's arguments. Suppliers often have experience that the purchaser lacks.
- Communication is real. The greatest problem with communication is the illusion that it has happened. Communication should lead to understanding. The purchaser needs the supplier to understand its requirements. The supplier needs the purchaser to understand the product or service being provided.

Relationships do not have to be equal to be good. Some management gurus like to proclaim the virtue of equality in business relationships, but in practice customer–supplier relationships are rarely equal. A small software house, 75% of whose business comes from one large multinational, is not dealing with that multinational on equal terms. In the same way, a small organization dealing with a large software company is not in the same bargaining position that a large multinational would be. Even so, dependency is not just a matter of relative size. A large IT user can find itself totally dependent on one small supplier who happens to supply one critical component of the IT systems.

It is sometimes said that the relationship between supplier and purchaser is a partnership and provided the meaning of the word 'partnership' is properly understood, this is true. A modern variant of this idea is called 'working together' where buyer and seller develop a close working relationship (either for a specific project or as a continuing long-term arrangement). However, while buyer and seller often have many interests in common, it should always be borne in mind that supplier relationships are not the same as normal business partnerships –

even when such sophisticated approaches as working together are used. The basic business fact is that suppliers makes their profits at the expense of the purchaser's profit (or in the case of the a non-profit making body, its resources).

In the commercial world, a company typically buys IT to increase its competitiveness and its profitability and/or to reduce its costs. If it can deal with its suppliers, including its IT suppliers, on more advantageous terms than its competitors can, then that will give it a cost advantage. On the other end, if it drives its suppliers to the extent that suppliers start to cut corners or, worse, go out of business, then considerable costs may arise from the subsequent problems and may put the purchaser at a considerable disadvantage. A purchaser's objective must, therefore, be to obtain the best sustainable cost advantage it can from its suppliers.

2.3 Poor supplier relationships

It is a rare organization that does not have a problem with one or more of its IT suppliers at some stage. There is a variety of symptoms of poor supplier relationships. These are not all necessarily problems on the part of the supplier.

2.3.1 Short-term/price-driven/exploitative

Some purchasers are obsessed by price. Such organizations tend to be aggressive in dealing with suppliers (in extreme cases, treating suppliers roughly becomes part of the company culture). They sometimes change supplier at regular intervals, make suppliers continuously re-bid for business or deliberately invite their competitors to bid against them. This policy may work in a highly competitive market and can be used selectively to great effect (see Case history 2.2). However, it can be a short-sighted strategy. Continually focusing on price rather than value in IT purchasing can lead to higher long-term costs. This is particularly true of software suppliers, systems integrators and custom software suppliers. These suppliers need to develop a good understanding of the purchaser's operations in order to be effective. This experience is sometimes built up over many years. Changing suppliers means that a new supplier goes through this learning curve all over again.

Case history 2.1: Penny wise, pound foolish

A small public sector organization which dealt with a particular social problem invited a software company in to review their computer systems. They bargained hard on price as their resources were limited. The software company took the view this was a small job and that, even if the job was not profitable, at least the loss would be small and it was in a good cause. The company was having a good year elsewhere and could afford to do a respectable job, even at a modest loss, and not worry too much.

No sooner had the job started than the Director of the organization started sniping at the company's work – claiming that they were not doing good work here, they had not delivered what he had expected there, and so on. It soon became clear that the reason for this was that the Director was manoeuvring himself into a position whereby he could say he was not going to pay the whole of the fairly small fee that he had negotiated on the grounds that he was not satisfied with the work.

When the software company's management realized this, they decided to cut their losses and offered to terminate the engagement on the spot for around half the fee, even through the work was only partially completed and of little value in its current state. The Director was only too delighted and congratulated himself on having saved the taxpayers a few thousand pounds. In fact all he had achieved was to waste a few thousand pounds of the taxpayers' money for no real return and in the process forfeited maybe twice as much in work that would have been done free on a goodwill basis.

Case history 2.1 is an extreme example of this type of short-term thinking and its consequences, but similar, if less dramatic examples can be found every day in the IT industry. This is not to say that a purchaser should always take the current supplier's price without question. However, there are ways of ensuring that current suppliers are competitive without changing them every month. The guiding principle in dealing with suppliers should be long-term value for money.

2.3.2 Unhealthy dependence

One symptom of a poor relationship is an unhealthy dependence by a supplier on a customer or vice versa. This can easily happen with software where an organization has heavily customized systems. Over time, the customer can become wholly dependent on the supplier to maintain the system and be at the mercy of the supplier's competence and goodwill (and honesty).

Case history 2.2: Exploiting the customer

A local authority had a customized system developed by a small software house to handle rents from its housing stock.

From the start there were problems with the project. The specification was not clear, the design was poor and the quality of the programming indifferent. After much effort the system eventually worked but, due to the inadequacy of the specification, needed continual modification to deal with day-to-day business requirements that had not been foreseen in the original design. As the programming was poor, and poorly documented, the Authority had no choice but to go back to the software house who charged them over £1000 a day for programming modifications (at a time when the average commercial rates for equivalent programmers was £350).

The Authority called in another larger and more professional software house to review the system. They concluded that the system was so badly designed that it was not worth fixing and recommended that it be re-written from scratch at a cost of £50 000. The department manager was unable to get approval for this on the grounds that he had already spent over £60 000 on the system and the Finance Department was unwilling to sanction further major expenditure. The Authority had little choice but to continue paying up.

Sometimes it can be difficult to avoid such relationships. A small supplier may have exactly the product or skill set required or have specialist industry expertise. The best strategy with such suppliers is to vet them carefully beforehand.

2.3.3 Uncontrolled

An uncontrolled relationship occurs where a purchaser really does not understand enough about the service being provided to manage the supplier effectively. This can result in the purchaser having to take the supplier's word on everything and meekly follow the supplier's advice. In effect, the purchaser has abdicated responsibility for purchasing decisions without even the formal protection of an outsourcing contract or agreement. Case history 2.3 is a familiar tale.

Case history 2.3: Supplier colonization

Many organizations take deliberate decisions to outsource some or sometimes all of their IT operations (see Chapter 2), but some organizations end up with 'outsourcing by stealth'. This is particularly true in the public sector where headcounts are tightly controlled, but IT budgets are not.

A good example occurred some years ago in a government department that decided to integrate a number of its heretofore silo systems. This started out as an internal project. Within about six minths, it had become clear that the scale and complexities of the project were much more formidable than had been thought. The department asked their software suppliers and consultants for technical advice. The first thing the consultants pointed out (reasonably enough) were not just flaws in the design, but, more seriously problems with the whole approach to the development. They had experience and they could bring it to bear – for a modest fee of course. One thing led to another and within a short time not only were almost the entire free IT resources of the department tied up in the project, there were also close to a hundred consultants and contractors working on the system. By this time too much had been invested to turn back and a system originally planned to cost £3 million ended up costing over £25 million. At least it worked.

2.3.4 Confrontational

The course of supplier relationships, like true love, does not always run smooth. It is almost inevitable that there will be disagreements from time to time and tempers may be lost (even as a matter of negotiating strategy!). The occasional argument does not necessarily mean that a relationship has a major problem. However, if there is a continuing feeling of discomfort or unease about a supplier relationship then it should be addressed, and if it cannot be sorted out then the purchaser should seek another supplier.

Poor supplier relationships can be remarkably durable. It is not uncommon to find an uneasy or even a hostile relationship that has lasted many years. If supplier relationships are poor, the problems should be sorted out or the relationship terminated.

2.4 Joint development

Sometimes a purchaser may decide to develop a customized software package which it feels may lead to a potentially saleable product in its own right. In these circumstances, it may be attractive to enter into an agreement with a supplier to develop the system jointly with a view to the supplier then selling on the software to third parties. This can have a number of attractions from the purchaser's viewpoint, including:

- The purchaser will get the software developed at a lower cost because the software supplier will be contributing to the cost.
- If the product sells, the purchaser will receive a royalty.
- The nature of the project will mean that supplier and purchaser must work closely together with all the beneficial effects of close co-operation.

There are, however, several drawbacks which should be considered before entering into this type of agreement:

- The cost savings may be wiped out by the necessity to put in features which the purchaser does not need, but which are required if the product is to be sold to a wider market.
- Any competitive advantage that the purchaser gains from the software may be foregone if their competitors buy the package.
- If a competitor buys the package, the supplier's ability to maintain confidentiality may be compromised.
- Maintenance of the package, once it builds up a user base, may involve the purchaser in ongoing commitments.

If such an arrangement is being considered, then the contractual arrangements need to be tight and, in particular, intellectual property rights must be protected.

As a cost reduction (and possibly profit-making) strategy, joint development of customized software is always worth considering if the issue of competitive advantage is not a barrier. If a commercial arrangement of this nature is being considered, professional legal and marketing advice should be sought.

2.5 Good suppliers

Good suppliers are a valuable asset to any organization. Good suppliers have some or all of the following characteristics:

- Technical expertise. Unless the purchaser is quite sophisticated, this is a *sine qua non* in most IT suppliers. Suppliers must have technical expertise in the products or services that they are selling. This is not something to be taken for granted. Many smaller firms and dealers do not fully understand the products they sell.
- A businesslike attitude. With larger suppliers this is not an issue. In practice, many IT products and services are supplied by small, often local, organizations, some of whom may have only been in business for a few years. Many of these firms are technology driven, i.e. they have a product and an evangelical fervour about its potential, but little real experience or appreciation of what real life is like in an office or on a factory floor.
- Reliability. The implications and scale of supplier reliability vary widely. For example, it is one thing to order half-a-dozen modem cards for delivery next week, another to ask for a 20 man-year software development project to be delivered on schedule at the start of June next year. A good supplier will deliver on time and will deliver what was ordered.
- Support strength. All but the most basic IT products require postsales support. Support does not have to come directly from the supplier. It can come from various sources including the manufacturer, the dealer, licensed third parties, unlicensed third parties or the buyer's internal resources.
- Stability. It is in the interest of the customer that suppliers, particularly of mission-critical software, are financially stable and well managed. The failure rate amongst IT businesses is high. Many smaller firms, particularly software firms, lack basic business skills. Having a key IT supplier go out of business can be a big problem. Good software systems may last seven to ten years (or more) and will need continuing support during that time.

- Responsiveness. A good supplier will be responsive in a number of ways. Simple tests of a supplier's responsiveness are:
  - When you call them, do you get to the right person quickly?
  - Do they return calls in a reasonable time?
  - When there is a problem, do they respond immediately?
  - Do they have a clear escalation procedure when problems are reported?
  - When they say they will send something or write, do they do so quickly?
  - Are they willing to respond to call-out emergencies during anti-social hours such as evenings and weekends?
- Good relationships with their own suppliers. Suppliers may be manufacturers/direct suppliers, dealers, other equipment manufacturers (OEMs), vendors, agents, system integrators or other entities. The majority of IT suppliers are not the developers, manufacturers or owners of most (or even any) of the products they sell. In such circumstances, the relationship of suppliers with their own sources/suppliers is important. Questions to ask are:
  - What exactly is their relationship with their own supplier?
  - Are they an official stockist or agent?
  - Do they have any certification (such as trained and approved engineers)?
  - How long has the relationship been in existence?
  - Is it a permanent arrangement or a contract for this particular project?

  The latter question is important. In the IT industry, there is a continuous process of forming and dissolving different relationships and alliances. It is common for strategic partnerships announced with a great fanfare to break up quietly (and sometimes not so quietly) some years (or even months) later.
- A responsible attitude. A good supplier will have a business-like and responsible attitude to problems. Poor suppliers will instinctively seek to apportion blame to everyone else when problem occurs, even seeking to hide behind the small print in the contract. A good supplier will sort out the problem first and worry about whose responsibility it is afterwards.
- An interest in the customer's business. Good suppliers take an (appropriate) interest in the customer's business. A good IT supplier will be aware of its customer's business dynamics and how it can help it (and naturally in so doing, help its own business). Good suppliers will understand the purchaser's needs and this can only be achieved by some level of understanding of the customer's operations. A good supplier will be in regular contact with its customers, presenting them

with new ideas, keeping them up to date with developments in its product or product range and suggesting how such products might be used to the customer's business advantage.

- A sound reputation. A good supplier will acquire a good reputation. The IT industry has an extensive trade press and a supplier's reputation (like its financial status) can easily be checked out. Existing customers are a good source of information.
- An acknowledged quality standard such as ISO 9001. Many suppliers now have ISO 9001 or equivalent certification (e.g. BS 5750). The value of this varies – it is more meaningful in hardware and maintenance companies, for example, than it is in software companies. It does, however, indicate an attitude of mind which is a sign of good management.

2.6 Supplier management strategies

Unless an organization chooses to outsource its entire IT operations (see below) or employ a systems integrator, it will have to deal with a number of suppliers. These may vary from major suppliers (for example its enterprise resource planning (ERP) system supplier) to minor suppliers (for example, computer paper suppliers). There are four basic ways of managing suppliers:

1 directly
2 using lead contractors
3 using systems integrators
4 complete outsourcing.

In practice many organizations use the first approach, direct management, with lead contractors or systems integrators being used for specific larger projects. The term 'complete outsourcing' is here used to distinguish between outsourcing of certain services and outsourcing of the whole IT/IS operation.

2.6.1 Direct management of suppliers

Most (though by no means all) organizations choose to manage their suppliers directly. When this approach is used, two immediate questions are what qualities to seek in a supplier and, where there is a choice, should single or multiple suppliers be used? The first of these questions has already been addressed. The second question is answered in the following paragraphs.

While in much purchasing it is advantageous to have multiple suppliers, it only makes sense where it is economically and technically sensible to do so. Having multiple suppliers for the sake of it only creates unnecessary administrative overheads and political hassle. In many areas of IT it is neither economically nor technically advantageous to have multiple suppliers. That said, there are some advantages of having multiple suppliers, including:

- It discourages supplier complacency. Suppliers who have too cosy a relationship with a purchaser can, over time, become easy-going about the level of service to be provided. The fact that there is a competitor with whom their customer is doing business can have an inspiring effect on the performance of suppliers.
- It helps to keep prices keen. While the IT industry is highly competitive, it is no less prone to anti-consumer business practices than any other. Before the emergence of Open Systems, customer lock-in was often exploited by suppliers who, having taken a loss-leader to become established, could then make fat margins from a customer who was not in a position to shop around.
- It eliminates the risk of single supplier dependency. Having multiple suppliers is not always a practical short-term option. Some suppliers cannot be replaced at short notice. Others may be replaceable, but replacement suppliers may face a formidable learning curve before they can be productive.
- No supplier can meet all a customer's needs. Short of out-sourcing, and except for the simplest of customers, no supplier can ever provide a 'total solution' to all a customer's IT needs. Even where they can, it is highly unlikely that they will be able to provide a good solution to all needs (see next point).
- It is improbable that any one supplier will be the 'best of breed' in everything. To be fair, few companies today claim that they do (though some did in years gone by). While 'best of breed' purchasing should be treated with caution, it is a useful policy for certain requirements.
- It provides a basis for comparison. One way to check up on suppliers' price performance is to get multiple quotations for everything.

With skilful management, an organization can get exceptional value from its suppliers by playing them off against one another. Some organizations have been known to tell suppliers something like: 'I will guarantee both you and your competitor 20%

of the business. The remaining 60% you have to fight for!'. The following story, from the public sector, is a simple example of how the natural competitiveness of suppliers can be used to get exceptional value.

Case history 2.4: Exploiting the competitive instinct

A large public sector body needed to replace its general ledger and put out a call for tender for consultants to undertake the first stage of a three-part project, namely to review the existing ledger and prepare a statement of requirements and outline design. Two large and fiercely competitive consultancy firms, A and B were shortlisted. Firm A was awarded the contract in a tight finish.

After a number of months, Firm A came up with a recommendation that the existing system be replaced. They produced an outline design for the new system and confirmed the view that this be followed by two further stages: detailed design stage and package selection/implementation. Naturally Firm A expected to get this work.

The Finance manager in the Department felt that Firm B, having lost the bid for the initial review, might be particularly keen to restore their pride so he invited them to bid for the second detailed design phase against Firm A. Firm A were not too happy about this, but they nevertheless bid aggressively for the contract. Firm B, however, were still sore over the loss of the first contract and were determined to win the second stage contract at any cost. They therefore bid well under cost for the second stage, which of course they won. They calculated that they could recover this loss and make a profit on the much larger third (implementation) stage.

Unfortunately for them, the Finance manager decided that it might be an interesting idea to put the third stage out to a third tender to the same two firms. Firm A, again, bid quite aggressively. Firm B's sales team, faced with a large loss on the current contract, was told by its senior management to put in a more commercial bid this time. Firm A won the contract. Firm B were left with a large loss and the Finance manager was pleased with having saved a large amount of taxpayers' money while still getting a first class job from two leading consultancy firms.

Tactics such as those used in Case history 2.4 will work where the suppliers are large and can take the loss. Using this type of tactic with smaller firms can be riskier. If a key supplier suffers a major loss, the implications can cause serious problems for the customer if the supplier gets into financial difficulty.

While multiple IT suppliers are a fact of life for most organizations, there are disadvantages in having to deal with them. The drawbacks of a multiple supplier policy are:

- Multiple suppliers are more complex to manage. Life is simpler when choices are limited. If the customer's IT choices are limited to what one supplier can offer, then at least the customer does not have to use complex evaluation and decision-making techniques to select the best course of action.
- It increases the risk of system compatibility problems. The more suppliers there are, the greater the number of interfaces between one supplier's product and another.
- There is a greater management and administrative overhead. Modern distributed systems often have hardware from several suppliers, multiple operating systems, several communications protocols and many software packages running. This is frequently the result of unplanned, spur of the moment, consortium or 'best of breed' purchasing.
- When problems arise, suppliers tend to blame each other rather than address the problems. Good suppliers will take ownership for a problem and co-operate with each other to solve it. Some suppliers, however, take a defensive attitude and their first reaction is to try and insulate themselves from blame, usually by trying to shift the blame to someone else.

A number of factors govern the question of where and when to use multiple suppliers. These factors include the size of the organization, the internal IT resources and skills available, the nature of the product or service being purchased and, of course, availability of such suppliers. Handling multiple suppliers requires management resources and skill. For smaller organizations both of these can be in short supply. For such organizations, the advantages of multiple suppliers are usually outweighed by the risks and the cost of the level of effort necessary to manage the resulting complexity. One solution for such organizations is to employ a contract project manager or systems integrator to assist or to look after specific systems.

Even in larger organizations with limited IT resources, management of multiple suppliers can be a problem. Again it is sometimes necessary to bring in consultants or specialist advisers to cope with the complexities that can arise. For smaller organizations, the relative size of the risks and the management effort involved usually outweigh the benefits of multiple suppliers. Larger suppliers often find it quite inefficient to deal with smaller buyers and the level of service tends to reflect this. In these circumstances, selective outsourcing, systems integrators and lead contractors may be more attractive options.

2.6.2 Using multiple suppliers

For larger purchasers (where, say, the total annual IT spend is greater than £100 000 per annum) multiple suppliers can be used for:

- most hardware including servers, PCs, printers, and so on
- communications equipment such as routers, modems, cabling, etc.
- consumables and office items (paper, diskettes, etc.)
- certain types of operational consultancy services such as systems specification and performance reviews.

The feasibility will depend on volume of purchases and simple practicality.

Software is different. The growth in standards and the decline of processor-specific operating systems and communication protocols has meant that processing, storage, output and communications hardware are all increasingly interchangeable. It is no great administrative or technical problem to have two server suppliers or three printer suppliers. The same is *not* true of software and the issue of multiple software suppliers demands careful consideration and planning. IT strategy impacts on software purchasing policy in a way that is not true for hardware. To illustrate this point, consider the following two hypothetical statements of policy:

'All PCs must be Pentiums 4s with a clock speed of at least 700 MHz, 256 MB of RAM and a minimum 40 GB of hard disk.'

'All word processing packages must provide reasonable functionality and run on Windows 2000 or higher.'

The former policy is not likely to give rise to any compatibility problems – even through it is fairly general and there are well over a dozen brands of PC which could be purchased under this guideline. The latter could cause major difficulties even if there are only half-a-dozen word processing packages which meet this need. To obtain uniformity of purchase with word processing, it is necessary to specify a particular package such as WordPerfect or Word. A consequence of this is that when it comes to software, purchasing policy must be subservient to IT policy in a way that is not normally necessary for hardware.

The use of multiple suppliers of software is something that should be approached with caution. Multiple software is often unnecessary. An organization should only require one payroll package, one accounting suite or one spreadsheet system. Unfortunately in diversified organizations individual divisions and departments make their own purchase decisions, often without reference to central IT management (if it exists). In the absence of a firm software policy, the result can be an electronic tower of Babel.

The following are the major software types and their suitability for multiple suppliers:

- System software. This includes operating systems and communications protocols. Most modern systems of any size use multiple operating systems and communications protocols, usually from a number of different hardware and software suppliers. Multiple suppliers are probably inevitable today in all but the smallest operations.
- Middleware. This category includes computer languages and data management systems and utilities. With the development of Open Systems and distributed computing, middleware has rapidly grown in importance. It is increasingly common for organizations to have, say, two or three different database management or systems languages in use. As with system software, multiple suppliers are often a fact of life, but IT management should try to keep the number to a minimum.
- Enterprise application software. These are the key organization-wide or multi-department business systems such as the general ledger, order processing or inventory control. It is highly desirable to keep such systems confined to single suppliers if at all possible. Major problems can arise from having to build and maintain complex interfaces between a large number of enterprise software systems.
- End user software. This includes desktop applications such as word-processing, spreadsheets and e-mail. Here single suppliers are always preferable. Any advantages of mixing and matching 'best' products in this area are generally overwhelmed by the ease of operation achieved when all products are from the one supplier.

There are areas of IT where it is either impractical, uneconomic or plain inconvenient to have multiple suppliers. These areas include one-off and infrequent purchases, most enterprise software and any situation where changing a supplier is difficult or expensive. Examples of such areas include mainframe and mid-range hardware, enterprise software and end user software.

2.6.3 Lead contractors

Where specific systems or sub-systems are required, a lead contractor can be a useful supplier-management approach. Twenty-five years ago, a purchaser with a systems need would have gone to its mainframe or minicomputer supplier for a solution. Today the wheel is going full circle with traditional mainframe suppliers such as IBM and Fujitsu transforming themselves into service companies that mix and match components from themselves and other suppliers to provide a solution to a customer's needs. In this case, there is a *de facto* lead contractor. However, on other occasions, IT solutions are put forward by *ad hoc* consortia of suppliers providing a mix of some or all of hardware, packaged software, custom software, communications and project management.

A lead contractor approach places the contract for delivery and implementation of the system with one and only one member of such a consortium. The lead contractor subcontracts with whatever other suppliers are needed to provide the necessary equipment, software or services. This process is often referred to as systems integration, but there is a subtle difference between lead contracting and true systems integration (see below). The advantages of lead contracting are:

- It simplifies supplier management. The purchaser signs only one contract. The lead contractor is contracted to deliver the required system. Any problems with other suppliers are the lead contractor's problems and not the purchaser's.
- It reduces risk. On the assumption that the lead supplier is competent and of a sufficient size, the approach reduces (though it does not eliminate) the risks arising from suppliers not delivering or small suppliers going out of business.
- It provides project management expertise. This is particularly useful if the purchaser does not have such skills or cannot make them available to the project.

There are three disadvantages to lead contracting:

- Cost. In taking on contractual responsibility, the lead contractor is assuming not just its own risk, but also the risk associated with the subcontractors. Generally there will be a financial premium to be paid for this.
- Lack of control. The purchaser is dependent on the lead contractor and may have little control of what is happening. The purchaser must rely on the lead contractor's reports which may not always be objective.
- Conflicts of interest. By definition, a lead contractor is also providing some component parts of the project. If there are problems, there may be a tendency for the lead contractor to blame sub-contractors. It may be difficult for the purchaser to detect where the real truth lies.

Despite these limitations, lead contracting is recommended for multi-vendor contracts.

2.6.4 Systems integrators

Where the project is large and complicated, or the purchaser feels that there is a risk of the lead contractor having a conflict of interest, then the use of a systems integrator should be considered. Systems integration is where the purchaser employs a supplier or individual to manage the other suppliers on a project. True systems integrators are independent, i.e. they do not have a vested interest in any other part of the project. This is desirable for several reasons which can be summarized as the characteristics that one should seek in a systems integrator. The systems integrator (organization or individual):

- Should have no conflicts of interest. The only responsibility of the systems integrator should be to its customer.
- Should be neutral. In most projects there will be problems at some stage and this risk is greatly amplified where many suppliers are involved. When disputes arise, it is imperative that the systems integrator be impartial and is seen to be impartial.
- Should be multi-skilled. Systems integration needs a wide variety of skills and broad technical awareness. A systems integrator must be able to communicate with all parties effectively, at least within the terms of the project in hand.

Good systems integrators do not come cheap. Typically systems integrators are highly experienced senior IT consultants or teams of consultants who come with a corresponding price tag (sometimes several thousand pounds a day). Nonetheless, they can be used selectively to great effect. Systems integration services are provided by most of the major IT consultancy firms.

2.7 Handling salesmen

Sales staff are trained to make a potential purchaser (known in sales jargon as 'the prospect') want to buy their product or service. A skilled salesman (or, increasingly, woman, but in the IT industry most of them are still male) will be able to manipulate a potential purchaser in ways of which the purchaser may not always be aware. IT managers or staff who have never before sat through a series of sales presentations are sometimes surprised by the fact that at the end of each session they are convinced that the product they have just considered is the only one to buy. Experienced buyers, who have seen this type of presentation many times, are less readily impressed.

For the salesman, IT has the advantage of being a complicated product. Most products have a number of strong features which can be emphasized while conveniently overlooking their less endearing features. When listening to a sales presentation the following should be borne in mind:

- The salesman will always highlight those aspects of the system that are strongest.

  Comment: Salesmen play to their product's strengths. The corollary of this is that they gloss over or do not mention weak points.

  Purchaser tactic: Try to hear what the salesman doesn't say. Ask about those features that have not been mentioned. Ask how his product is better than that of its competitors and (if you are feeling really mean) follow this by asking where he feels its competitors' product might be better.

- Salesmen sometimes have limited technical knowledge.

  Comment: It is not a safe assumption for all salesmen, but many IT salesmen have only a superficial knowledge of the technology that they sell. They are adept at using jargon, buzzwords and acronyms (see Case history 2.5) to impress customers, but it is surprising how quickly they will back off if challenged on specific technical issues.

  Purchaser tactic: Do not be intimidated by jargon. Even experienced IT managers can feel intimidated by emergent technology or areas of technology with which they are not yet familiar. Learn the key buzz words – it is surprising how judicious use of an in piece of jargon or two can derail a bluffing salesman. Even a 'bluffer's' knowledge on the part of the purchaser can be enough to make a salesman more cautious about what he or she says and, as a consequence, less liable to mislead.

Case history 2.5: TLA is a TLA

An interesting illustration of how liberally IT salesmen use jargon they probably do not understand can be seen in the following story which happened in the early 1990s when Open Systems were a big issue in IT.

An IT manager was attending a sales seminar on Open Systems presented by a leading supplier. As he had heard much of the sales line before, his attention soon drifted off to other things until he noticed the extraordinary number of three letter acronyms (TLAs) being used by the speakers. They ranged from OSI to IBM and TCP to XPG. Fascinated, he started to jot them down and, by the end of the morning he had assembled a grand total of 87.

When he got back to his own office he set out to decipher as many of the TLAs as he could. After consulting several colleagues and a number of references, he managed to translate 60 of them. The remaining 27 defied translation.

As a further experiment, he persuaded a computer magazine to run the 60 TLAs as a Christmas quiz with a substantial prize for the person who could identify the most. The highest scoring entry was 52 and the next after that 45.

- Salesmen are often technically rather than business oriented.

Comment: Many salesmen, especially younger ones (who are in the majority), take refuge in technical matters where they are more at home. They are often reluctant to get into business specifics. Good, more experienced, salesmen often stand out simply because of their business expertise. Never forget the dot.com bust.

Purchaser tactic: Focus on your needs. Keep asking what will this do for my business or department. Do not be technology driven. Unless your business or organization has a need to be at the forefront of IT, do not be seduced by the desire simply to impress customers or clients with technology.

● Salesmen are boundlessly confident.

Comment: Salesmen who survive are optimists. Everything is possible and problems, if they exist at all, are only minor. This can be quite overwhelming, even to experienced buyers.

Purchaser tactic: Discount much of what you hear. It may be that the sales talk is fully justified and that this product is the technology breakthrough the world has been waiting for, but never take the salesman's word for this without question.

● The killer question.

Comment: Professional salesmen will often ask questions designed to 'hook' the purchaser. For example:

'Is there anything that you need that our system cannot provide?'

'Is there anything else that we need to do to get the business?'

'Are you happy with the price?'

These, and similar 'sale closing' questions, are designed to move the purchaser from looking into buying mode. By entering into a discussion of any of the above, the purchaser can start to become psychologically committed to the supplier.

Purchaser tactic: Watch out for such questions and fend them off politely. Evasive answers to the above three questions might be:

Question: 'Is there anything that you need that our system cannot meet?'

Answer: 'No, but several of the systems we have looked at meet the needs.'

Question: 'Is there anything else that we need to do to get the business?'

Answer: 'I won't know the answer to that until I have talked to the other bidders.'

Question: 'Are you happy with the price?'

Answer: 'We'll talk about that if we decide to do business with you.'

It is important to stay objective at all times. Understanding how a sales team tries to manipulate the purchaser is a key part of this.

2.8 Negotiating

Big organizations have a considerable advantage when buying. By virtue of the scale of their purchases, they can often obtain discounts and deals which are not available to the smaller buyer. Subsidiaries of multinationals can take advantage of world-wide deals and many public sector bodies often get hefty discounts. This often leaves the smaller commercial organization paying the highest price.

Nevertheless there are tactics which all organizations, including the smallest, can use to get better value for money. The following are strategies which can be used to drive a harder bargain. Some of these will always be applicable when buying IT.

- Find out as much as possible about a supplier's economics and use this information. If the purchaser knows the supplier's margins, this may help in gauging how much discount can be obtained. Service companies which sell time by the man-hour (such as software houses and consultancies) prefer block bookings for which they will give discounts.
- Use (or threaten to use) competitive bidding. This is an effective tactic, but it must be used judiciously. Continually threatening suppliers or making them continuously re-quote for business can be counterproductive in the longer term.
- Take advantage of first or advance customer offers. Some-times, when companies are trying to get a new product moving or to break into a new market, they are willing to buy market share. An astute purchaser can take advantage of this to get a good bargain. This can involve risk, but this need not be excessive – especially if it is a proven product for which a good supplier is seeking some local reference sites.
- Offer to be a reference site. This is a variant of the preceding tactic. It can be useful where new technology is being introduced or where a supplier wants a flagship site. Being a reference site can be a nuisance. It can mean a steady stream of the supplier's potential customers coming to look at the

purchaser's IT system, which can be disruptive as well as time consuming.

- Take advantage of loss leaders. Suppliers are often willing to use loss leaders to gain a foothold with a customer (see Case history 2.4). The skill here is to take advantage of this while still obtaining good value from the supplier in the longer term. With a good contract and careful management, a buyer can take advantage of the initial bargain without having to pay a premium later on.

- Use a consultant or systems integrator to do the negotiating. Aggressive negotiation can be inimical to a good long term relationship. A way around this problem is to employ a consultant to help in the negotiations. With two parties, it is possible to use 'hard man, soft man' tactics with the consultant playing for a hard bargain and the user being more willing to compromise or vice versa.

- Consider a long term agreement. Competitive bidding and tendering is expensive. Over time, a good IT supplier will expect to win around one competitive bid in every four. The cost of the three failed bids can be high and the supplier's margin on the successful bid must cover this cost. Where suppliers do not have to bid, they can sometimes be persuaded to pass some of this risk margin back to customers by way of a reduced price.

- Short-term timing. Many computer salesmen work on a commission basis. This is based on targets or quotas which have to be hit within certain time periods. As the end of year or quarter approaches, sales teams are often anxious to reach quota and deals can be struck. This normally requires that the purchaser has the finance available and can take the product. The latter is not always essential as the following case history reveals.

Case history 2.6: A virtual bargain

A manufacturing company was in the process of negotiating the acquisition of a large tranche of hardware (PCs, terminals, printers and disk storage units) from its supplier. The company was in no hurry for the equipment, it was to be used for a new software system which was still in development and would not be ready for several months. In addition it was coming up to Christmas and no-one was interested in installing a large amount of equipment until after the holiday break.

The hardware supplier's account executive on the other hand was anxious to close the deal. The supplier's year end was 31 December and although the salesman had made his quota for the year, the supplier company, which was a subsidiary of a large multinational, was, as a whole, significantly under quota. The pressure was on to make up the numbers.

Under the supplier's quota scheme, an order was not sufficient. Quotas were measured on cash received. This latter rule presented the salesman with another problem. Not all of the required products were in stock due to production delays in the factory. So, even if he could close the sale, he could not deliver any product.

What the supplier did have was plenty of linerboard boxes. The customer's Finance manager became aware of this and, assessing the supplier as a good risk, made the salesman an enterprising offer. If the supplier would give a 15% discount on the order, the purchaser would buy and pay for the product before the end of December. To comply with the customer's purchasing procedures, the supplier would deliver a large number of boxes which the purchaser would not open. Some time in February of the following year, the boxes would be quietly replaced with another set of boxes which would be opened to reveal the actual equipment ordered. The salesman accepted immediately and the deal was closed with both parties satisfied.

How the salesman dealt with this internally, the customer did not ask!

- Long-term timing. All IT companies, but particularly service companies, have cyclical business patterns. IT service companies tend to lead the economic cycle. When there is a downturn in the economy, they will feel it first. When there is an upturn, they are amongst the first to benefit as deferred IT expenditure plans are re-activated. Rises and falls in staff numbers during the cycle are a common phenomenon and daily charge-out rates and contract prices follow this pattern closely. If a purchaser can time the buying of required services to a low point in the IT economic cycle, it can often obtain good value for money.
- Joint development. Finally, for software, joint development can be considered. The advantages and disadvantages of this are discussed below.

All of the above tactics are useful. Many depend on timing and circumstance, but the shrewd purchaser will always be on the look-out for such opportunities. Whatever tactics are used, it is important that they do not damage the supplier relationship as this may not be in the purchaser's long-term interest.

2.9 Using formal tenders

The value of competitive tendering as a purchasing tactic has already been discussed. The process of formal tendering is widely used in the public sector, but is less common in the private sector. One reason for this is the time and effort involved which are considerable (see below). Nevertheless for major purchases, it makes good business sense to seek formal bids from a number of suppliers. Invitations to tender or requests for proposal (the distinction is defined below) are mandatory for public sector purchasing of anything beyond relatively modest levels of external expenditure. Seeking and evaluating formal bids is an expensive and time consuming process. Despite this, there are strong arguments for seeking competitive bids. These include:

- Cost effectiveness. Because it is competitive, this approach will usually lead to a more cost-effective solution. It will certainly give a good picture of market prices and the purchaser can judge the relative cost and value of the selected system.
- Information. It gives an overview of the market and the various possible solutions. It reduces the risk of missing opportunities arising from new technology or innovative approaches.
- Clear decision making. The submission of tenders and the need to compare like with like systematically introduces a clear procedure into the decision-making system. If the further discipline of explaining to unsuccessful suppliers why they did not get the business is included, it focuses the purchaser's mind on why it is rejecting a bid.
- Risk reduction. All purchasing involves risk and this increases with complexity and scale. Formal tenders are a useful risk reduction strategy.

Formal requests for proposals or invitations to tender may be open or restricted to a limited number of bidders. In an open tender a public advertisement and/or a web procurement site invites all qualified suppliers to bid.

The process involved for this type of formal purchasing needs to be understood in context. The steps in the full project/process are:

1 Specification of requirements.
2 Issuing and management of the Invitation to Tender/Request for Proposal.
3 Evaluation and selection.
4 Contract.

The second of these topics is considered here. The others are discussed in Chapters 6, 9 and 11 respectively. Seeking and evaluating formal bids is a project in its own right. A large invitation to tender, evaluation, selection and contract negotiation procedure will typically take four to six months and can take up to a year. A typical schedule might be:

Time	Activity
Week 1	Advertise tender
Weeks 1–2	Send out documentation to interested suppliers
Weeks 3–8	Meetings with suppliers
	Suppliers prepare submissions
Week 9	Receipt of bids
Weeks 10–11	Preliminary evaluation
	Shortlisting
	Informing suppliers eliminated at this stage
Weeks 12–13	Detailed evaluation of short list
	Clarification with suppliers of points of fact/detail
	Presentations from suppliers
Week 15	Tentative decision on winning bid
Weeks 16–17	Visits to reference sites
Weeks 18–19	Contract negotiations
Week 20	Contract signed

The above timescales are realistic for a moderately complex project (say £250 000 to £1 000 000 expenditure) involving hardware and software bids.

It is important to allow time for this process to be effective. Unless the requirements are simple, a *minimum* of four weeks should be provided for suppliers to prepare bids. Six or seven is better. EU regulations for public sector tenders specify that suppliers must be given a minimum response time of 52 days from the time the advertisement is first sent to the Official Journal.

2.9.1 Invitations to tender and requests for proposal

Formal bids fall into two broad categories:

- Invitations to tender. An invitation to tender (ITT), sometimes called a request for tender (RFT), asks suppliers to quote for a list of specified products or services. It is appropriate when the requirements are known and how they are to be met has been determined. Suppliers are not given discretion (or are given very little discretion) in what is quoted. ITTs are quite common in the purchase of hardware, consumables, basic support services (such as hardware maintenance) and off-the-shelf software.
- Requests for proposal. A request for proposal (RFP) is a more open-ended document which states the user requirement, usually in business rather than technical terms. Suppliers are invited to propose how they would meet this need. Responses to RFPs will be more varied and the price range can be correspondingly wide depending on how suppliers interpret the needs.

Broadly speaking the same procedures apply to ITTs and RFPs.

A ITT/RFP should contain the following:

- Any necessary background information. It is good practice to provide suppliers with background material on both the organization, the nature of its business/operations, its current IT systems and the equipment, software and/or system(s) being sought. This will assist the suppliers in preparing their tenders/proposals correctly and save time later in not having to repeat this information several times.
- The statement or specification of requirements. A clear specification of requirements is essential. If the specification of requirements is not clear, there is a distinct possibility that some or all of the tenders/proposals received will be inappropriate.
- The formal invitation to tender/proposal. Example 2.1 shows how to do this.
- Tendering terms and conditions. This is a formal statement of all instructions and any conditions applying to the tender. A common and simple approach is a letter backed up by a formal schedule. The following should be included in either the letter (as below) and/or the schedule:
  - the legal entity requesting the tender
  - a brief description of the goods being sought

Example 2.1: Invitation to tender

Date

Acme Computing Ltd.
21 The High Street
Chesham
Surrey

Dear Sirs,

Re: New Computer System for Example Trading Company plc.

You are invited to tender for the supply of hardware, systems software and local area networking for Example Trading Company plc (hereafter referred to as ETC or the Company). The new system will replace the existing systems currently in use in ETC.

Accompanying this letter are:

(1) A statement of requirements;
(2) Terms and conditions of this tender;
(3) The criteria which will be used to select the successful supplier;
(4) The required format for responses.

Three copies of the tender should be submitted in sealed, plain envelopes to:

Ms. Jane Doe
Project Manager
Example Trading Company
Example House
Manstead

to arrive no later than 5.00 p.m. on 25 June 200X

The successful supplier(s) will the one(s) who, in the view of the Company and its advisers, best meets the stated selection criteria. While this invitation to tender is made in good faith, the Company reserves the right not to choose the least cost tender and the right not to accept any tender.

The Company will not be responsible for any expenses or costs incurred by suppliers either in formulating their tenders or in making equipment or software available for demonstration or evaluation purposes.

All proposals in response to this document will be taken as contractually binding subject to the conditions in part (2) of the accompanying documentation.

The Company reserves the right to alter, update or amend any details contained in the document up to the deadline for submission of tenders.

Every effort has been made to ensure that the enclosed documentation contains all the necessary information for completion of tenders. If you require clarification of any aspect of the documentation, you may call Jane Doe at (01234–98765) extension 123.

Yours faithfully

A.N. Other
IT Manager

- the name, address and telephone number of the person in charge of the tender
- a contact name for further information (if different from the above)
- where the goods are to be delivered
- the place of delivery for the tender document
- the deadline for delivery of the tender document
- the number of copies of the tender documentation required (note it is a good idea to ask for one copy of the tender in loose leaf form to facilitate subsequent copying)
- payment terms and conditions
- for how long the prices quoted are expected to remain valid
- any conditions or regulations with which the supplier must comply. For public sector bodies, this may include the condition that a supplier has a tax clearance certificate and complies with certain EU regulations.

- Selection criteria. These are discussed in Chapter 9.
- The format for responses. A format for responses should be specified. This simplifies later comparison and evaluation. The format for responses should state the information required, how the information should be provided and the order in which it is to be provided. Above all, always ask for a management summary and a cost summary. The ITT should always stipulate that:
  - a summary of all costs (in one place!) be provided
  - all costs are clearly identified
  - one-off costs and continuing costs are clearly distinguished
  - where applicable, incremental costs are stated.

The evaluation of RFP/ITT responses is covered in Chapter 9.

2.10 Total outsourcing

Total outsourcing is the contracting out of all IT/IS services to a third party (the term total outsourcing is applied as the word 'outsourcing' is often used to mean partial outsourcing). In the past decade there have been many prominent outsourcing contracts signed, including companies such as BP and public sector bodies such as the Inland Revenue. The argument was broadly that 'Our company/local authority is not in the IT business. We don't clean our own windows or build our own buildings, why should we do our own IT?'.

In recent years there has been a reaction to this trend and the emergence of what is termed 'insourcing'. The strategic aspects of out- and insourcing and the financial implications are discussed in Chapter 3. This section deals with the advantages and disadvantages of outsourcing, the management of out-source suppliers and characteristics to look for in an outsource supplier

The advantages of outsourcing are:

- Less administration. Outsourcing eliminates a large amount of administrative work in paying salaries, recruitment, training, technology management, IT purchasing and so on.
- Better technology/competitive advantage. Because of their scale and their technical expertise, outsourcing suppliers should, in theory, have better technology and be able to keep it up to date more easily than the customer could.
- Lower costs. Because of their greater purchasing power and their size, outsourcing suppliers can achieve economies of scale which an internal IT unit may not be able to match. Expensive resources (such as wide area communications networks) can be shared with others.
- It enables the organization to 'stick to the knitting'. Relieved of the burden and problems of managing the IT function, management can concentrate on running the business. Valu-able management resources are freed up.
- Flexibility. IT services requirements can be turned on and off at will. If additional resources are needed for a temporary period, they can be purchased without the long-term commit-ment of hiring staff or the problems of managing consultants or contractors.
- One-stop shopping. The larger outsourcing suppliers can offer a comprehensive range of services either directly or indirectly.

A number of these advantages have been challenged. In particular, the cost advantages are not always as great as they may appear and, in many instances, outsourcing may actually cost more money than a well-managed internal IT department.

There are also disadvantages of outsourcing, some of which are a direct contradiction of the advantages listed above. Dis-advantages include:

- Loss of control. For an increasing number of organizations, IT is a strategic asset and a key part of the business. The advisability of having such a key asset run by a third party is open to question.

- Loss of flexibility. While there are gains in some types of flexibility, there are losses in others. For example, the outsourcing supplier may be using older technology and may be unwilling to upgrade it in the short-term just because one of its customers wants to change to a more modern environment.
- Longer-term costs. Signing a long-term IT contract with an outsourcing supplier can involve making a number of assumptions about the future direction of technology and of the purchaser's organization. A contract signed on the basis of today's technology and operations might be unsuitable or expensive in a number of years' time.
- High marginal costs. If the contract with the outsourcing supplier is for a fixed price for a predetermined level of service, additional services can be expensive.
- Transition problems. Personnel problems can arise if an internal IT department (particularly a public sector IT department) is passed wholesale to an outsourcing company. This can lead to a range of issues to be resolved from holiday entitlements to pension arrangements.
- Ownership of data. A particularly sensitive issue is ownership of data. This needs to be clearly defined in the contract.
- Protection of intellectual property. This needs particular care. See Chapter 11.

Research suggests that quite a number of outsourcing deals eventually fall through, and that when this happens it is expensive. So this is a strategy that needs to be contemplated carefully.

2.10.1 Managing outsourcing

Total outsourcing of all IT services is a major decision and the terms and conditions of an outsourcing contract need to be drawn up with particular care. The key issues involved are discussed in Chapter 11. For management of outsource suppliers, the following are some guidelines:

- Put in place appropriate internal IT resources. It is not desirable to abdicate all responsibility for IT to the outsourcing supplier. At least a skeleton IT staff should be retained in-house.
- Establish clear performance monitoring arrangements. Outsource contracts must contain clear performance commitments and guarantees. These need to be monitored and measured.

- Hold regular meetings with outsourcing supplier management. Senior management in the organization should take a close interest in IT whether it is internally or externally sourced.
- Monitor the supplier's security and 'Chinese walls'. Outsourcing suppliers may well be providing services to organizations in direct commercial competition. If an organization is in a position where effective use of IT is central to its competitive position, the security arrangements within the outsourcing supplier need to be watertight.

2.10.2 Selecting an outsourcing supplier

When selecting an outsourcing supplier the following should be taken into consideration:

- Range of services offered. As well as managing the running of the existing systems, these should include such services as system development, maintenance and strategic planning.
- Geographic spread. Suppliers should be in a position to provide local support where and when it is needed.
- Purchasing power/scale. This matters if cost savings are to be realised.
- Independence. It is important that the outsource supplier be truly independent from its parent and not a vehicle for selling more hardware to the customer.
- Suitable skills and technology. Outsourcing companies cannot be all things to all men. The nature of some outsourcing companies' personnel skills and technology expertise may match a purchaser's organization's needs better than others.
- Financial stability. Financial stability is desirable with all suppliers. For an outsourcing supplier it is essential. Financial failure of an outsourcing supplier could have catastrophic consequences.
- Flexibility. An outsourcing supplier needs to be flexible. If, for example, it does not have the best solution to a customer requirement, it should be willing to work with third party suppliers to deliver what is needed.

Outsourcing is not without its critics. Before totally outsourcing its IT, an organization should consider both insourcing and selective outsourcing approaches such as lead contracting. A full discussion of the wider implications of outsourcing is contained in Chapter 3.

2.11 Sources of supplier information

Finding out about a supplier or a potential supplier is important. Information on suppliers can be obtained from many sources. The following is a good list of such sources:

- The trade press (e.g. *Computer Weekly, Computing,* etc.). For serious comment avoid the hobby-type publications, which can be pretty superficial in their judgments and advice.
- Computer user associations. Most major products have user associations, although the same is not, unfortunately, true for service organizations.
- Software directories such as the *Computer Users Yearbook*.
- Value added networks such as the *Financial Times* databases, and Dun and Bradstreet.
- The world-wide web. The web is a great resource, particularly for comparing prices and finding out what is available. Be careful of comment, however, which is frequently lacking in objectivity. Some data, such as hardware benchmarks, are freely available on the web.
- Industry analysts. There are many organizations which sell research. These include organizations such as Datapro, Paine Webber, Xephon, Forrester Research, IDC, Gartner Group and several others.

There is much information freely available as well as much you can buy. Purchased research can be expensive, but well worth it if the investment is large.

3

IT costs and cost management

Various surveys over the years suggest that companies spend between four and seven percent of their turnover on information technology. Surveys of the financial services industry show up to one third of firms reporting that IT costs were over 20% of their cost base. It is not, therefore, surprising that IT and senior managers are perennially faced with the following five questions:

1 What exactly are we spending on IT?
2 Are we spending the right amount on IT?
3 Are we spending what we do spend in the right areas?
4 Are we getting value for money for what we spend?
5 How do we measure the effectiveness of IT expenditure?

In many of these surveys, 100% of respondents replied that value for money and effectiveness of IT spend were major management issues. The five questions above are addressed in this chapter and the two following chapters. This chapter is concerned with IT costs and specifically with the dynamics of IT cost growth, the components of IT cost and identifying and controlling semi-visible and invisible costs.

3.1 Are we getting value from IT?

The question of whether organizations are obtaining value from IT is a vexed one. IT value is one of the most controversial and often amongst the least understood of subjects in finance and business management. In recent years much research, debate and effort has gone into trying to:

- establish whether organizations are obtaining value for money from IT expenditure
- find ways of controlling IT costs
- find ways of reducing IT costs
- develop methods for assessing the real return on IT investments.

Efforts to do this have been hampered and/or complicated by a number of problems including:

- Senior managers often regard IT simply as an overhead expense and not as an investment on which there should be a return. This distorts management thinking, makes proper evaluation of IT expenditure difficult and leads to poor decision making.
- Inadequate understanding of the dynamics of IT cost growth.
- Inadequate understanding of the nature and scope of IT costs.
- Insufficient or inadequate cost information.
- Non-IT costs being classified as IT costs.
- Uncertainty about what the benefits of IT are.
- Lack of ways of, and data for, measuring benefits.
- Use of inappropriate evaluation methods.

Efficient and effective management of IT costs must address these problems. Intuitively most managers know that IT is essential. Despite this, many non-IT senior managers have the nagging feeling that while they have to spend money on IT, they don't like doing it and that it is poor value for money. IT managers are often on the receiving end of this perception.

Before embarking on an examination of costs, there are two important principles that must be stated at the outset. The first is that *achieving effective IT cost management is a process*. Although one-off savings on IT costs are often possible, in general there is no one magic solution to the problem of reducing or controlling IT costs. Control of IT costs is achieved through good procedures, proper management and suitable information systems used consistently over time. Secondly, a *key to successful cost management is to develop an asset view of IT*. Some organizations regard IT as an annual expense. Most IT, and in particular IT infrastructure, needs to be regarded as an asset and such IT expenditure should be regarded as a long-term investment. By viewing IT as an asset, it is easier for management to make correct investment decisions.

3.2 The dynamics of IT cost growth

IT costs sometimes seem to move in only one direction – upwards. A simple model for understanding cost dynamics is to break down IT costs into three headings:

1 Development (including enhancement). This includes specification, design, acquisition and/or development and implementation of new systems. Within a single project, this cost is a one-off.
2 Maintenance (including modification). Maintenance refers to the process of keeping existing systems in operation and up to date.
3 Production (including support and operational costs). This covers the day-to-day cost of running the systems.

Two useful rules of thumb generally borne out by experience for these three costs are:

1 Every £1 spent on systems development generates an average ongoing annual cost of £0.40 in maintenance costs and £0.20 in production costs over the following 5 years.
2 Maintenance costs tend to rise over time.

Three immediate consequences follow from the above rules of thumb. First, if development expenditure is constant, the level of IT expenditure over time will grow linearly. This simple mathematical fact lies behind much of the alarm at IT costs which are apparently spiralling out of control. Secondly, if the level of IT expenditure is fixed, a diminishing amount of expenditure will be on new systems. In fact, eventually all new development will cease as all of the existing budget will be used up in maintenance. Thirdly, if development cost is kept at a constant percentage of the IT budget, the IT budget will grow exponentially.

The best way to see these points is to use a series of simple examples. In these examples, the numbers have been kept small for clarity.

Example 3.1: IT cost growth – constant investment

A small engineering business currently has a steady annual turnover of £1.75 million, an annual ongoing IT expenditure of £60 000 and invests £20 000 in new systems each year. Its current cash expenditure on IT is therefore £80 000. Over 5 years its expenditure will grow as shown in Table 3.1.

Table 3.1 Constant investment cost growth (£'000s)

Heading	Year				
	1	2	3	4	5
Development	20	20	20	20	20
Maintenance	40	48	56	64	72
Operations	20	24	28	32	36
Total	80	92	104	116	128
Cumulative growth		15.0%	30.0%	45.0%	60.0%
Turnover	1750	1750	1750	1750	1750
IT as % of T/O	4.6%	5.3%	5.9%	6.6%	7.3%

Without any growth in the business, IT expenditure has risen from 4.6% to 7.3% of turnover.

This is illustrated in Figure 3.1.

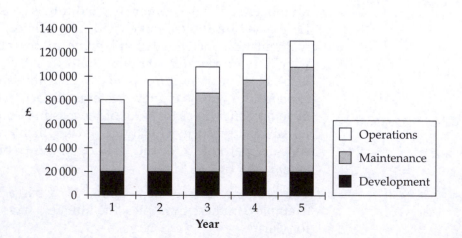

Figure 3.1
Constant investment

Example 3.2 shows what happens if the budget is limited to a fixed ceiling.

Example 3.2: IT cost growth – constant expenditure

Suppose now that the company decides to freeze IT expenditure at £80 000 per annum. The picture will then change as shown in Table 3.2.

Table 3.2 Constant expenditure cost growth (£'000s)

Heading	Year				
	1	2	3	4	5
Development	20.0	8.0	3.2	1.3	0.5
Maintenance	40.0	48.0	51.2	52.5	53.0
Operations	20.0	24.0	25.6	26.2	26.496
Total	80.0	80.0	80.0	80.0	80.0
Cumulative growth		0.0%	0.0%	0.0%	0.0%
Turnover	1750	1750	1750	1750	1750
IT as % of T/O	4.6%	4.6%	4.6%	4.6%	4.6%

Under this policy, the Company's investment in new systems tails off as maintenance and operations consume more and more of the budget.

This is shown in Figure 3.2.

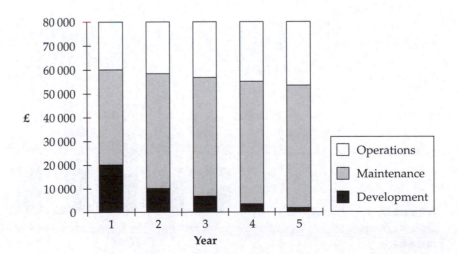

Figure 3.2
Constant expenditure

A third option might be to keep investment constant as a percentage. The impact of this is shown in Example 3.3.

Example 3.3: IT cost growth – constant investment percentage

Now suppose the company decides to maintain its development expenditure as a fixed percentage of IT expenditure (i.e. £20 000 as a percentage of £80 000 = 25%). Then the 5 year expenditure pattern would be as shown in Table 3.3.

Table 3.3 Constant investment percentage cost growth (£000s)

Heading	Year				
	1	2	3	4	5
Development	20.0	24.0	28.8	34.6	41.5
Maintenance	40.0	48.0	57.6	69.1	82.9
Operations	20.0	24.0	28.8	34.6	41.5
Total	80.0	96.0	115.2	138.3	165.9
Cumulative growth		20.0%	44.0%	72.8%	107.4%
Turnover	1750	1750	1750	1750	1750
IT as % of T/O	4.6%	5.5%	6.6%	7.9%	9.5%

This gives an exponentially increasing cost rising from 4.6% to 9.5% of turnover.

This is illustrated graphically in Figure 3.3.

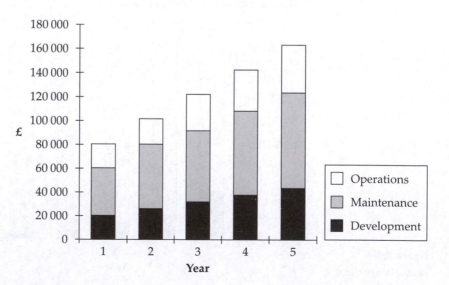

Figure 3.3
Constant investment percentage

There is nothing profound about the above calculations. The mathematics are simple. However, most senior non-IT management and even some IT management do not understand (or more likely have just never realized) the dynamics explicit in the above examples. IT costs seem to grow in a way that takes management by surprise. The result can be panic measures such as freezing expenditure, cutting expenditure arbitrarily or adoption of IT harvesting strategies (i.e. get the most out of what we have before we spend any more) all of which create risks, including the risk of incurring still greater expenditure in the longer term. Clearly IT costs cannot be allowed to rise faster than an organization can absorb them. To avoid this, understanding as well as good management is required.

3.2.1 Refinements to the simple cost model

The simple model described above can be refined to take account of three further effects. The first is *development knock-on*. This is the effect whereby new systems and developments tend to generate a demand for yet more development – be this enhancements or modifications. There are two reasons why this can happen. The first is structural change. The development changes the nature of the organization's operations in a way that in itself demands more IT resources. One of the most common causes of such change is an operating system upgrade which can necessitate additional disk and memory on PCs. Another effect is growth in user awareness This is particularly true where new systems are installed. For example, a new user enquiry system is installed to provide a number of reports. As soon as users realize what can be done, they immediately ask for more reports to be written using the package. This may lead to increased demand on the server which may require an upgrade to cope with the additional load.

A second refinement to take into account is *business growth*. If there is growth in the level of the organization's operations or business then IT expenditure will tend to grow with it. The following example illustrates this phenomenon (bearing in mind that the costs used are for illustrative purposes only).

Example 3.4: IT costs in a growing organization

Suppose now that Company A is growing at 10% a year. Assume that business growth is reflected in a pro rata growth in development, maintenance and operational IT costs. Over 5 years Company A's IT expenditure will be as shown in Table 3.4.

Table 3.4 IT costs in a growing organization (£'000s)

Heading	Year				
	1	2	3	4	5
Development	20.0	22.0	24.2	26.6	29.3
Maintenance	40.0	52.0	66.0	82.2	101.2
Operations	20.0	26.0	33.0	41.1	50.6
Total	80.0	100.0	123.2	150.0	181.0
Cumulative growth		25.0%	54.0%	87.6%	126.3%
Turnover	1750	1925	2117	2329	2562
IT as % of T/O	4.6%	5.2%	5.8%	6.4%	7.1%

Here IT grows as a percentage of total turnover, and cumulatively at 126%!

Graphically this can be seen more dramatically, as shown in Figure 3.4.

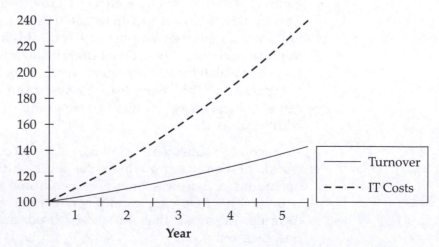

Figure 3.4
Growth in IT costs and turnover in a growing organization

Business growth can give rise to demand for new systems, thus giving a further twist to the cost spiral. For example, technology changes can leave an organization with no choice but to upgrade if only to keep up with competitors. Upgrades can give rise to two types of cost. An upgrade in itself can be expensive – particularly with development or packaged software upgrades where the upgrade path is not simple. This is not common in the PC world where software (and hardware) tend to be upwards-compatible. It is, however, an issue in the world of larger systems where, for example, major application software package upgrades can cause upheavals in the user base at regular intervals. An upgrade to one part of a system can lead to consequential effects elsewhere. Sometimes this can arise from internal organizational actions. Case history 3.1 illustrates this point.

Case history 3.1: A question of colour

A small research company that undertook economic analysis for business customers produced reports prepared by several authors/departments. These were printed by the respective departments following a company standard format. The various sections were then compiled centrally into one final document. The guidelines were tight so that the final collated product looked and felt the same throughout. The effort in final editing was therefore minimal.

Departments printed their final contributions using a specified resolution on inkjet printers which produced high quality colour, but was slow. Where multiple copies were requested, they usually ran off the second and subsequent copies on the much faster monochrome laser.

One of the departments decided that it would like to have all versions in colour so it bought a colour laser. This caused two problems. First, the other departments had to move to colour for additional copies, but also, because the colour quality on the laser was slightly different from that on the inkjets, the whole printing process had to move to colour laser. This involved buying several expensive machines.

To control IT costs it is essential to understand their dynamics. IT development expenditure will generate ongoing costs, and even where there is no development the costs of operations and maintenance grow over time. These insights can be used for more effective planning and costing of IT investment.

3.3 Identifying IT costs

Most IT costs are easy to identify, but some are not. There are various reasons why IT costs can be difficult to spot. These include IT goods and services which are purchased under other non-IT headings. IT costs can also be indirect and even hidden. To help to identify IT costs, it is useful to look at them from a number of different perspectives. The following three approaches provide frameworks for thinking about this issue.

One way to look at IT costs is to divide them into *hard costs and soft costs*. Hard costs are those which require a specific and direct payment. Mostly, but not exclusively, these will be to third parties (i.e. suppliers) or staff (wages, overtime, expenses, etc.). However, they could be from, for example, internal transfers between departments. Soft costs are not so easily identifiable because they are either non-cash costs and/or are indirect costs. They include learning time, disruption and the costs of a system failure.

A second perspective is to divide IT costs into *infrastructural and business unit costs*. Infrastructural costs include the cost of providing the framework within which the IT systems operate, i.e. things such as networks, network management systems, security, contingency planning and so on. Business unit costs are the costs of the business or functional applications. They include amongst other items end user computing, application packages, custom built applications and local support. There are some items where the distinction may not be clear (for example servers). A simple classification test is to ask, does the item provide a direct business function or not? The distinction between infrastructure and business unit costs is important when considering charge-back policies (see below) and IT investment decisions (see Chapter 4).

A third way to view costs is as *one-off or continuing*. In some organizations, the bulk of IT costs are one-off. One-off costs include most hardware, most software and some services. One-off purchases are best defined as items that do not normally need to be replaced or replenished at regular intervals or at intervals of less than a couple of years. Continuing costs include salaries and wages, licences, contract fees, insurance, etc. Most one-off costs give rise to continuing costs.

All three frameworks are useful when assessing whether all IT costs are being identified or not.

3.4 Managing hidden costs

Hidden costs are a major problem in IT. Hidden IT costs can be defined as costs which are not perceived at the time the expenditure is made and/or the IT department does not pay directly and/or for which the user does not incur a direct cash cost. Hidden costs may be semi-visible. Semi-visible (for want of a better term) costs are costs which are visible (which normally, but not necessarily, means they are explicit cash costs), but are either not recognized as IT costs and/or not measured properly and/or overlooked when costing a project or system. Hidden costs can also be invisible. These are costs which are perceived (for example, coded in the accounts) as being non-IT costs or are not measured (or are not separately identified) by the accounting system or are not easily measurable at all.

There is a number of costs that fall into the category of the semi-visible. The most important are:

- training
- maintenance
- support
- testing
- installation/implementation.

These costs and how they can be controlled are examined in the following paragraphs.

3.5 Training costs

Research has shown that the two of the most effective ways of reducing and/or containing IT costs are proper training and proper procedures. IT generates constant training requirements. The scope and cost of training may not always be immediately obvious. For example, if a new document management system is installed, then training will be required for users, support staff and administrators.

Training may consist of:

- externally attended courses
- externally provided courses given in-house
- computer based training (CBT) courses

- internal courses
- self-instruction from manuals or textbooks
- on-the-job training.

The first two of these, and possibly the third, incur a direct and visible cash cost. The cost of the third and fourth may or may not be identified by the accounting systems. The final two will almost certainly not be tracked as costs at all.

To compute the full investment costs of any training, it is necessary to include not only the cash costs but also the time-cost of the people attending the course, the productivity cost of their absence and the productivity cost in gaining familiarity with the new system.

There is a number of costing issues that ensue, as Examples 3.5 and 3.6 illustrate.

Example 3.5: Training cost

A company sends its database administrator (DBA) on a four-day course. The total cost of this is:

Cost of course	£1600
Cost of DBA's time 4 days @ £100 per day	£400
Cost of overtime for staff covering her absence	£200
Cost of additional time incurred by disruption to others because of DBA's absence	£250
Expenses and miscellaneous	£50
Total	£2500

This example is worthy of comment because it highlights a number of important costing issues. The organization is investing in the DBA's skills. If the database were a new system, this would be regarded as part of the implementation cost. However, if the database is an established system, most organizations will treat this as an expense and would not regard the DBA's salary cost of £400, for example, as a real training cost (some would not even regard it as a system cost).

The point being made in the example is the justification of the cost will be based on what causes this expense to be incurred.

In any assessment of return on IT investment, this must be included. Tracking such costs is also important if techniques such as charge-back are to be used.

The following, more complex example illustrates this point further.

Example 3.6: New database training programme

The following is a simplified description of a new database installation in a professional law practice. In this organization the average salary cost of the 12 professional staff is £25 per hour or £200 per day. The average cost of the support technician and the Database Administrator is £15 per hour or £120 per day. The support technician provides in-house training. Four key users will be sent on an external course. The remainder will be trained internally by the technician. Both user groups will also use self-instruction and on-the-job learning to bring themselves up to full productivity.

Using the same approach as above, the total training cost can be calculated as follows:

Technician training course (5 days)	1 person × £1000	£1000
Attendance at course	1 person × 5 days × £120	£600
DBA introductory course (3 days)	1 person × £900	£900
DBA advanced course (3 days)	1 person × £1050	£1050
DBA security course (2 days)	1 person × £600	£600
DBA course attendance	1 person × 8 days × £120	£960
External user course		
External user training courses (2 days)	4 persons × £600	£2400
Participants' time	4 persons × 2 days × £200	£1600
Internal user 3 day course		
Trainer time including preparation	1 person × 5 days × £120	£600
Materials		£200
Participants' time	8 persons × 2 days × £200	£3200
Self-instruction time	12 persons × 1 day × £200	£2400
On-the-job training		
Cost of support time	12 person days × £120	£1440
Cost of users' time	12 persons × 1 day × £200	£2400
Total		£19350

A more extreme view of this would be to extend the concept to opportunity cost. In this instance, the professional staff have a charge-out rate of £120 per hour. If this figure were to be used instead of £25, the total cost would rise to £54 780

A more accurate way to use opportunity cost is to allow for the probability of professional staff having work. Suppose this is 70%. Then the expected opportunity cost per staff member is then (70% × £120) = £84 per hour. Using this figure for staff time, the total cost is £40 956.

We can see from the above example that, no matter which measure is used, the cost of training is substantial and that not all of the costs are measurable in cash paid out. Some of the costs may be in income/profit foregone. Clearly, how staff are costed will depend on circumstances and how critical the work of the person(s) involved is. Where staff have to be replaced by temporary staff hired in to do their work, or where the staff are fee-earning (as in the above example) the cost is visible. In other circumstances it may be less easy to see.

It is an irony that training costs often need little control as most organizations underspend on IT training. During a recession, training is often the first item on the budget to be cut. During a boom, everybody is too busy to attend courses. Control apart, there are ways of maximizing the value for the training budget. The following strategies should be considered.

The first step is to determine what training is required. A useful device is to compile a skills matrix. This should be the skills required at different staff levels. The following is an example.

Example 3.7: Skills matrix

	DB Administrator	Programmer	Systems analyst
Database administration	Yes	No	No
SQL basics	Yes	Yes	Yes
SQL advanced	Yes	Yes	No
Database design	Yes	No	Yes
Object oriented design	No	No	Yes

A skills matrix can be extended to make a skills gap or skills shortage matrix, which can be used for determining training requirements.

Next, identify what is expected from each training course and decide the most appropriate form of training. This may vary from formal courses through self-instruction to on-the-job training. For each course there should be a clear set of objectives for the participant(s) and these should be checked carefully against the course objectives. This should include checking that the training methods employed are appropriate for developing the skills required. When this is done, an IT training budget can be assembled. This should be clearly distinguishable within any overall company training budget.

An important aspect of training cost management is timing. Newly acquired skills should be used as soon as possible. There are few more frustrating experiences in training than arriving back from a course to discover that it will be several weeks or months before one's new skills can be put into practice. IT training expenditure is often wasted in such circumstances. Try to avoid a policy which assigns people to training solely on the basis of their slack periods (however, see next point). Of course where training is generic or related to day-to-day work, it make sense to schedule training for periods of low activity.

Another way of keeping training costs down is to buy in bulk. Most training organizations are willing to run in-house courses or special sessions for customers. If an organization has ten people to send on a course on its new development language, it should be able to obtain a group rate or a fixed cost. For example, some training organizations will run a course for a fixed fee (say £5000) and allow the customer to send as many participants as the customer wishes (within reason). For some technical skills, such as programming, consider the use of computer-based training (CBT). CBT has been around for some time, but with the evolution of DVD technology interactive CBT is becoming increasingly effective and popular. CBT is efficient for certain types of training (such as programming and operational skills). The issue is often one of scale. CBT can be expensive if only one person needs to be trained, but inexpensive if ten people need to be trained.

For larger organizations, it may be worth building an in-house training capability. Training the trainer is one of the best ways of reducing training costs. By sending one person on a course and getting them to train everybody else when they return, considerable savings can be realized. For this to work the putative trainer must be competent and the organization must have suitable training facilities. The subject must, of course, be amenable to the type of training in question.

One of the most common forms of IT training is on-the-job training. This is an excellent method of training, but there is an illusion that it is cheap because it does not involve writing a cheque. On-the-job training is a valuable supplement to other training but as a total training strategy is it potentially expensive – especially if the person being trained makes mistakes that damage the business. Much on-the-job training also takes up the time of two people – the trainee and the guide.

Finally, never forget to negotiate on price. Like hotels and consultancy, training is a time-based product. Unsold course places are permanently foregone income and the marginal cost of additional participants is often low. While many larger training organizations are unbending on price, some organizations will negotiate – especially if the purchaser is offering to take up a number of places.

3.6 Managing maintenance and support costs

Maintenance is the process of keeping systems functional (as opposed to functioning). Maintenance covers:

- fixing of bugs in software
- fixing of hardware problems
- modifications to the software
- enhancements to the software
- data cleaning and checking.

Although they are often similar in scope, it is useful to distinguish between modifications and enhancements.

Modifications are small changes or additions to the existing system and are part of the routine expense of running the system. Modifications might include changing the size of a field in a database or changing the payroll to take account of tax changes announced by the Chancellor in the budget. They can be regarded as running costs. High modification costs are a symptom of one or more of the following:

- a dynamic business
- inadequate specification
- poor design
- inappropriate or old technology
- poor user discipline.

Enhancements are significant new features and are investments rather than expense decisions. Enhancements tend to be larger and require a greater effort. They should be regarded as capital costs. A high rate of unplanned enhancements is a symptom of one or more of:

- a dynamic business
- inadequate initial specification
- growing user awareness
- poor user discipline.

The distinction between modifications and enhancements cannot always be clinically defined and IT management will have to decide on a case-by-case basis into which category a particular expenditure falls.

The cost of maintenance may be external, i.e. when the work is carried out by a third party such as a software house or by consultants, or internal, i.e. done by IT and user staff. External costs are visible; internal costs are semi-visible. The organization knows that it is paying the staff, but often has little or no idea how much of their time is spent on this activity.

The first step in controlling maintenance costs is to understand where costs are being incurred. Tracking and analysing internal staff costs is fundamental. It applies in maintenance, support, system design and development, and in several other areas of IT activity. There are four ways of costing internal activity.

The first is to use a *time recording* system. Technically, this is relatively easy to do. All professional organizations operate on this basis. Time spent is recorded by staff on a timesheet (see Example 3.8) and analysed by activity according to a range of pre-determined codes. Usually time is recorded to the nearest quarter hour. There are many time recording systems available on the market for processing and analysing such data. There are also systems which use bar-coding and card-swipe technology to eliminate writing (and keying) up a paper timesheet. Analysing the resulting data needs to be done with care, see Example 3.9.

The advantages of this approach are that it provides detailed and accurate information on costs and it introduces a discipline into work patterns, making staff conscious of the time tasks really take. The drawbacks are that staff may resent it, especially in an organization where nobody else's time is recorded. Staff who are not used to such systems may feel that management is spying on them. It also costs time and money to administer. In order to make the data meaningful, the work done in the IT department has to be classified by project and/or activity. While professional organizations are used to this, it can be a difficult task for IT management in 'ordinary' organizations who have never tried it before. It is also difficult to enforce for non-IT/user staff. This may mean missing many hidden costs.

Example 3.8: Time recording form

Acme Ltd.

Time Sheet

Name   Week ending

Code		Description	Time	Cumulative	To Complete
Job	Task				

There are many job-recording and timesheet processing packages on the market which will process the above type of data.

Example 3.9: Job costing

The accounting systems and philosophy in organizations which are process-oriented may need to be adjusted to deal with job-costing systems. Job costing within an organization requires working out a rate per productive hour for all staff. This is not simply a question of dividing their salaries by the number of working hours or days in the year. It needs to take account of:

- cost overheads
- leave
- illness
- training
- time when there may be no work to do

and other 'non-productive' time. Management also needs to decide whether it wishes to try to recover the cost of all staff time or simply wants reasonably accurate indicative costs. Most of the time the latter is perfectly adequate and avoids having to have complex variance analyses and reconciliations. The following is a simple example.

Specialist programmers in an organization are paid a salary of £30 000. Overheads (social insurance, pension, other costs) add approximately one third to this, so their annual cost to the company is £40 000 each. Ignoring overtime, availability per programmer is calculated as follows:

Total hours	1880
Less holidays (4 weeks)	150
Less training (2 weeks)	75
Less provision for illness	30
Available hours	1625

Cost per productive hour = £40 000/1625 = £24.61

A job that will take 3 programmer-months will therefore cost (in programming time):

3 months × 21 days per month × 7.5 hours per day × £24.61 = £11 628

in programmer time. The total cost will include managerial time, user time, etc.

A variant on the above method requires staff to log time on *specific (but not all) activities*. The advantages of this approach are that it can yield good information about such operations and it is administratively simpler than full recording. It is also easier to get staff to cooperate and it is more suitable for end users. The disadvantage is that there is still a considerable administration requirement and it tends to be less accurate that the first method. Certain key information may also be missed or lost.

The third technique is to use a *survey*. Surveys have the advantage that as one-off exercises they can give a good snapshot of the current position. They also avoid most of the potential political problems with time recording. The drawback is that unless work patterns are constant, a sample will not be representative. Furthermore, it must be done properly which can mean a great deal of work for a one-off exercise.

A fourth approach is to ask staff to try to *self-analyse* where their own time has gone, if necessary by keeping private logs (some IT staff do this for themselves anyway). This has the great advantage of simplicity and, in the right circumstances, it can yield useful information. The obvious disadvantage is accuracy, or rather the lack of same. There is plenty of evidence that, even if staff are totally honest, their recollection and estimates of the time taken to do tasks can be way out.

Accurate knowledge of maintenance costs is essential to effective planning of IT and to reducing IT expenditure. Rational decisions on IT systems and proposed expenditure cannot be made without a good understanding of current costs. Such costs do not have to be known with absolute precision. It is better to have reasonably accurate costs that are easy to calculate and understand than convoluted costing systems which cause political problems. Several of the cost-reduction strategies outlined below including replacement can only be assessed if accurate information is available. IT management should therefore take steps to understand where all IT staff time is used and to compute accurate maintenance and support costs for all systems. To do this requires accurate recording of all external costs, sufficiently detailed analysis of internal costs and correct allocation of those costs to systems, applications and users.

For this reason, both the accounting and internal time-tracking systems must be adequate. This means that the accounting system (i.e. the account code) should be capable of analysing IT costs adequately and, in particular, be able to handle project costs. It is not always practical in organizations not based on a fee-charging/time-recording system to use the accounting system to allocate individual staff costs over a number of account headings except by using an allocation method, and this is difficult to do accurately for tasks such as maintenance. It can, however, be used for costs where staff are dedicated to a particular system or business unit.

One solution to this problem is to institute a charge-back system (see below).

The tracking and costing principles set out for maintenance can be applied in the same way to support activities and costs. Support staff help users in anything from how to use applications systems and helplines to installing new PCs. High support costs can be symptomatic of problems such as:

- poor implementation
- inadequate training
- inadequate documentation
- poorly designed systems
- unreliable systems
- poor support systems
- lack of self discipline by users.

Some support costs are clear. For example, in larger organizations, the help desk or the desk-top publishing may be separate cost centres and thus visible. Other parts, however, may be semi-visible. Examples of the latter include time spent by operations, maintenance or development staff in working with users in helping them out. Support costs should be distinguished from maintenance tasks.

3.7 Testing, installation and implementation

Testing, installation and implementation of systems can be another semi-visible cost. One reason for this is that a large part of the testing of a new system is often undertaken by users. It is important to identify this time as it represents part of the IT investment cost in a new system. In terms of workdays, user testing can be a multiple of IT staff and supplier time combined. Users may be involved in developing test packs or in any of unit, system or performance testing. They may also carry out an acceptance test. Good costing will incorporate testing time into the overall investment cost.

Implementation of systems almost invariably involves disruption to normal business operations. This may include transitional tasks such as parallel running, data conversion and the physical disruption of moving. Ideally, time spent on these activities should be logged by users. These costs usually only occur where a new system is being installed or a system is being enhanced. In these circumstances, they are investment costs and should be regarded as such.

Not all implementation costs are investment costs, as Case history 3.2 shows.

Case history 3.2: Data conversion – the hidden costs

During the implementation of a new system, the data conversion cost estimate often overlooks the cost of correcting problems in the existing data. This can be a significant cost where data is being converted from a manual or an older system where the validation controls were weak. The following is a pertinent example.

A professional organization was implementing a new, state-of-the-art membership system to replace an ageing computer-based system they had used for almost 10 years. A special program had been written to covert the data into a format suitable for the new package.

After the conversion program was run, an attempt was made to load the data into the new system and the validation rules on the new system rejected 80% of the incoming records as breaking the organization's business rules. On inspection of the data, it was found that, because of lax controls in the old system, users had systematically bent the rules as a result of which there were many inaccuracies and inconsistencies in the data.

A two-person team was set to work to clean up the data. It took them nearly three months before the new system would accept the last item of data as correct.

The cost of correcting the standing data is not an investment cost. It is a cost that is attributable to the old system and a running cost.

Implementation and testing costs, like training, maintenance and support are all real IT costs. They may be investment or expense costs, but they should be properly identified and tracked.

3.8 Invisible costs

There is a number of invisible costs incurred in IT. These are difficult to track down and difficult to put a value on. That does not make the costs any less real. The following is a list of such costs, their potential impact and strategies that can be used to control or reduce them.

Learning curves are time spent becoming familiar with a system (new or existing). During this time there may be a loss of productivity. It is not unusual for new operators to drop to 50% or less of normal productivity when adapting to a new system or product. Mistakes will also be made which may add to costs. Proper training and support is the best way to reduce learning curve costs.

Ineffective use of systems can create all sorts of invisible costs. An everyday example of this is staff who do not understand basic facilities on their word processor. Such minor inefficiencies add up. They may be small for any individual, but over a large number of people and a long period they can be significant. Here again properly timed training is the key. Also, consider having a skilled user review use of the system from time to time. It is surprising how, with a few simple tips, many users' productivity can be increased. Where appropriate set strict standards of usage and enforce them rigorously. Case history 3.3 is all too typical.

Case history 3.3: The cost of non-compliance

In a university department, all of the academic staff did their own typing using the same sophisticated word processing package. As many documents (such as examination papers), were written by more than one author, the departmental secretaries set standards for all (margins, fonts, line spacing, numbering, etc.).

Unfortunately, a couple of the staff felt that the secretaries were not taking full advantage of the advanced features of

---

the software and continually insisted on using features which nobody else used. Other members contended that they did not have time to learn the more basic techniques necessary to use the standard. The result was that merging documents was a nightmare and over the year dozens of hours were wasted while documents were brought to standard.

It took several years and much frustration and wasted time for the department to finally realize that there were virtues in all pulling together.

Inefficient systems are a common source of hidden costs. Systems can be inefficient for a number of reasons, the most common one being poor design. Where the computer system does not match the way the user or department works, then time is wasted while the user works around the system limitations – usually with the aid of enormous spreadsheets. The solution to this is often the application of common sense. For example, making sure that input screens and forms match. It is also important to review processes and workflow. If it is easy and cost effective, change workflow to match the systems. Otherwise consider modification or replacement of the system.

Poor system performance can lead to significant invisible (although occasionally all-too-visible) costs. One reason that these costs are hard to identify is that they are made up of hundreds of small delays. For example, a slow laser printer will have a steady stream of people standing by it during the day, waiting for it to finishing printing somebody else's work. If, on average, there is someone waiting by the printer for 2 hours of each day, this will cost 62 workdays per year or £8–10 000 at an average staff cost of (say) £30 000 p.a. Apart from loss of productivity, problems from under-performing systems include unnecessary overtime, user frustration and poor customer response and service. Systems which are under-powered should be replaced. It is a false economy to try to 'harvest' value from such systems.

Inappropriate systems are use of a product for an inappropriate purpose. Amongst the worst offenders here is so-called end user software. For example, using a spreadsheet as a database may work, but is likely to be inefficient. Problems often arise because users themselves are not aware of the alternatives. An associated problem is where users try to solve every computing problem themselves using the same tool. Amazingly, large organizations sometimes depend on such end user technology for key operational systems. This also gives rise to risks whereby critical information such as product pricing, customer analysis or costing are based on ad hoc and inadequately designed systems. All of this results in staff wasting their time and the organization's money. Using inappropriate software can also create business risks which can lead to high costs. To prevent this, there should be a periodic audit of all applications in the organization. Users should be policed.

Over specification can also incur unnecessary expense. Systems which are far more powerful or contain far more features than are required to do the job often end up wasting time and money. Costs here include not only additional capital expenditure on unnecessary systems, but distraction of users with features that are not relevant to the tasks they have to do. A good example is modern word processing which entices users to play around with fonts and formats and can thus actually reduce productivity when compared with older text-based systems. While it is better to err on the side of over- rather than under-specification, systems need to be specified appropriately.

Unnecessary duplication (re-inventing the wheel) is another common problem. Here time and money are wasted in doing the same thing twice (or even more times). This generally happens because people are not aware that somebody else has already done this. This can be ameliorated by better communications between users. Some organizations have an IT bulletin. Others use e-mail, a bulletin board or an intranet to inform people what is happening in the IT scene. Above all, discourage the 'not invented here' syndrome.

Non standard systems can lead to a variety of small and sometimes not so small inefficiencies. For example, when systems are not standardized there are conversion costs when data or files need to be transferred between them. Other costs include additional training costs and impediments to staff mobility. Standardization has drawbacks, but it saves money.

Poor ergonomics, i.e. poorly designed workplace or systems, poor lighting and badly designed furniture lead to indirect costs. Staff working in poor conditions tend to be less productive. Problems can vary from increased inaccuracy in data entry to more illness and days lost from work to problems such as repetitive strain injury.

Inappropriate use of systems occurs when staff use systems to do work that is not appropriate to their job. Common examples are senior executives doing their own printing and non-IT staff developing complex IT applications. The cost impact of this is subtle, but can be substantial (see Example 3.10).

Example 3.10: Super typists?

The following is a long-standing debate, but still relevant today.

Should senior managers do (or be allowed to do) their own typing?

An issue that IT management (and/or other management) sometimes has to confront is should executives be allowed to type their own letters and reports? This is a political as well as a technical and financial question. When senior staff become programmers and typists, a number of costs are incurred without any corresponding payback. Consider a middle ranking executive who chooses to do his own typing:

Executive

Gross salary	£80 000
Hours worked p.a.	2000
Cost per hour	£40.00
Typing speed words per minute (wpm)	40
Typing speed adjusted for corrections, wpm	25
Cost per page typed (400 words)	£10.67

Professional typist

Gross salary	£16 000
Hours worked p.a.	1800
Cost per hour	£8.88
Typing speed wpm	100
Typing speed adjusted wpm	80
Cost per page typed (400 words)	£0.74

A difference of £9.93 per page!

Against this must be set the time that the executive would take to get the letter ready for the typist (if, say, it was hand-written) and the advantage of using word processors for 'first thoughts' writing or 'brain dumping'. Unless the executive is a good typist, using a dictating machine may be a far more efficient use of his or her time. While in theory the total cost could be broadly similar, in practice, executives often waste time on formatting, fonts, etc. which drives up the cost even further.

One company addressed this issue by issuing an edict that only staff who had attended a formal course in typing and achieved certain speed and accuracy targets would be allowed to use word processors!

3.9 Charge-back

A seemingly simple and powerful way to encourage cost-effective IT usage is to charge for it. This process is known as *charge-back*. Charge-back is controversial, not because it is considered a bad idea, but because it is often exceedingly difficult to devise a system which simultaneously is fair, encourages users to use IT productively and discourages users from using IT unproductively.

These difficulties have been considerably amplified by the trend towards distributed processing where it is increasingly difficult to find simple measures of resource usage, although some modern network management tools are going some way towards solving this problem.

Despite the difficulties, charging users for the cost of IT is desirable for several reasons.

- It ensures that users fully understand the cost of their IT usage. It is a basic economic law that people do not tend to value goods that carry a low cost or are free, until such time as they are withdrawn or have to pay for them.
- It encourages effective use of IT and sensible IT spending. An immediate corollary of the previous point is that, faced with the cost, users will tend to concentrate their minds on spending money on IT where they really need it.
- It focuses users on service quality. When they have to pay for a service, users will be more aware of the quality of the service that they are receiving.
- It focuses attention on the IT department's efficiency. Because they are paying for the service, users will be more conscious of the efficiency of the IT department in delivering that service cost effectively. This should have a beneficial effect on the IT department's performance.
- It ensures that IT department is not taken for granted. IT services are often taken for granted and ignored until they fail to deliver. By highlighting the cost of IT, a charge-back system will remind users and management of the contribution IT makes to the business.

Charge-back has a number of potential disadvantages. These disadvantages tend to occur where the charge-back system is poor or is used in special circumstances (for example, where an organization is trying to encourage reluctant users to overcome their fear of technology). The risks include:

- It may discourage users from using IT. This may happen even when such usage is cost-effective from the organization's and even the user's viewpoint. Users can be quite irrational about IT costs.
- If it is not perceived to be fair it can give rise to internal battles. Where a user department feels that it is bearing a disproportionate cost, it may become aggrieved resulting in counterproductive poor relationships and ill will.
- If it is poorly designed, it may encourage waste. This can easily happen where, for example, the marginal cost to one user of additional resource usage is borne by all users.
- There is an administrative overhead. Logs and records must be kept. Systems must be in place to account for the internal transfers created. Time recording may be required.
- It can lead to users looking elsewhere for service. If users perceive that the IT service is too expensive or inefficient, they may argue that, if they have to pay for it anyway, they should have the right to use external suppliers. This can occur even where the use of an external supplier is a cost to the organization as a whole.
- Users may not understand the system. Charge-back allocations can depend on complex formulae incorporating processor usage, network usage, disk storage, staff time and so on. This can be difficult to explain and can lead to protracted discussions on the equity of the system used.

Despite the drawbacks, there are considerable merits in charge-back systems. If a charge-back system is to be implemented, its purpose must be to induce users of IT to behave in a rational and cost-effective way. It is easy to reduce IT costs by charging users large amounts for the service, but this defeats the purpose of the system.

3.9.1 Different approaches to charge-back

There are four approaches to passing IT costs to users:

1 Cost recovery (whole or partial).
2 A profit centre approach.
3 Insourcing.
4 Outsourcing.

The second and third items on the above list are similar. Although there are some differences, they will be regarded as being the same. Outsourcing is dealt with separately below.

● Cost recovery sets out to recover some or all of the cost of IT operations from users. To do this a cost allocation and/or charging mechanism is employed. While this is an internal accounting exercise, the costs to user departments are real. Cost recovery tends to be less politically contentious (or dangerous) than a profit centre approach. It should lead to more effective use of systems and it can be quite flexible. Where necessary, awkward issues can be avoided by designating certain costs as a centrally absorbed overhead which is not charged out to users. On the other hand, exact recovery of costs is difficult to achieve. Where cost recovery is partial, users may waste the non-charged centrally funded resources.

● The second approach is profit centre/insourcing. This is where the internal IT unit is treated as an organization within the organization. It seeks to run on a break-even or a small profit basis. Insourcing contracts are often arrived at by allowing the internal IT department to quote against an external provider. If insourcing is to work, it is best that the IT department be run on a profit-making basis. The advantages of a profit centre approach are that, like hanging, it concentrates the mind of IT management wonderfully and provides a clearer set of goals. In so doing, it encourages IT departments to be efficient because if their prices get out of line users will go elsewhere. On the negative side, users may object to an internal service making a profit at their expense and, of course, it invites comparisons with external suppliers. If the service has to be paid for, then internal IT should compete with outside vendors. This in itself is not a bad thing, but it may not be in the organization's overall interests if internal resources are under-used as a result.

3.9.2 Designing a charge-back system

Before outlining how to design a charge-back system, it is worthwhile reviewing the issues that must be addressed. The central requirement in charge-back is determination of the basis on which IT costs are allocated to users. Direct costs are straightforward, although even here there may be some complications. This is particularly true of central and infrastructure IT costs. For example, if a department acquires a server, users will accept the cost of the server because they can relate the product to the cost. When that server is connected to the network, they will accept the cost of the network card and the local cable. However, when IT management sends them a bill for network overheads and administration or central server support, they may balk. This leads to difficult questions. Consider the following.

- A company spends £100 000 in installing a new network system. Initially it is intended that the system will support 200 users but for the first year only 20 users will be connected. How much should each of the initial users be charged?
- A company has a hot-line support team of five people. Together, they cost £150 000 in salary and other costs per year. The company has 300 computer users in seven departments Some users use the support service all the time, others hardly at all. Over 50% of the calls come from two departments. Should the company charge departments on a per head or on a usage basis?

Poor charge-back policies can lead to behaviour which is counterproductive from the organization's viewpoint while perfectly logical for the user. This must be avoided. To do this requires planning, research and careful implementation.

3.9.3 Characteristics of a good charge-back system

A charge-back system should have the following characteristics. It should:

- encourage user behaviour which is optimal from an organizational perspective
- be fair
- be efficient
- be flexible.

With these principles in mind, the following paragraphs outline how to develop a charge-back system.

Charge-back is concerned with recovery of IT costs. For this purpose, costs usually included are:

- hardware
- software
- IT staff
- IT management
- licences, etc.
- security, back-up, insurance, etc.
- contractor and other third party costs (such as internet service providers)
- consumables.

The first step in setting up a charge-back system is to classify these IT costs under three headings.

Infrastructure. These are core services, host computers, servers, networks, communications systems and system software. It includes costs such as back-up, contingency and general IT management which benefit all users. The key characteristics of infrastructure costs is that they are used by all or nearly all users at some time, although the level of usage may vary by user. It is important to differentiate infrastructure costs which serve all users and services which serve only one user or user group (see below).

Infrastructure policy will normally be based on IT strategy and needs to be tightly defined. The policy should state what items are considered to be infrastructure costs as well as infrastructure standards. Users who require non-standard equipment should be charged the marginal cost of meeting their requirements. Such costs should be classified under application or direct user costs (see below). This avoids a major weakness of many charge-back systems whereby a request for a specific feature by one user is paid for by all users. For example, suppose an organization has decided that the standard server operating system will be Unix. A user who requires a Windows server will then be charged with the full cost of acquiring, installing and supporting the Windows server. In effect, this becomes a direct cost for that user.

Some organizations decide that infrastructure costs will not be charged out. Like the national road system, the cost is borne out of general expenditure. This is certainly simpler than allocating out such costs, but it requires good management to ensure that investment in infrastructure is at the right level.

Applications. These are costs which are specific to an application of the system. They may include:

- application software costs
- licence costs
- support and maintenance costs
- development or modification costs
- application-specific hardware, e.g. specialist printers, high speed scanners.

Some applications, e.g. e-mail, may be universally used. These should be classified under infrastructure costs. Applications costs refer to costs which are specific to a defined or definable group in the organization, for example, the sales forecasting system or the master production scheduling system. These are costs which, by definition, can be associated with a specific cost centre or centres.

A variant of this are systems which are used by 'horizontal' groups rather than by organizational units. With the growth of integrated/enterprise systems, this type of charge-back has become more complicated as it becomes more difficult to determine who uses what.

Direct user costs. These are costs that are solely incurred by one user or cost centre. These include personal computers, departmental printers, local systems support and so on.

3.9.4 Allocating infrastructure costs

Direct costs are easily assigned to users. However, with infrastructure and application costs there are problems to resolve. For each of these categories a different approach is required.

Where it is decided to charge for infrastructure, the basis of charging should be usage. Infrastructure costs are, by definition, shared costs. This should include usage of processors, networks, disk storage, archive storage and support. The simplest and fairest way to allocate infrastructure costs is to calculate a periodic standard charge as:

System cost / Projected level of usage

Level of usage may be measured in different ways including CPU usage, network traffic or staff costs of support. The projected level of usage is the normally expected level of demand for the service. Thus, for example, if the total network cost for the month is £2000 and the average traffic is expected to be 500 GB, then the standard charge is:

£2000/500 = £0.40 per GB.

Similarly, if the support centre employs three staff at a monthly cost of £6000 and the IT department expects them to spend a total of 500 man hours during the month working on user problems, then the standard charge is:

£6000/500 = £12 per hour.

Users are measured on and charged at the standard rate. Obviously, it will only be in a rare month that the actual network traffic or hours come out at, or even close to, the projected usage. In this case there will be a variance, which may be positive if usage is greater or negative if usage is lower than the projected level. If the cost and projected usage figures are accurate, over a long period (say a year) the cumulative variance should be small.

There are several advantages to this standard costing approach:

- users are charged pro rata with their level of usage
- users cannot play 'beggar my neighbour', i.e. incur expense for which other users have to pay
- users totally control their own costs
- services which are particularly heavily or lightly used are highlighted. This can, for example, show up services which are providing poor value for money.

The only drawbacks are that this system requires the IT department to decide and implement a suitable basis of usage measurement and, of course, to project usage using that basis.

As noted above it is essential that cost drivers be clear. Where one user or department generates an IT cost that would otherwise not be incurred, then that user should bear the full cost of the service. Case history 3.4 is an example.

Case history 3.4: Special requirements

Company G ran a complex distributed IT system in its main office with many local area networks linked together. The central infrastructure costs, including back-up and off site storage of back-up, were absorbed centrally and not charged out to users.

After a security review, one department decided that it needed a 'cold site' disaster recovery service, i.e. it needed a separate computer system set up some distance from the company's offices, ready to be used in the event of a disaster such as a fire at the main computer site. None of the other user departments felt the need for such a service. They had a back-to-back arrangement with another company to share computer services in the event of a disaster and this was satisfactory for them.

> The cost of the cold site, including office rental, equipment, maintenance and support was estimated at £37 000 per annum. Although, in the case of a disaster, all users stood to benefit from the cold site, they were unwilling to share in the cost.
>
> It was therefore agreed that the department requiring the cold site would bear the full cost of the system. However, in the event of a disaster and a move to the cold site, it could recover some of this cost by charging other departments for its use.

3.9.5 Alternative approaches to infrastructure cost allocation

Sometimes it is not possible to measure usage of the system. This may be because an organization does not have the facilities or because there are insufficient resources to carry out the necessary administrative work. In these circumstances, infrastructure costs can be allocated on a number of other possible bases including the number of users, the number of workstations or the number of attached devices. None of these are perfect but they can give a rough approximation of usage in some circumstances.

3.9.6 Allocating application and direct costs

Application costs are for software and support of software applications used by more than one user and/or applications specifically designed for a particular user. Examples are:

- sales order processing
- payroll
- accounting systems
- personnel systems

and so on. Where an application is used by a single department, clearly the cost should be allocated to that department. The issue of whether that cost is in turned passed on to other departments should be a separate question for the user department concerned. For example, the cost of the payroll system will be borne by the Finance Department. The fact that every Department in the organization benefits from the payroll is not an issue that the charge-back system should try to handle. Where an application is used by virtually all departments, it should be considered as an infrastructural cost and charged for accordingly. Direct costs can and should be directly charged to users. If a user purchases a memory upgrade for her PC, then she or her department should be billed with that cost.

3.10 Outsourcing

Outsourcing has become a major issue in IT cost management and there are many good books available on the topic. The following is a summary of important issues and factors to bear in mind when looking at the possibility of outsourcing IT.

The first thing to be aware of with outsourcing is that its effectiveness is critically dependent on the outsource contract. Outsourcing contracts are complex. Some of the issues involved are touched on in Chapter 11. Outsourcing bids should be the subject of a formal Request for Tender which is carefully thought out and rigorously evaluated.

Secondly, and despite what the hyperbole would have you believe, an outsource supplier is not a true business partner. The Boeing corporation use the concept of 'working together' to describe such relationships. This is a better notion than partnership. The outsource vendor's profit is made at the expense of the customer. While such suppliers may provide an excellent service, they will taking a margin for profit and risk. It is a mistake to regard them as partners as their interests may not always be the same as the customer's.

Thirdly, outsourcing may impose constraints on the business. The commercial imperatives that drive the supplier may not be the same as those for the customer. If, for example, a number of customers share resources (be these hardware, software or people), then a decision by one customer to change strategy may be difficult for a supplier to accommodate. It may not be cost-effective for it to support one customer who wants to be different.

Fourthly, outsourcing may limit opportunities for competitive advantage. Unless the outsource vendor is a 'captive' supplier, i.e. the user is his only customer in fact or in effect, then it may be difficult to make the type of strategic moves that will give the purchaser a major competitive advantage. How feasible such moves are will depend very much on the flexibility of the supplier.

Fifthly, deviations from normal operations can be expensive. Outsource contracts make a large number of assumptions about levels of service, long-term requirements and strategic direction. Contracts will allow for additional services, but these are often at a high marginal cost, and often at prices which are well above open market rates.

Sixthly, outsource contracts are long-term and can become expensive over time. Outsourcing contracts are typically for five to ten years. It is difficult to foresee the direction of technological change over that time period and unless the contract is well designed, the customer can find itself locked into an expensive solution.

3.10.1 Guidelines for outsourcing

When outsourcing, the following guidelines should be adopted.

Decide the extent to which the IT systems are to be outsourced. It may make sense to use selective outsourcing. Candidates for this include:

- mainframe/minicomputer/server operations
- data centres
- system design and development
- hardware maintenance (normally outsourced)
- end user software support
- software maintenance
- Certain software applications (e.g. payroll).

Draw up a detailed statement of requirements. This needs to be thorough and carefully worded. See Chapters 6–8.

Issue a formal request for tender/proposal to a number of suppliers. Formal evaluation techniques should be used to select the winning bid (see Chapter 9).

Consider carefully any long term business plans. These will need to be reflected in the contract. In negotiations with any potential supplier, assess how effective they are likely to be in developing innovative or strategic IT applications.

Invite the internal IT department to bid against the outsource vendors. This should be done on a level-playing-field basis. The internal department should be allowed to use its natural advantages (system knowledge, lower profit expectations) and given the opportunity to overcome its possible natural disadvantages (overstaffing, poorer management structures, etc.). It should also be allowed to put forward any restructuring and/or downsizing proposal as part of its bid. In other words, do not compare current internal costs with proposed external costs, compare proposed internal costs with proposed external costs.

Consider carefully the flexibility and marginal costs. It is important that the purchaser is not bound into unnecessarily restrictive behaviour. An outsource supplier may not be able to provide all services or even the best of any service. The purchaser should have some flexibility to select specialist or 'best of breed' services from elsewhere if it wishes.

Outsourcing has some powerful attractions. However, it is not an unmitigated good and has several drawbacks. Before outsourcing, the full range of benefits and disadvantages should be carefully weighted up. For many organizations, the experience of outsourcing is not as rosy as many media reports have made it out to be.

3.11 IT asset statements

A useful (and often first step) in managing IT finances is to prepare an IT asset statement. The purpose of building an IT asset statement is twofold. Firstly to establish exactly what the current investment in IT is and secondly, if it does not already exist, to compile an inventory of IT assets. Many companies do not have a central register of even IT hardware.

An IT asset statement is one contribution to putting IT's role in an organization into perspective. The scale of IT investments can easily be underestimated, especially with the growth of end user computing. Case history 3.5, though it took place many years ago, illustrates this point.

Case history 3.5: Unseen IT investments

In the early 1980s, around the time PCs became affordable in large numbers, a moderately sized insurance company had a mainframe computer system supported by an IT staff of 20 including management, analysts, programmers and support staff. For some time, IT management had been aware that there was a continuing steady growth in the

---

number of stand-alone PCs in the organization, but because it was focused on the central systems and had a substantial backlog of work, IT management tended to ignore the PCs on the grounds that they were departmental expenditure and distracted users from adding further requests to the backlog. In response to a request from general management, they had assigned a junior member of staff to support the PC population on a half-time basis (i.e. half of his time was dedicated to PC user support).

Matters came to a head when an underwriter was (literally) hit by a bus shortly before Christmas one year. He had written a quotation system on a PC using a popular end user tool, but there was neither documentation nor user instructions to be found. As the system had become a key tool in the Department, there was a certain amount of panic and the IT department had to throw in considerable resources to get the system back into operation (with the aid of a couple of visits to the hospital!).

Prompted into action, the IT department decided to survey the overall position. To put this in perspective, at the time, the two mainframes they possessed had 120 terminals and 5 gigabytes of disk (a moderately large system at that time). To their horror, IT management discovered that the organization had somehow acquired 80 PCs with a cumulative disk space of just over 2.5 gigabytes and that the total investment in PCs (including software) was approaching 60% of that of the central systems.

They decided fairly quickly that a junior staff member for a half-day a week was rather less than an adequate response and took action to establish proper controls over and support for all non-central systems.

An IT asset statement is made up of four parts:

1 Hardware.
2 Software.
3 Infrastructure.
4 Data.

The asset statement does not normally include intangibles such as staff skills or expertise, although it may be appropriate to include these under certain circumstances.

An IT asset statement is not intended for the Annual Report or the auditors. It does not need to be absolutely correct. However, it should be sufficiently accurate to be useful. The steps in preparing an IT asset statement are as follows.

The first step is to prepare an inventory of *hardware*. Many organizations do not keep such an inventory. If the organization does not have one, it should be compiled. If the organization is small, a spreadsheet or simple PC database package can be used for keeping the list. For larger organizations there are special packages available. Once the list has been prepared, it should be kept up to date.

Next, estimate the value of each component. This information is for internal management, not for the financial accounts, so it should be done realistically and need not necessarily comply with the company's formal accounting policy. For example, PC hardware loses value rapidly. Some organizations take an aggressive view and expense PCs at the time of purchase. This does not mean that they are worthless the day after they are purchased. There are four options for this valuation:

- The book value. This is appropriate if accounting policies are based on realistic value write-off and not either deliberately aggressive or conservative.
- Replacement cost. This is accurate if the machine is still fairly new. However, most older equipment is unlikely to be replaced by the same machine today so this valuation may not be meaningful.
- Market value. With some hardware, this is reasonably realistic.
- Subjective value to the business. If none of the above methods is satisfactory, it may be appropriate for management to form a view of the device's value to the organization.

Values should be computed for all hardware devices.

Software is somewhat trickier to value. As before, the first step is to compile an inventory. This may be quite difficult, especially in distributed systems and where there are stand-alone devices. Software is not immediately visible and may even be deliberately hidden by users. Unless the organization has quite strict policies, some bootleg software will turn up in the inventory. All such illegal or unlicensed software should be removed. Another problem can be the personal software that users sometimes put on their machines. This may or may not be legal and permission to do so may or may not be organizational policy. Either way, they are not part of the assets.

While you are at this, it is a good idea to remove 'dead' software, i.e. software that is no longer used or useful. It is pointless using up disk space and administrative effort in holding onto such software.

Valuing software is the most difficult part of preparing an IT asset statement. Much end user software is written-off as an expense and therefore has no value in the books. Enterprise packaged software may be written-off on purchase or may be depreciated over a number of years. Custom software may or may not have been capitalized. Ways to value software include:

- At book value. This may not be realistic (and will not be if the software has been expensed). However, even if the accounts have taken an unrealistic view of software depreciation, it can still be re-calculated for management purposes.
- At replacement cost. If the software is up-to-date, for example, if all upgrade licences have been paid, then it is arguable that the software is worth what a new replacement would cost today. This is not necessarily true, but may be a valid basis.
- Subjective value to the business. In practice, it may be appropriate to 'form a view' of the worth of software. This may take into account both of the above factors.

Market value has little relevance to software as it cannot usually be sold to third parties.

Again, costs should be analysed by headings such as system software, application software, etc.

Physical infrastructure includes such items as special building work (including fire protection systems), air conditioning systems, power supply systems and cabling. This might be quite a large investment (for example, on a dispersed site, it might include digging, installing ducting and running cables). Again, valuing these items can be done as:

- Book value. This is appropriate for items such as air conditioning that have a limited physical life, or older cabling which may have a limited technical life. The caveats for hardware also apply here.
- Replacement value. This may be appropriate for items such as fibre-optic cabling which has a long expected useful life.
- Subjective valuation. As above, this may be used to supplement other methods.

Finally, it is essential to estimate a value for *data*. The first step here is to prepare a list of commercially valuable data in the business. All organizations with an IT system, however modest, gather data. While some data may be transient, some of this data accumulates over time to become a valuable, or in some cases, a critical resource. Examples of such data include customer records, past sales patterns, precedents, product records and standard documents (letters, contracts, quotations, etc.). Valuing the data is tricky. Unless the information systems are very good indeed, often the only way that this can be done is subjectively. The value of knowing customer buying patterns or having standard letters available can be difficult to compute. Even the pure assembly cost of the data may be difficult to estimate. Occasionally data that has been bought in or converted will be easy to value. Example 3.11 is a simple example of such a statement.

Example 3.11: An IT asset statement

Company D is a distribution company specializing in selling high quality goods from catalogues. Customers mostly phone in orders, but they can send in written orders on a form supplied with the catalogue.

They employ 43 people including management, teleordering staff and warehouse/postroom staff. They run a highly fault-tolerant system with mirrored servers using a separate high specification RAID unit.

Hardware	£
Servers (4)	15 000
PCs (38)	57 000
Storage network	18 000
Laser printers (6)	6000
Other printers (4)	2000
Communications equipment	8000
Subtotal Hardware	106 000

Software	£
Financial reporting system	15 000
Telemarketing system (incl. mods.)	40 000
Payroll	3000
Distribution system	12 000
Other software	10 000
End user software	18 000
Total software	98 000

Physical infrastructure	£
Computer room	5000
Fire extinguishing system	5000
Cabling	4000
Subtotal	14 000
Data	£
Sales database	20 000
Customer information	30 000
Other data	10 000
Total data	60 000
Grand total	278 000
IT investment per employee	6465

The IT asset statement tells the organization what its current investment in IT is. With this information, it can make a realistic assessment of the management resources required/justified, assess the return on the investment and assess key ratios such as investment per employee.

A major advantage is that it can bring home to senior management the importance of IT to the organization. This is often lost, particularly if IT is regarded as an expense and written-off at the point of acquisition. Management can see the building and physical plant. IT is often much less visible because it is dispersed throughout the organization or is in non-visible forms such as software or data.

Evaluating and reviewing IT investments

4.1 Principles of IT evaluation

While skilful negotiation, sound supplier management and good budgetary procedures are critical to day-to-day IT cost control, long term control of IT costs and benefits requires investment in management, and this requires proper evaluation, approval, monitoring and review/assessment procedures. In particular:

- clear identification of all costs
- clear identification of benefits
- ways of measuring costs
- ways of measuring benefits
- methods of evaluating proposed expenditure
- appropriate evaluation measures and techniques.

Research consistently shows that, when it comes to IT, in many organizations neither costs nor benefits are well understood. The preceding chapter described the types of IT cost and how to identify them. The other side of this coin is benefits.

4.2 IT benefits

Just as all the costs of IT are not always fully realized, so the benefits of IT are not always fully known or measured. Sensible evaluation of IT expenditure, be it current or proposed, can only be done if the benefits are fully understood. IT offers a wide range of potential benefits, including:

- Competitive advantage. IT was originally seen as a mechanism for reducing costs by automating routine tasks. Reducing costs is one important way of achieving competitive advantage.

However, when applied in an IT evaluation, competitive advantage is also seen as being able to provide a product or service that competitors (at least temporarily) cannot match. This may vary from something quite sophisticated (such as home banking) to basic business improvements such as shortened delivery times.

- Added product value. IT may be able to add value to an existing product – even a mundane one. An everyday example of this is discount cards and 'club' cards. Such systems have the dual effect of encouraging customer loyalty and gathering valuable information about buying patterns.

- New products or services. IT can sometimes create, or facilitate creation of, new products. For example, some professional tax advisors now sell systems for calculating various types of tax. Estate agencies offer on-line virtual tours.

- Reduced costs. This is one of the most frequently cited benefits of IT. However, while cost reductions are sometimes clear (e.g. the company needs ten less staff or there is a reduction in inventory or working capital costs), they are not always simple to compute and hidden costs may diminish their effectiveness. Care is therefore needed when estimating such costs.

- Increased productivity. IT can increase productivity in a variety of ways – by eliminating manual chores, by removing steps in a process and by automating procedures. Increased productivity does not necessarily mean a reduction in total cost. It can mean increased service or an improved level of customer service. It is a feature of IT that sometimes the benefits may not accrue to the organization, but rather to its customers.

- Improved product delivery. IT can improve delivery of products in several ways. For certain products (such as financial products), electronic delivery is much more efficient and effective. Use of powerful IT scheduling systems and on-line information about ship and air timetables, traffic computers and so on, all speed up delivery times.

- Avoided future costs. This is one of the more important benefits of IT and also one of the most difficult to quantify. IT often enables an organization to provide the same level of production or service without additional staffing.

- Better customer service. Better customer service incorporates a whole range of potential benefits. For example, in the public sector, the time it takes to receive a benefit cheque or get a new driving licence are both items which can be or have been improved with effective use of information technology. In e-business process re-engineering can radically improve customer services in everything from obtaining a new price list to settlement of an insurance claim.

- Better decision making. Management information systems, decision support systems and executive information systems provides management with an increasing proportion of the information it needs to run the organization. This is an intangible, but nonetheless valuable benefit.

- Improved company or product image. Improved corporate image is a classic intangible benefit, but one which may matter to certain types of organization. Use of information technology to simply present a dynamic or innovative image of the organization to the public can be important.

- Improved communication. IT can improve communications in many ways. This not only include tools such as e-mail and the world-wide web, but more subtle uses. For example, some companies use networked PCs in meetings to enable staff to make anonymous comments. This encourages the flow of ideas which might otherwise go unstated because of staff fear of looking silly or of management displeasure.

- Business survival. Survival is not mandatory. Technology can change the economics of a whole industry overnight and IT is no exception. There are many examples of great companies failing to move with the times and going into a long term decline. In this case, conventional measures of IT return on investment can be positively dangerous. See Case history 4.1.

- Job enrichment. While IT can impoverish certain jobs and make some skills redundant, it can enhance and enrich many other jobs. This may be important in motivating employees, attracting and retaining staff of a suitable calibre and increasing productivity.

- Reduction in errors. IT systems make less errors than people. The cost of errors can be high and even a small reduction in, say, errors in customer delivery can yield major cost savings.

4.3 Why IT expenditure is difficult to evaluate

While some of the above benefits of IT are tangible and easy to measure, others are not and techniques to assess them are not always easy to agree on. One of the problems in evaluating IT is that conventional return on investment/assets measurements are frequently not only difficult to apply, they may also be inappropriate or even misleading. This is because IT, like other technologies, can shift the economics of a market. Case history 4.1 illustrates this point.

Case history 4.1: Where's the pay-back?

Company A is a professional services company which operates in a highly competitive market. While it had had central IT systems for administration for many years, like its competitors, it spent heavily on end user IT from the mid 1980s onwards.

After 10 years, the management of the organization took stock. They had spent hugely on technology. Currently technology spend was heading for £15 000 per professional staff member in capital and infrastructural costs alone. Yet, although there had been some shift towards more senior (and therefore more profitable) staff, the average time charged per annum was still where it had been in the mid 1980s, market share was roughly the same and, after adjustment for inflation, turnover per employee and profitability were not a great deal different. It was true that output had increased dramatically, but they had been unable to convert this into higher prices because of market pressures on charge-out rates. Return on investment looked, if anything, negative.

Looking back on 10 years of investment, some members of senior management were heard to mutter that it would have been better to pay the money to the shareholders or to have invested it elsewhere.

However the key question in this instance was where would the company be if they had not invested in IT? The answer was simple – they would have been out of business. Their competitors would have undercut them and they would not have been able to attract good people into the company. For company A, the IT investment was mandatory – it was invest or die. The real beneficiaries were their clients who were getting better value for money and the staff who had more interesting and rewarding jobs.

The phenomenon described in Case history 4.1 has been described as the 'Red Queen' syndrome. In *Alice Through the Looking Glass*, the Red Queen has to run faster and faster in order to stay in the same place. This phenomenon is quite common in IT and is one of the most difficult concepts for many managers to understand. That does not make it any the less real.

4.4 Methods of evaluating IT expenditure

Evaluation of IT expenditure may be done before the expenditure is made (sometimes called *ex ante* evaluation) and/or in retrospect (sometimes called *ex post* evaluation). A variety of tools and methods are available for this task. Conventional/traditional measures of return on IT investments include:

- Annual return on investment (or, in certain circumstances, return on assets).
- Standard capital budgeting techniques, including:
  - payback (simple and discounted)
  - net present value
  - internal rate of return
  - full return on investment
  - discounted return on investment.
- Cost–benefit analysis.

In recent years, other methods, some of them quite innovative, have been proposed. These include:

- return on management
- anchor measurements
- benchmarks
- multi-criteria decision methods
- return on time invested
- information economics
- value chain analysis.

Some of these methods are quite theoretical and their value in a practice is yet to be demonstrated. The methods most commonly used in practice are covered in this chapter.

There are several methods of evaluating investment projects from a financial viewpoint. Most can be applied to IT projects in that same way as to any other project. The following are the basic principles of these methods with examples.

4.4.1 Annual return on investment

Return on investment (ROI) is based on the assumption that all expenditure and benefits can be expressed in cash terms. This is not always easy to do and can be misleading. However, where costs are simple it is an effective method. Annual ROI looks at the annual savings and/or additional revenue as measured against the initial outlay. This may, of course, vary from year to year, but in some situations where there is a continuing and more or less constant saving, it will be a constant figure. Example 4.1 is a simple example of this technique.

Example 4.1: Simple annual ROI

Company B, a small printing company, was considering investing in new typesetting technology. The new technology was simpler and more powerful than the older machines they currently used. Two of the typesetting staff were in their late fifties and were willing to take a package to retire early. The company also calculated that, due to the faster production method, it could increase its turnover by 12% (approximately £100 000) without any additional cost. Profit margin on new business would be approximately 14%. It computed the ROI as follows:

PCs	£50 000
LAN	£10 000
Printers	£12 000
Training	£8000
Retirement package costs	£73 000
Total	£153 000
Annual running costs	
Support	£9000
Additional insurance	£500
Annual savings	
Maintenance of current systems	£14 500
Wages	£35 000
Add	
Additional business margin	£14 000
Net savings plus income	£54 000
Return on investment	35%

This method has all the attraction of simplicity, but it is only applicable in a limited number of situations. It works well in Example 4.1 because the costs and savings are clear and the annual continuing impact is easy to assess (though even in this example a number of issues are conveniently simplified). This is not usually the case and to tackle more complex investment decisions more sophisticated methods are needed.

4.4.2 Capital budgeting methods

On the assumption that all revenues, costs and cost savings are expressible in cash terms, there is a number of more refined investment analysis techniques available for evaluating the cash flows from proposed IT investments. The following are summary descriptions of commonly used techniques.

Net present value. Net present value (NPV) is computed by the process of discounting. The underlying principle is that money today is worth more than money in the future. All other things being equal, the further in the future a cash flow occurs, the less important it is. This reduction in impact is expressed by using a *discount rate*, expressed as a percentage figure, and using this to generate a series of discount factors. This is done using the formula:

$$\text{Discount factor} = (1 / (1 + \text{Discount rate} / 100))^n$$

Where n is the number of years being discounted. Conventionally, year 1 is not discounted. For example, if the discount factor is 10% per annum, the discount factors for years 1–5 would be:

Year 1		$= 1.00$
Year 2	$1/(1 + 10/100)$	$= 0.91$
Year 3	$(1/(1 + 10/100))^2$	$= 0.83$
Year 4	$(1/(1 + 10/100))^3$	$= 0.75$
Year 5	$(1/(1 + 10/100))^4$	$= 0.68$

The NPV is the sum of all net cash flows discounted for the years in which they occur and is a money value. The net present value is today's cash value of the proposed investment. Example 4.2 illustrates this approach

Example 4.2: Net present value

Company C is evaluating whether or not it should replace its current inventory control system. The new system will cost £100 000 in year 1 and an additional £5000 per annum to maintain. It is estimated that, by reducing inventory, the company will save £5000 per year in interest charges and that losses from shrinkage and product deterioration will save £25 000 per annum. Using a discount rate of 10% the NPV of this proposal over 5 years is:

Year	Cash out	Cash in	Net cash	Discount factor	NPV cash
1	100 000	30 000	(70 000)	1.00	(70 000)
2	5000	30 000	25 000	0.91	22 730
3	5000	30 000	25 000	0.83	20 660
4	5000	30 000	25 000	0.75	18 780
5	5000	30 000	25 000	0.68	17 080
Total					9250

As the NPV is positive (+£9250), the company should make the investment.

The discount rate chosen is critical and will be determined by the company's cost of capital, the rate of inflation, the level of risk (the higher the risk, the higher the discount rate) and company standard discount rates for investment projects. In broad terms, if NPV is greater than zero, the investment is a good one. For a given discount rate, the higher the NPV value the better the investment or return.

The advantages of the NPV approach include that it is simple to understand as well as being unambiguous. It takes into account the timing of the cash flows and can take into account risk factors. It also obliges the user to quantify the discount rate. There are some drawbacks. Two are that the meaning of the monetary value is not always understood and the answer will vary with the discount rate chosen, so many answers are possible. Despite these drawbacks, the NPV is the most reliable and least questionable measure of investment return.

Pay-back. Pay-back is the amount of time that a project takes to recover the original investment. It comes in two forms, simple and discounted. Simple pay-back measures the time that it takes the cumulative cash flow to become positive. Discounted pay-back is the time the discounted cash flows take to become positive. Pay-back is the amount of time it takes to get back the original investment. These are shown in Examples 4.3 and and 4.4.

Example 4.3: Pay-back

Using the data in Example 4.2, the payback calculation is as follows:

Year	Cash out	Cash in	Net cash	Cumulative cash flow
1	100 000	30 000	(70 000)	(70 000)
2	5000	30 000	25 000	(45 000)
3	5000	30 000	25 000	(20 000)
4	5000	30 000	25 000	5000
5	5000	30 000	25 000	30 000

As the cumulative cash flow becomes positive in year 4, the pay-back is 4 years.

Example 4.4: Discounted pay-back

Using the data in Example 4.2 and a 10% discount rate, the payback calculation is:

Year	Cash out	Cash in	Net cash	Discount factor	NPV cash	Cumulative cash flow
1	100 000	30 000	(70 000)	1.00	(70 000)	(70 000)
2	5000	30 000	25 000	0.91	22 730	(47 270)
3	5000	30 000	25 000	0.83	20 660	(26 610)
4	5000	30 000	25 000	0.75	18 780	(7830)
5	5000	30 000	25 000	0.68	17 080	9250

The discounted pay-back is 5 years.

The advantages of pay-back are that is easy to calculate and understand. When discounted, it at least partially takes into account time and risk factors. On the down side, it ignores

109

events after the pay-back point and it does not always give a clear or accurate signal. The first of these drawbacks is a potentially disastrous flaw. If there is a large outflow immediately after the pay-back point, the project could be a bad investment (see Example 4.5).

Example 4.5: Risks in using pay-back

This example shows the potential problem in using pay-back with late negative cash flows.

Year	Cash out	Cash in	Net cash	Cumulative cash flow
1	100 000	30 000	(70 000)	(70 000)
2	5000	30 000	25 000	(45 000)
3	5000	30 000	25 000	(20 000)
4	5000	30 000	25 000	5000
5	10 000	0	(10 000)	(5000)

This has a pay-back of 4 years, but in year 5, the project is back into a cumulative loss.

Internal rate of return. The internal rate of return (IRR) is the discount rate that will discount a cash flow to give a net present value of zero. The IRR cannot be calculated by formula and must be found by trial and error. All spreadsheets have a function for computing an IRR. In Example 4.3, the IRR can be computed as 16% giving the following discount factors:

Year 1 1 $= 1.00$

Year 2 $1 / (1 + 16/100)$ $= 0.86$

Year 3 $(1 / (1 + 16 / 100))^2$ $= 0.74$

Year 4 $(1 / (1 + 16 / 100))^3$ $= 0.64$

Year 5 $(1 / (1 + 16 / 100))^4$ $= 0.55$

Applying these to Example 4.3 gives (with some rounding) the results in Example 4.6.

Example 4.6: Internal rate of return

Using the data in Example 4.2, the internal rate of return is approximately 16%.

Year	Cash out	Cash in	Net cash	Discount factor	NPV cash
1	100 000	30 000	(70 000)	1.00	(70 000)
2	5000	30 000	25 000	0.86	21 560
3	5000	30 000	25 000	0.74	18 590
4	5000	30 000	25 000	0.64	16 030
5	5000	30 000	25 000	0.55	13 820
Total					0

The advantages of the IRR are that it gives a single answer and it returns a percentage answer, which is seemingly easier to interpret than an NPV. There are, however, several weaknesses in the IRR. One is that in certain circumstances it can give more than one answer. More seriously, it assumes that surplus cash at any point can be reinvested at the IRR rate. This is highly unlikely to be the case. There are other theoretical disadvantages of the IRR which need not concern us here. For these reasons, the IRR is best avoided as an evaluation tool in IT projects.

Return on investment (ROI). There are a number of ways of computing this. One common definition is:

$$\frac{\text{Total net cash surplus over the project life}}{\text{Total expenditure at outset}} \times 100$$

In simple cases, this can be expressed as an amount per year (see Example 4.2). Unlike an annual ROI, full ROI is calculated over the life of an investment. For example, if it is assumed that the inventory control system in Company C has a 5 year life, then the return on investment is

£30 000 / £100 000 × 100 = 30%

Discounted ROI is the same as ROI except it uses the NPV divided by the total initial expenditure. In effect, discounted ROI is:

$$\frac{\text{Net present value of investment}}{\text{Total Expenditure at outset}} \times 100$$

This gives:

$$£9250 / £100\,000 \times 100 = 9.25\%$$

ROI can become complicated to compute and interpret when the investment is continuing, i.e. it does not all take place at the start of the project. In such cases, it can become difficult to separate out the investment cost from all the other cash flows. One of the advantages of net present value is that it overcomes this problem.

In all of the above we have ignored the issue of risk except in as much as the discount rate reflects risk. Refinement of the above methods to take account of risk are covered in Chapter 10.

4.4.3 Cost–benefit analysis

Cost–benefit analysis matches the costs of the system to the benefits using money as a metric. It is a widely used technique, though not without its problems (see below). Cost–benefit analysis requires all benefits as well as all costs be translated into financial amounts in order to make the comparison. This is not always simple to do. While it is straightforward to translate a saving in staff numbers into a cash equivalent, other benefits and costs require special techniques and sometimes several assumptions in order to convert them to a monetary equivalent. The principal examples of these are described in the following paragraphs.

The following are common benefits and how to translate them into financial terms.

Productivity. For the purposes of IT investment evaluation, productivity can be defined as the unit of output per employee (or sometimes per work unit). Output can be measured in a wide variety of ways. Examples of productivity measures are income per employee, units produced per employee, claims processed per employee, sales calls per employee, and so on.

Productivity gains from investment can usually be translated into financial equivalents by working out the level of staffing necessary to sustain the volume of activity before and after an IT investment. This is given by the formula:

$$\text{Staff saving} = \left(\frac{\text{New volume}}{\text{Old volume}} \times \text{Old staffing level} \right)$$

$$- \text{New staffing level}$$

This computes the level of staffing that would have been required to meet the new level of activity had the previous output per employee been maintained, and subtracts from it the (presumably lower) actual or projected number of employees after implementation of the new system. This difference is the labour saved by the IT system. This can be converted into an ongoing cash saving by multiplying it by the marginal cost of labour.

However, in some cases the effect may be more subtle. For example, where employee productivity results in increased revenue rather than reduced headcount, the greater output per employee is not always a simple figure to compute. This is illustrated in Case history 4.2.

Case history 4.2: Measuring improved productivity

Company D operated a tele-ordering system staffed by 12 operators. Between them they handled between 2000 and 2500 calls per day.

Customers who rang in were answered by an answering machine and put into an automatic telephone queuing system. The average waiting time for an answer was 60 seconds and the average time to process an order was 2.25 minutes, some of which was due to a relatively slow response by the computer. IT management estimated that an upgrade to the computer might reduce this time by at least 45 seconds, but would cost £25 000 with an additional continuing annual maintenance cost of £3000.

To evaluate this potential investment, the company instal-led a monitor on the telephone system to measure how many customers per day hung up before they were answered and decided that, if they could reduce the waiting time to 15 seconds, they would (after allowing for some people who would call back) gain over 100 additional sales per day. The average profit margin on a sale was £1.25 which would yield £125 per day, approximately £30 000 per year or a net £27 000 after allowing for the additional maintenance costs. Their first-cut computations were as follows:

Cost of new system	£25 000
Training	£2000
Implementation costs	£5000
Total initial cost	£32 000
Additional orders per week	700
Average gross profit per order	£1.25
Additional gross profit per year	£30 000
Less additional maintenance costs	£3000
Net contribution	£27 000

Thus the system seemingly had a potential pay-back time of just over one year.

However, computing the impact of the new system was not quite this simple. The additional order levels were based on the assumption that there would always be a customer waiting and that there would be no 'idle time'. While it was estimated that the new system could reduce the average transaction time (i.e. the time taken to process an order) to 1.75 minutes, it took some sophisticated operations research work and some assumptions about demand levels to estimate that this would reduce the average waiting time for customers to 15 seconds, and to confirm that the additional 700 orders per week could be achieved.

In fact, the additional order level turned out to be of the order of 450 per week, enough to justify the investment but not as spectacular a return as the initial calculations had projected.

Although calculating the potential contribution of IT is not always simple and sometimes requires the use of statistical and/ or operations research techniques, the financial principles remain the same. There is an increased revenue from the effect of the better IT system and this needs to be quantified.

Projecting the increased productivity in processes is not always easy to do, particularly where a process has a number of stages which are dependent on each other. In such cases, improvements in productivity have to be coordinated over the entire process – otherwise bottlenecks will develop which may squander much of the productivity gain. Many processes in organizations are of the multiple-queue multiple-server type as illustrated in Figure 4.1.

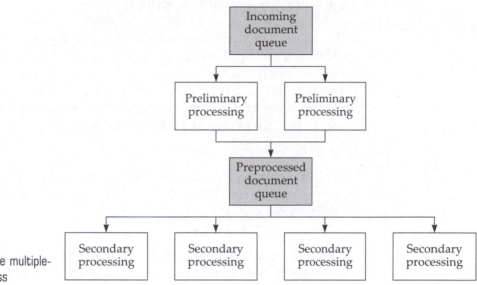

Figure 4.1
Multiple-queue multiple-server process

In order to analyse the impact of improved productivity in one component on the whole operation, a complex operations research analysis or simulation of the system may be required. A common problem is to solve a processing problem in one area only to create one somewhere else. This can lead to a never-ending circle of problems. It is better to tackle the process as a whole.

Increased throughput. Where an increased volume of activity can be handled without increasing staff levels, the same approach as in productivity can be used with a slight modification such that the formula is now:

$$\text{Staff saving} = \left(\frac{\text{New volume}}{\text{Old volume}} \times \text{Current staffing level} \right) - \text{Current staffing level}$$

This staff saving can be converted to a financial figure.

Increased market share/sales. To evaluate the benefits from increased market share or increased sales accurately requires (1) that the increase in sales/market share that can be attributed to the IT investment can be isolated, and (2) that the value of the increase in market share be quantified. Both of these present difficulties. In the case of the first, it is essential that, when the objectives are being set, the anticipated increase in market share due to IT and the anticipated increase due to other factors is agreed in advance. If this is not done, then there will be disputes afterwards over what that effect was.

The second requires computing the marginal profitability on additional sales. This is a straightforward cost accounting exercise, but it must be done properly. It is not unheard of for the cost of gaining market share to be greater than the increased net income generated. Simply going after market share for its own sake is not always good business sense.

Reduced inventory. Reduction (or in the case of just-in-time processing, elimination) of inventory by use of IT leads to several cost savings:

- As inventory must be financed (money is tied up in the stock), a reduction in inventory can immediately be translated into a reduction in borrowing (or an increase in cash). This can be multiplied by the borrowing (or earnings) rate to compute an annual saving.
- Some products deteriorate when stored. A reduction in storage time will reduce this and may eliminate this cost completely.
- Products and raw materials can be damaged in storage. The longer they are stored and the more of the product that is stored, the greater the losses from damage. This saving can usually be quantified.
- Reduction in inventory may also reduce losses through shrinkage (theft).

All of the above factors should be computed when evaluating the impact of IT on inventory reduction. Example 4.7 illustrates this.

Example 4.7: Saving on inventory

Company F was looking at implementing a new forecasting system which would enable it to reduce inventories. The proposed investment was substantial and included links to customers sales forecasting systems as well as some sophisticated software. The total cost was estimated to be around £180 000. Running costs would be minimal.

The company calculated that with the new system it could reduce its finished goods inventory by £500 000. Currently it made provisions as follows:

Damage to stock   1% of stock value per quarter
Theft   0.25% of stock value per quarter

The company's products did not deteriorate in the normal storage period and its cost of borrowing was 5%. The company reasoned that a reduction in stock would not affect the rate of theft, but would reduce damage, probably pro rata with the reduction in stock value. While the reduced stock would save on warehouse space, they did not feel that they could realize any financial savings or additional income from this. Their calculations were therefore as follows:

Annual savings from damage	£500 000 × 1% × 4	£20 000
Savings on theft		£0
Interest savings	£500 000 × 5%	£25 000
Total savings		£45 000

In this instance, as the savings were ongoing, pay-back was felt to be the most useful method for assessing the return. On this basis, payback was four years and the investment was approved.

Faster turnaround. Where IT facilitates faster turnaround of operations, there may be several savings. For example, shortened production processes and/or better production planning can increase the return on and utilization of plant, faster turnaround (or elimination) of paperwork can reduce backlogs, saving storage, reducing overtime and raising staff morale, and faster response may also lead to higher sales.

Quality of service. Quality of service is an important benefit of IT, but one where the financial benefit to the organization may be very circuitous indeed. For example, it is doubtful whether the introduction of automatic teller machines into the banking system could have been cost justified using short term financial criteria (long term would be different). ATMs are, in fact, a classic case of a strategic move by one bank that immediately becomes a mandatory response for its competitors. Quality of service can be converted to money by either getting users to put a value on it or by assessing the indirect impact of the improvement. For example, a new electronic banking service may generate demand for other products such as loans or insurance. Quality of service should, if it is of any value at all, increase (or at least sustain) long term revenue and profitability. Case history 4.3 is a good example.

Case history 4.3: Competing with service

A chain of small 'mini market' type groceries shops needed to compete with the supermarkets. While it could use its collective buying power to compete on price at the point of purchase, its ordering and distribution costs were higher because it had many hundreds of relatively small outlets whereas the supermarket chains, which only operated in the larger towns and cities, had a relatively small number of drop points.

To overcome this disadvantage they developed an ordering system using hand held terminals which were given to the shop proprietors and franchisees. These could be used to enter orders. At night they were left connected to a modem which would read the orders (and incidentally update the terminal with any price changes). Prior to this, customers had 'phoned in their orders.

Using this system, the company was able to schedule the order and delivery process into an efficient cycle which, although still not as low cost as the supermarkets, was close enough to avoid a major competitive disadvantage. The company also saved money because it was able to reduce its telephone ordering department to a much smaller size which dealt with rush orders only.

Intangibles. In practice, the only effective way to measure intangible benefits is to ask those who receive the benefit (or who are seeking it) to put a value on it. Thus, for example, a company may see a benefit from providing larger screens on their PCs, but may be unable to show any direct measurable benefit. A simple device is to ask them what they would pay for this. The following case history shows a somewhat devious, but effective, use of this method.

Case history 4.4: Measuring intangible benefits

Company E was considering building a corporate planning model. The project did not have a readily measurable financial return. It was to be used for exploring the potential impact of a number of expansion plans on Group cash-flow.

The IT department were unsure as to how to value the benefits from this proposed investment. Possible ways of constructing such a measure were:

- working out the saving in management time in doing the calculations by hand, or
- measuring the savings from bad decisions avoided.

The first was not meaningful as the calculations would simply not have been done by hand if that was the only choice. The second was clearly not calculable. While the users could identify several benefits from the model (such as the ability to explore the effect on cash flow of various growth strategies), none of these was readily quantifiable into a money figure.

To overcome this problem, IT management first prepared an estimate of how much it would cost to build. The model required was complex and the cost was estimated at approximately £50 000. IT management then asked users what they were prepared to pay for the model. Over a period of a couple of weeks, IT and the users 'negotiated' a price for the model of £45 000. To do this IT management cheated by pretending that the model would probably have to be developed by contract staff and that it would therefore be a direct cost. This was not actually true, but it had the effect of concentrating the minds of the users. Senior management were then asked to decide whether or not, given this user valuation of the model, the project should proceed.

The process described in Case history 4.4 is instructive. The users were forced to quantify how much they were prepared to pay in hard cash. Had they been paying an external developer or an outsource supplier to develop the model they would have had to agree a price in advance. Because the model was internal, users did not place a 'real' value on it.

Where IT is part of a larger investment, separating out the benefits realized from IT can be difficult if not impossible. When a complex business investment or improvement project includes, for example, other technology investments, management changes, process changes and factors such as advertising it may not even be meaningful to ask the question. Where IT is part of a much larger project involving a range of other costs, the project should be viewed as a whole and not an 'IT Investment'.

4.4.4 Anchor values

Another approach to IT investment evaluation is to use anchor values. Anchor values set a metric or metrics that the organization can use to measure the impact of IT expenditure. Typical metrics include productivity and similar measures, for example:

- sales per employee
- market share
- average customer waiting time
- profit per customer
- transactions per employee.

In certain circumstances, anchor values can be more meaningful than conventional return on investment or return on asset measures as they can be designed to take into account changes in the level of activity. They can also be a useful counterweight to conventional measures. Anchor values can be used to measure intangible benefits or items which may benefit the customer rather than the provider of the product or service.

The advantages of anchor values are that they are generally easy to measure and to understand. If data are available, they can sometimes be compared with performance in peer organizations. However, they may not give a clear indication as to whether the impact is worth the investment and they can give mixed signals. Example 4.8 illustrates this point.

Example 4.8: Conflicting signals

A company invests in a major upgrade to its IT systems with the objective of increasing its market share and reducing the number of people it employs. The results are as follows:

	Year 1	Year 5
Assets	£70 million	£77 million
Sales	£182 million	£236 million
Profit	£14 million	£15.1 million
Market share	8.73%	10.25%
Number of employees	1042	760
Return on assets	20%	19.61
Profit % of turnover	7.69%	6.40%
Sales/employee	£175 000	£310 000
Profit/employee	£13 435	£19 868

What is happening here? Two indicators, return on assets and profit percentage are showing a deterioration in the company's performance. Three, market share, profit and turnover per employee are showing a significant improvement.

To interpret the figures, the company needs to know more. For example, there could have been a marked decline in prices over the period due to greater competition. Alternatively, the increase in market share might have been achieved by price cutting or increased promotion costs and so on.

The moral of this example is that using indicators of any sort in isolation is risky. All analysis of IT investment needs to be looked at in context and holistically.

In practice anchor measures are best used as a supplement to other evaluation techniques.

4.4.5 Return on time invested

Time is money, but it can often be more meaningful to users to express return on investment in time rather than money terms. In some IT projects, the major outlays and the major savings are in time rather than capital. Rather than going into the complications of translating time into money, the investment can be evaluated using time as the metric. For example, it has been established that proper training in end user computing tools will save users a large multiple of the time invested in training in the first year of software usage. Example 4.9 illustrates this technique.

Example 4.9: Investing time to save time

Company Q did a considerable amount of internal system development and had a team of 20 staff employed full-time on development of new systems. Over the years it had evolved its own style of system development in an ad hoc manner. This method was not great and tended to result in a high level of post-delivery modification of systems due to inadequate specification and weak design methods.

The IT manager felt that the development group should move to a modern system of development methods and chose a leading structured methodology. As there were plenty of self tutoring manuals available on the market, he reckoned that they could teach themselves without the necessity for formal courses and at a minimum capital outlay (he was something of an optimist!).

The IT manager then estimated that the total time required for this would be approximately 6 man-weeks per staff member, allowing for:

- initial self tuition
- learning curve.

In addition, he estimated that around 6 man-months (say 26 man-weeks) would be required for planning and managing the change. The new approach would be used on new projects only – it was not intended to try to retro-fit the technique to existing systems. His total time investment would therefore be:

$$(6 \times 20) + 26 = 146 \text{ man-weeks.}$$

He then estimated (conservatively) that, by using this methodology, he could save approximately 10% on current development times and, on average, one full-time person equivalent on modification and maintenance. Assuming that his development team worked a 44 week year, his annual 'return' was therefore

$$10\% \text{ of } 20 \times 44 + 44 = 132 \text{ man-weeks}$$

a payback period of a little over a year.

Although the above method does not take into account the relative costs of the individuals' time (on a strictly financial basis, it can be shown that the payback would take slightly longer), it is accurate enough for all practical purposes.

4.4.6 When to use particular methods of evaluation

Not every evaluation technique is suitable for every type of IT project. In order to decide the method of evaluation which is most suitable, it is necessary to categorize types of investment. Justifications for IT investments may be categorized in various ways.

Mandatory expenditure may be driven by the need for business survival or by regulation or legislation. In this case, it may not be necessary to evaluate the project/expenditure at all as the money has to be spent anyway. However, it may be appropriate for management to ask whether the organization should stay in a market at all. If the IT investment entry costs (or the cost of staying in) are too high to make the proposition viable, then it should be avoided.

Where the rationale behind the expenditure is *cost saving*, it should be possible to identify the cost savings to be made both in advance and in retrospect. It is essential that specific savings be identified. Avoid vague statements such as 'we expect to make savings of £50–70 000 per year'. Cost savings should be specific such as:

- 'Reduction in average inventory of finished goods product of £100 000 giving rise to an average interest saving of £5500 per annum starting next year.'
- 'Immediate reduction in the number of counter staff required by 3 giving a continuing saving of £55 000 per annum.'

Cost savings should identify not only the gross and net savings anticipated, but how these savings will be realized. It should be clear whether the savings will be one-off or continuing and any risk to the project should be stated (i.e. what is the likelihood that the savings will be realized). Cost savings which cannot be identified and for which firm estimates cannot be made should be ignored.

Cost avoidance is similar to cost saving, but the results are not as readily measurable in advance (or even in retrospect) and therefore have to be estimated. This can give rise to problems of perception and opinion, for example disputes as to how many staff it would have taken to provide a service or whether, if it had been going to cost that much anyway, the organization would have spent the money in the first place. Senior management can be remarkably reluctant to acknowledge avoided costs, even where the organization would have had no choice but to spend the money. Case history 4.5 is a good example.

Case history 4.5: Sometimes you cannot win . . .!

The senior management of an organization were complaining bitterly about the cost of a highly successful IT system. The system had cost more than planned, largely because users kept adding to the features required while it was being built. Now senior managers were under pressure from the Board to justify the cost.

As it happened, the IT system had enabled the organization to meet a change in the regulatory environment in which they worked, with relative ease. Without the computer, it was estimated the organization would have needed to hire around ten additional staff to cope with the demands and the problems with which they were faced.

Even having admitted this fact to the IT manager, the CEO still complained that the system had cost too much and questioned its value. While his head acknowledged the essential nature of the system, his heart could not reconcile itself to what was perceived as a high cost.

Even an unexpected and important benefit of the system was not fully acknowledged.

Cost avoidance must be quantified. Justifications should identify where future costs would have been incurred and the likelihood that they will be incurred. They should show why and how these costs will be avoided and whether this is one-off or continuing. Predicting future cost savings is a process which is naturally open to question by sceptical management. It is not always possible to be certain that costs will be saved. In this case, the concept of an expected future cost saving can be used. This is discussed in Chapter 10.

Revenue generating IT expenditure should, in theory, be easy to project and assess. Revenue enhancement may come from many sources, from increased sales volumes to ability to raise prices through added value or faster customer payment. Once again it is important to be specific. For example:

- 'The system will enable the company to sell an additional 5000 units per annum.'
- 'We expect, on the basis of this new direct customer booking system, to increase occupancy in the hotel by 2 percentage points next year and by 5 percentage points in subsequent years.'

One of the difficulties with revenue generating (and to a certain extent with cost saving) IT investments is that it can be difficult to isolate the effect of IT investment. An increase in sales may be put down to many factors, including an economic upturn, new sales management, better advertising and so on. The key here is to identify those responsible for revenue generation and ask them to estimate how much revenue will increase if the IT investment is not made. This baseline can then be used to assess the marginal impact of the IT investment. It is essential that this be done in advance. Otherwise one can end up in fruitless arguments about the impact of different factors.

Information generation/decision support is another common justification. Most IT systems provide information as a by-product. However some systems are designed purely to gather, manipulate and present information. Examples include query systems, executive information and decision support systems. Such systems often cannot be economically justified by conventional return-on-investment means. In these cases, the only effective form of evaluation is to ask the executives or managers involved to put a subjective value on the system.

Service enhancement. Sometimes, and quite frequently in public sector or non-profit making organizations, the benefit from an IT investment accrues not to the organization, but rather in *service enhancement* to its customers or clients. For example, the return on a new system which reduces waiting times in Local Government offices cannot readily be measured in normal financial terms. In such instances, anchor measures such as average waiting time or speed of response are more meaningful.

Case history 4.6: Anchor measures

In a survey of IT benefits, one telephone company measured its improvements from IT and IT-related investment over a 5 year period as follows:

	Year 0	Year 5
Number of employees	246 000	172 000
Residential orders completed in 8 working days	62%	86%
Faults cleared in 2 working days	90%	99%
Directory enquiries answered in 15 seconds or less	81%	92%
Operator assistance calls answered in 15 seconds or less	87%	95%
Call failure rate due to local factors	1.9%	0.2%

For this organization, the purpose of the exercise was twofold; cost reduction and service improvement. To measure this, several different anchor values were used.

Usually, the objectives in IT projects of this nature are to set a target in improved service levels for which the organization is prepared to invest a certain amount. Measurements of effectiveness used in marketing and advertising (such as customer satisfaction surveys, market research and opinion polls) may be used to set objectives and to evaluate the effectiveness of the investment.

Strategic Some IT investments are designed to transform the company or give it a major market advantage. Although such projects will tend to be on a large scale, the benefits of the proposed investment must be clearly stated in measurable terms. Conventional return on investment measurements can be used, as can appropriate anchor measures such as market share, sales per employee or percentage gross margin.

Image. Occasionally organizations install computer systems for *image* reasons. For example, financial institutions, brokers and estate agents often have PCs sitting around in public areas. Sometimes these machines are barely used. They are there to give a feeling that this is a 'high tech' organization. Where systems are developed for marketing or similar reasons, evaluation must be done with great care. It may be that such expenditure should not be classified as IT expenditure at all, but rather as a marketing cost. Such systems are often installed at the whim of senior management (see below) and occasionally just to satisfy the ego of some executive. In such circumstances it can be difficult for IT management to apply normal rules of expenditure control.

Case history 4.7: Never mind the quality, feel the width

Company F was in a business that made extensive use of computer technology both in its production and in the management information systems. Some of the production systems were old and in much need of overhaul. Senior management did not have a good understanding of information technology and were generally critical of the quality of information provided by the system.

At an industry conference, one of the senior management team saw a demonstration of an Executive Information System. This, he decided, was the answer to the company's problems. Not only would it provide all the missing information, it would also project a state of the art image of the company's systems to visitors.

Without considering the broader implications, or the root causes of the problems of acquiring information, the executive committee ordered the system (at a starting cost of over £100 000). Management also assumed (on the basis of the sales presentation) that the system was self-explanatory and that little formal training was needed. This turned out to be a serious misjudgment.

Worse, the problems in the underlying systems had not gone away. As they were unable to produce the information (or were unable to produce it quickly enough or accurately enough) to feed the EIS, the latter was effectively useless and after an initial burst of enthusiasm, it died a quiet (and expensive) death.

4.4.7 Summary

In summary therefore, to assess an IT investment, the following should be done:

- The reason for the investment should be spelled out.
- All costs, both initial and continuing, direct and hidden should be identified and phased.
- All benefits should be identified.
- Timings of each benefit should be projected.
- Where the reason for the investment is mandatory, it may not be necessary to justify expenditure.
- Where applicable, additional revenue, cost savings and cost avoidance should be identified.
- Where there are intangible benefits, these should be expressed in financial form using one of the techniques outlined above. Users should be forced to quantify such benefits.
- Other techniques such as return on time invested can be considered in special circumstances.

4.5 IT expenditure benchmarking

One of the most common questions that organizations ask about IT is 'are we spending the right amount on IT?'. At one level this question is essentially no different from 'are we spending the right amount on marketing?'. Comparative tables are produced for many industries. These tables, while interesting, are often a poor guideline for company spending for several reasons:

- They may not be accurate. If the method of measurement is not standardized in some way (for example, it is specific and well defined), the figures quoted may be misleading.
- They may not be relevant. For example, an organization with large legacy systems needing high maintenance may have the same level of ongoing expenditure as a company which is developing brand new systems, but the nature of that expenditure is entirely different.
- There is no measure of effectiveness. They do not indicate how cost effectively the money is being spent. Measures of effectiveness of expenditure can only be comparable if the same level of service is being provided.
- The herd is not always right. There are many example of the IT equivalent of panic buying. This was nowhere better illustrated than during the dot.com boom of the late 1990s.

Nevertheless, provided care and judgment are exercised, it can be useful to measure IT performance against peer organizations. The following is a list of benchmarking metrics which are all useful in various contexts:

- IT expenditure as a percentage of turnover
- IT expenditure per employee
- IT expenditure per user
- IT assets per employee
- IT assets per user
- IT assets as a percentage of total assets
- IT headcount as a percentage of total headcount
- IT management to staff ratio
- disk storage per user
- system utilization
- network availability
- IT staff turnover rates
- average age of systems
- number of programming languages supported
- number of operating systems supported
- number of data management systems supported
- length of application delivery backlog (in years or man-years)
- ratio of custom to packaged applications
- cost per unit of performance
- cost per line of code
- cost per function point.

4.6 Reviewing and auditing IT systems

All IT systems eventually need upgrading or replacement. Sometimes organizations are reluctant to face up to this. IT systems can represent an emotional as well as a financial investment. Users may be slow to risk giving up a tried and true system, no matter how unwieldy, for something new and untried. The philosophy of 'if it ain't broke, don't fix it' prevails.

This reluctance to address ageing, inefficient and/or unproductive systems can have serious consequences, including incurring unnecessary direct and indirect costs, user frustration and loss of both competitiveness and business opportunities. Case history 4.8, from the strange but true department, is a good case in point.

Case history 4.8: What? No trade in?

A company in the rag trade had a very old minicomputer on which it ran a simple accounting system. The model dated from the 1960s, occupied a moderately sized room and supported a single user and one printer. It was a credit to the design and manufacture of the machine that it still worked almost 20 years after it had been built, although there were occasional problems. These came to a head one day when the machine suffered a disk head crash. After scouring the world, the supplier managed to find a replacement disk in an old machine in California which was cannibalized and flown in to replace the faulty disk.

The incident had the effect of finally persuading management that it was time to upgrade and they negotiated a deal for a new machine. Being the rag trade, the MD of the company was not one to give away anything and called in the computer salesman to haggle over the deal. Having taken a few more pounds off the price, the MD played his trump card and asked how much the supplier would allow as a trade in on the old machine.

One can only imagine his disappointment when the salesman said that his best offer was not to charge for carting it away.

To avoid such traps, all systems should be periodically reviewed. Where there is an ongoing strategic IT planning process, reviews of existing systems will (or should) be part and parcel of this process. Alternatively it might be part of a wider IT health check. Where neither of these are applicable, good management should undertake a review/audit of all systems at regular intervals. Target systems for review might be identified during budget preparation, but this should be a separate exercise from the budget itself.

A system's efficiency and effectiveness review can be based on a series of questions. The key questions to ask are as follows.

● What are the maintenance costs?

Case history 4.9 illustrates this point.

Case history 4.9: The high cost of inertia

Company X had been one of the first companies in Europe to make use of laser printing technology. However, nearly 15 years after they first introduced the lasers, they were still using and maintaining their original printers. This was a credit to the robustness of the printer design and build quality, but the annual cost of the maintenance contract was the equivalent of the cost of three modern (and faster) lasers.

Even when this was pointed out to a highly conservative senior management, they were reluctant to change because of an irrational fear that the new technology might cause compatibility problems or might be less reliable.

- Are maintenance costs rising and if so why? Maintenance costs tend to rise with time. Rapidly rising costs are an early warning that problems are building up.
- Is the underlying technology appropriate? Many so called 'legacy' systems were built over 15 years ago. IT has advanced phenomenally over the intervening years and major opportunities are being missed by many organizations because of lack of flexibility in their systems.
- What are the major problems with this system? It can be useful to list known problems with the system. It is also useful to know if this list is stable or growing.
- What are the major shortcomings of this system? This is a more useful question than the preceding one. With few exceptions, IT systems are continually being upgraded, modified and enhanced. If the backlog of such requests is increasing it may be that the problem can be solved by upgrading the technology or replacing the system.
- What is the expected lifetime of this system? Most IT systems and components have relatively short useful lives. This does not always prevent organizations from harvesting technology beyond a point where it is sensible to do so. A simple and common example is organizations who use 5 or 6 year-old PCs which lack the power to run modern office software efficiently. It is often bad IT management to hold on to an IT system merely in order to extract every last ounce of value from the investment. Management must look at the full costs, both financial and opportunity, of each system.

- What are the alternatives? Simply deciding that a system is not efficient is not sufficient cause to replace it. There have to be alternative(s) which are better and which can be cost-justified in terms of savings, income or improved productivity or services.
- What would be the return on an upgrade or replacement of this system? This question should be asked periodically of all systems which are over 5 years old. Although some systems last 20 years or more, most systems tend to have a life of 5 to 10 years.
- How could new technology be used to change the way things are done? Last, but by no means least, systems should be reviewed in the context of the organization's operations. Organizations often adapt their behaviour to their IT systems rather than the other way around. This is particularly true with older technologies which were less agile than today's.

A review should recommend whether the system being reviewed should be retained, upgraded, scrapped or replaced. Reviews must be hard-headed. A common phenomenon is for users, sometimes with the connivance of IT management, to ignore the need for investment in nuts and bolts systems and become fascinated by glitzy, but less economically sound projects. Decisions about IT investment should be made on the basis of where the best benefits will be realized, not on what may be the most glamorous project currently being considered.

5 | IT budgeting, accounting and cost control

5.1 Introduction

Budgeting is a fundamental management discipline. Budgets and reporting against budget are key financial and day-to-day management control mechanisms. Despite this, some organizations do not prepare proper IT budgets. IT budgets are relegated to subsections of other budgets or expressed as global numbers without any underlying analysis. Given the size and complexity of modern IT expenditure, this is not a satisfactory approach. Control of IT costs requires that proper IT budgets be prepared and proper IT budgetary control exercised. This chapter provides a structure for IT budgeting and a set of steps to follow when preparing an IT budget.

Budgeting deals with measurable and reportable costs. The more subtle problems described in Chapter 3 must be dealt with by more direct management action. It should be borne in mind that while budgeting is a critical component of IT cost management and control, it is not the only tool available. Other tools and techniques are discussed elsewhere in this book.

In this chapter it is assumed, unless otherwise stated, that budgeting is an annual process and that budgets are prepared for a financial or operating year. Phasing of budgets is specifically addressed in Section 5.12.

IT budgeting presents particular challenges to management at all levels and not just to IT management. For most of the past 30 years, IT budgets have risen inexorably, both in absolute terms and as a proportion of turnover. In their struggle to control burgeoning IT budgets, organizations have adopted a variety of cost control and reduction measures. These include:

- indiscriminate across-the-board cuts
- extending the life of existing systems
- buying from the lowest cost vendor irregardless of other considerations
- cutting back on maintenance
- cutting back on training
- cancelling development of new systems

and so on. Other organizations have attempted to solve this problem by use of outsourcing (see Chapter 4). Unfortunately, because of lack of understanding of the nature of IT costs and cost drivers, these methods are often ineffective and are sometimes counterproductive. Amongst the problems indiscriminate budget cutting can cause are:

- Loss of, or deterioration in, services to users. This is often the first effect of budget cuts. Users find that it takes longer to obtain answers to queries and/or that changes are put on hold for long periods. The system and/or the level of service is perceived by users to 'run down'.
- Loss of, or deterioration in, service to customers. This can manifest itself in a variety of ways. Longer telephone response times, longer order lead times, longer queues. etc.
- Shifting of costs from one area to another. This is one of the most common effects. IT is perceived by many non-IT managers as an overhead cost. It is often possible, by reducing IT costs, to shift effort and costs elsewhere – thus giving the illusion of a cost saving. Another problem is the shifting of visible IT costs to other headings, as illustrated in Case history 5.1 (which is a composite of a number of such examples).
- Generation of greater, but hidden, costs. Not spending on an IT system can be a false economy. A system that responds slowly to users or is poorly designed may result in huge hidden costs. Example 5.1 is a simple case in point.
- Loss of staff morale. Poor systems, lack of systems and out of date technology can lead to low staff morale and an inability to attract or retain the best workers.

Across the board cuts are a last resort in organizational management. They should only be used where there is a real emergency and there is insufficient time to make more refined cuts. Across the board cuts in IT are usually an admission that management does not really understand the costs that it is

---

Case history 5.1: The illusion of reduced IT costs

Organization A was a large non-profit making organization with a centralized mainframe computer system.

Concerned about rising IT costs, the company announced a moratorium on the development of new systems and told users that they would have to live with the current systems for some time.

Unfortunately for the organization, the IT budget was mainframe-oriented and IT costs were perceived by management as being only those directly associated with the mainframe and its surrounding operations. Personal computers and their associated costs were treated as departmental expenditure under a variety of headings (including office furniture!).

At the time there were a few PCs in the organization. When the ban on new developments was announced, users, faced with even longer delays in meeting their requirements, turned to personal computers which were purchased in large numbers. This did not show up in the IT costs. While senior management congratulated themselves on keeping IT costs under control, real IT costs were rising dramatically and a long term maintenance and support problem was being built up.

Example 5.1: False economies

A telephone sales order system is operated by three staff working an 8 hour day. The time taken to take an order is normally 3 minutes so the staff can (in theory at least) process 480 orders per day. If, because of an underpowered system server (say), the response time were to deteriorate to 4 minutes per order, then the total orders per day would drop to 360 per day. To handle the same number of orders per day would then require another full-time salesperson. The cost of this, even over a single year, is likely to be significantly greater than the cost of, say, upgrading the server.

cutting. There is an assumption that there is over-expenditure and inefficiency in the system and that it can easily be eliminated by users and IT management. This is not true in all cases and the result can be damage that is out of all proportion to the money saved – if indeed there are any savings at all.

Good budgeting and reporting systems should therefore give management an accurate and appropriately detailed picture of current expenditure to enable them not only to control expenditure, but to make decisions on cuts, additional expenditure or reallocation of resources as and when necessary.

5.2 Prerequisites for good IT budgeting

Good budgeting involves ensuring that essential and business-justified user demands are met whilst simultaneously keeping users financially disciplined. It follows that effective IT budget management, be it aimed at cost reduction, cost containment or cost management, demands a full understanding of IT cost structures, cost drivers and the ways that the organization is supported by IT. In particular it is important to be aware of the knock-on impact of decisions.

This chapter covers each of these issues at a detailed level and provides a set of guidelines for budget preparation, management and reporting. The chapter is divided into three main parts.

1 The first part covers budgeting and budget preparation and sets out the principles of good budgeting in general. It looks at why IT budgeting is different and examines a number of approaches to IT budgeting. A straightforward set of procedures is described including how to allocate staff costs and how to present a budget properly.
2 The second part covers monitoring and reporting against budget and provides guidelines on how to monitor costs. The various reported ways to do this are described, as is the nature of the 'actuals' data that needed for reporting. There is a brief review of audit techniques.
3 The third part is a short outline of formal accounting for IT. It describes the differences between capital and current expenditure and provides guidelines on when to capitalize expenditure. It looks at the different ways of depreciating/writing down IT assets and gives guidelines on depreciation polices for different types of IT components.

Finally there is a checklist of actions for IT cost control.

5.3 Why good budgeting is important

Budgeting is good management practice for several reasons:

- it forces the management to formalize its plans
- it brings to the surface underlying business assumptions
- it places a financial discipline and structure on business plans
- it acts as a communication mechanism between users and managers
- it provides a basis for control against which expenditure can be monitored
- it provides a mechanism for allocating responsibility.

It is not unheard of for IT to be just another budget heading in a departmental or function budget – along with light, heat and office cleaning. However, there are strong reasons why a separate IT budget should be prepared. For a start, the size of much IT expenditure alone justifies its own budget. There is also a significant risk of duplication of effort and/or systems if IT budgeting is not properly coordinated. IT costs should be visible both within organizational units and across the organization as a whole, as should the factors driving IT costs. IT expenditure needs to be coordinated if best value for money is to be obtained.

While even a departmental budget with IT as a subheading is better than no IT budget, for an IT budget to be an effective management tool it must be properly thought out, planned and executed. Good IT budgeting:

- reflects the business needs
- has underlying assumptions that are explicit and understood
- is realistic
- is attainable
- is fair
- has the commitment of managers at all levels
- is integrated with other budgets
- is at an appropriate level of detail
- is measurable
- is flexible.

Budgeting which does not meet the above criteria can lead to various problems, including the following.

Bringing the management and control process into discredit. Unrealistic budgeting will undermine management credibility. There is little point in preparing a budget if performance against the budget is either unachievable or cannot be measured.

137

Evasion. Users are adept at finding ways of hiding or burying IT expenditure under other headings.

Passing of the blame for problems onto others. A major problem with unrealistic budgets is users disowning them ('I didn't draw up this budget – it's not my fault that there is a problem'). Ownership is an important principle in good budgeting.

Internal manoeuvres and battles. Unfair allocations of central and/or infrastructural costs can lead to unproductive inter-departmental battles. This can in turn lead to much ill will and lack of co-operation.

Inflexible rules. For example, a department may have budgeted for IT training which it does not need and have no money for a printer which it needs desperately, yet not be allowed to transfer the funds to make the printer purchase possible. This problem can be a particularly pernicious problem in the public sector, where sometimes budgets must be spent within a given time period, irrespective of whether this is a logical thing to do or not.

Poor control. If a budget is not at an appropriate level of detail, it can be difficult to control expenditure effectively afterwards. For example, setting a budget for 'hardware' of £50 000, while providing a ceiling on expenditure, gives no insight into the nature of the hardware expenditure and potential knock-on and/or hidden costs.

5.4 Four basic approaches to budgeting

There are four basic ways of building a budget. Budgeting may be:

1 Incremental.
2 Zero-based.
3 Top-down.
4 Bottom-up.

These are not mutually exclusive. In an IT budgeting process, elements of each may be used. It is, however, important to know when each is appropriate and how to combine them effectively. In preparing the IT budget, it is also necessary to consider the issue of dimensions. To control IT effectively, the total IT expenditure across the organization must be consolidated. The concept of dimensions is discussed in detail below.

5.4.1 Incremental budgeting

Incremental budgeting starts from the assumption that next year's requirements will not differ materially from this year's outturn. An incremental budget is built up by making selective adjustments to the prior year's figures. Frequently this is done by 'adding on a bit for inflation' or putting in a 'growth factor'. The advantages of incremental budgeting are that it is simple and takes relatively little time to prepare. If the organization is in a fairly stable environment this approach may be satisfactory provided there is a thorough review from time to time.

There are, however, drawbacks. First, it does not take account of structural changes in costs (for example, a rapid drop in hardware prices) and it will perpetuate any structural errors that there may be in the budget. It also discourages fresh thinking, especially about any changes into the nature of the organization's operations.

As a general rule, incremental budgeting is poor practice. It is conducive to sloppy thinking and should generally be avoided except for a small number of items for which it makes sense, for example some wage and salary costs and minor costs which are fairly stable such as certain consumables (e.g. paper, toner).

5.4.2 Zero-based budgeting

Zero-based budgeting seeks to build a budget from scratch. While zero-based budgeting takes into account existing equipment and systems, it assesses the business need for each item of expenditure. In theory, zero-based budgeting can be used to review all expenditure – even seemingly committed continuing expenditure. While it is good practice to review all expenditure from time to time, the annual budgeting process is not necessarily the best vehicle for so doing. A better method is to use a review and audit technique (see Chapter 4)

The advantages of zero-based budgeting are that it forces management to review regularly the entire cost base and, in parallel, it encourages management and users to look critically at current expenditure. Zero-based budgeting is good at highlighting cost drivers and control weaknesses needs such as the 'burying of fat' in the budget.

The main disadvantage of zero-based budgeting is it is time consuming and users may (sometimes rightly) feel that they are re-inventing the wheel every year. It can also waste user time in justifying and re-justifying the same expenditure year after year.

Zero-based budgeting starts from core assumptions such as units, hours, staff numbers and service response levels. Example 5.2 illustrates this point.

In theory, zero-based budgeting *can* go back to the fundamentals of the organization's operations. In Example 5.2 a totally zero-based budgeting approach might go back to questions such as what tasks do the operations staff perform and how many staff

---

Example 5.2: Incremental versus zero-based budgeting

An IT Department wants to budget for operations support staff. There are seven staff, five operatives (grade 1) and two supervisors (grade 2).

Incremental approach

Item	This year actual	Inflation	Growth	Next year budget
Staff costs	£100 000	5%	10%	£115 500

Zero-based approach

Grade 1

Numbers	5
Salary	£12 000
Base salary cost	£60 000
Overtime hours	500
Overtime cost/hour	£20
Cost of O/T	£10 000
Other pay costs	£10 000
Total cost Grade 1	£80 000

Grade 2

Numbers	2
Salary	£15 000
Base salary cost	£30 000
Overtime hours	100
Overtime cost/hour	£30
Cost of O/T	£3000
Other pay costs	£7000
Total cost grade 2	£40 000

	This years actual	Next year budget
Total staff cost	£100 000	£120 000

are needed for this operation? Such questions can raise issues about operations which may lead into other areas such as process re-design. While a good budgeting system may provoke such questions, it is not the function of the budget process to explore such issues in depth.

5.4.3 Top-down budgeting

Top-down budgeting is the process whereby senior management sets levels of expenditure within which the organization must operate for the year. This may be a global figure (for example, the increase in budget expenditure must be kept to under 5%) or may set certain specific limits (for example, limiting pay increases or capital expenditure).

The advantages of top-down budgeting are that is it driven by business realities. Firstly, top-down budgets will be determined by management's perceptions of growth, turnover or margins (or in the public sector by anticipated public demand or cash limits) during the forthcoming year. Secondly, it sends a simple and clear signal to users. Users sometimes seem to have an almost insatiable appetite for IT expenditure. Top-down budgeting ensures that users have a realistic view of what is reasonable. Thirdly, it sets enterprise-wide parameters. Such parameters may include assumptions about inflation, wage rate increases, overtime limits, etc.

The disadvantages of top-down budgeting are that it can lead to a subsequent lack of sufficient detail for reporting purposes. An allied problem can be the absence of adequate analysis of 'why', as in 'why are we spending this?' Opportunities may be missed as timing is driven by factors that do not relate to IT needs. When business is booming and margins are good, IT spending is generous and, conversely, when there is a recession IT is cut back. In certain circumstances, both of these policies may be wrong. It is important to know when.

5.4.4 Bottom-up budgeting

Bottom-up budgeting starts from the needs at the lowest level in the organization and consolidates these up into a compete budget. Fully zero-based budgeting is, by definition, bottom-up, but the converse is not true. The level at which bottom-up budgeting is started is determined by a number of factors including the organization structure, corporate culture, control needs and the materiality of the expenditure.

141

A key advantage of bottom-up budgeting is that it gets users involved in the process. User commitment and ownership are important contributors to good budgeting. Bottom-up budgeting is more likely to be based on a detailed analysis of needs and consequently to provide an information base for later management decisions. It also takes into account the operational needs of the organization, something which neither top-down nor incremental budgeting do. As a result it provides a strong basis for subsequent control.

It does have drawbacks. Like zero-based budgeting, it is time consuming and this problem is aggravated by the complex communications needed to ensure that users, IT management and general management understand each other's positions. In this, there is a danger that the overall picture can be lost. This can happen if there is no top-down view to balance the bottom-up estimates (see below). Because it can be difficult to see the wood for the trees, potential synergies from sharing of systems, training and other services can be missed. This type of budgeting is not particularly suitable for strategic or infra-structural projects which need a wide vision. Bottom-up budgeting is a good discipline and is to be recommended, but it needs to be matched with some top-down controls.

5.4.5 Combined bottom-up and top-down

Almost invariably the costs computed from a bottom-up budgeting procedure are greater than the equivalent top-down budget figures. When this happens, management at all levels has to determine where the correct balance between the two numbers lies. Priorities will be, in approximate order:

- Committed IT expenditure. Committed expenditure must be the first priority unless management are willing to shut down (or run down) existing systems. Periodic reviews of existing systems are important, but the budget cycle may not be the best place to do this.
- Self-financing expenditure. IT expenditure which is self financing in cash terms within the budget horizon requires no further justification.
- Business priorities. Business priorities may be driven by legal and regulatory requirements, market demand, customer requirements or by competitive necessity.
- Technical imperatives. These can arise, for example, where a supplier withdraws support for a current piece of hardware

or software or a supplier goes out of business. Likewise, a key standard to which the organization must comply may be changed.

● Return on investment. Once expenditures meeting the above criteria have been met, further projects should be considered in terms of their return to the business.

In extreme cases, when difficult choices have to be made, risk management and scoring methods such as those outlined in Chapter 10 may be used.

5.5 Ownership

Central to good budgeting is the concept of ownership. An owner (sometimes called a budget holder) is a person who sets and takes responsibility for, and management of, some part of the budget. Budget ownership goes hand-in-hand with delegated management responsibility. Responsibility without authority is bad budgeting practice (although the reverse situation is worse). If ownership of a budget is to be effective then the budget owner must be involved in the development of the budget. When involved and consulted, managers and users can be encouraged to 'sign on' to a budget and will be motivated to manage that budget properly, including living with any constraints that it may impose. Budgets which are imposed from above may be complied with, but may be resented or used as an excuse for other problems. Furthermore, the owner should control, directly or indirectly, the subsequent expenditure. This is self-evident, but it is surprising how many organizations do not put this simple rule into practice.

Case history 5.2: Overdoing the controls

A large services company suddenly became alarmed at the amount of money being spent on IT and decided to take drastic measures to get it under control. Hitherto IT budgeting had been done by each department in the company as part of the overall budget and had not received any special attention. As part of the new regime, the company set up an IT steering group of senior managers to review all spending. This group instituted a highly formalized planning system whereby IT budgets were submitted to the Steering Group, reviewed, sent back for changes, re-submitted and so on until a final budget was agreed.

The results of this exercise were highly beneficial. Budgets became rigorous and were properly checked and coordinated. Unfortunately the company also decided to institute a further control whereby each time a user wanted to spend money, even on a budgeted item, it had to be re-approved by the Steering Group. Apart from the waste of time and resources this involved, the result was long delays in decisions as the Steering Group only met monthly and sometimes did not get through the full agenda, leaving some requests over to the following meeting. An expenditure request could, in extreme cases, take 3 months to be approved and even more if the Steering Group queried the request.

As a result, the departmental managers became extremely frustrated. IT management, who were caught in the middle of this paper trail, were subjected to increasing abuse as users vented their frustration at both having to go through the same loop twice and at the delays.

Much of the good achieved from the tighter budget procedures was dissipated by the resulting user disrespect for the process.

5.6 Practical rules for budget ownership

There is a number of important practical caveats to the general principles of budget ownership set out in the preceding section. Owners must be able to control the costs for which they have responsibility. This means that:

- Owners should control IT budgets covering the operations and only the operations for which they have responsibility. This means that IT spending authority runs parallel with other spending authority. Budget owners should be at the appropriate managerial level.
- Budget owners should not be allowed to change the nature of items purchased without authority. A common stratagem in budgeting is to budget for one thing, but to purchase another. It is key to proper control that users are not allowed to purchase arbitrary IT products and services simply because they have the money. However, flexibility is important (see below).
- Subject to the preceding caveat, budget owners should be authorized to spend up to their agreed budget level without further reference upwards. It is important that owners take

budget preparation seriously. It is not unknown for organizations, having spent a large amount of time reviewing and agreeing budgets, to then make budget holders repeat the entire justification process when they wish to spend the money (see Case history 5.2). Apart from being a waste of time, this brings the budget process into disrepute and discourages users from taking it seriously.

- All expenditure must be notified to both financial and IT management. This should happen even where the expenditure is according to the agreed plan and within budget.

In summary, ownership and authority are key to good budgetary control. Failure to gain budget ownership leads to a lack of discipline, overspending, shifting blame to others when the budget overruns, lack of interest in the budget and all that this implies. Once the IT plan has been agreed and the budget approved, users (i.e. user management) should own and be responsible for all application expenditure. The IT manager should be responsible for all infrastructural expenditure, and financial management should monitor and control the overall position.

5.7 The scope of IT budgeting

The scale and scope of IT budgeting is surprisingly large and often not fully appreciated. For example, in organizations which do not sell IT as a service, the following might be a common perception of IT budgeting:

> *'IT budgeting is the process of setting short-term (usually one year) targets for all IT expenditure.'*

This definition is only partially complete. A better definition is:

> *'IT budgeting is the process of converting the (physical) corporate and departmental IT plans into corporate and departmental financial plans which can be used as one of the methods of monitoring and controlling IT expenditure.'*

The rationale for this long winded definition is to stress the close relationship between the IT plan and the IT budget on the one hand and IT budget and financial control on the other. Most IT budgeting is about expenditure, and this is made up of the costs of:

- continuing support of current systems
- continuing maintenance of current systems

- enhancement to current systems
- replacement of current systems
- new systems.

The development of an IT budget needs to take into account each of these. It also needs to take account of the integrated nature of IT.

The above picture is complicated by a number of factors. First, some IT expenditure is infrastructural in nature. Not all IT expenditure can be mapped directly onto a particular user, department or even application. For example, a decision to replace the current coaxial cabling in the local area network with fibre optic cable may affect every system, new and old in the building. Some expenditure is enterprise-wide and, as a consequence, IT budgets have many dimensions. Figure 5.1 illustrates this principle.

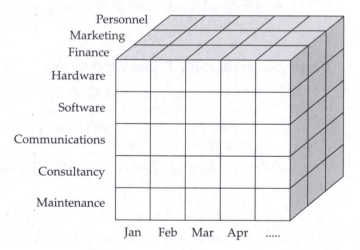

Figure 5.1

Even Figure 5.1 does not represent the full picture. IT expenditure may be analysed by:

- expenditure heading (e.g. staff costs, insurance, licences, etc.)
- type (i.e. hardware, software, communications, etc.)
- department
- time
- scenario (budget, actual, forecast)
- source (i.e. internal costs, external costs, etc.).

The depth of analysis required will depend on the scale of the expenditure and the nature of the organization's IT operations. Handling this type of analysis needs good tools. For smaller organizations, spreadsheets are probably sufficient, but for larger organizations more sophisticated tools such as multi-dimensional database management systems may be needed.

5.8 Roles in the IT budgeting process

There are three principal parties involved in every IT budget decision:

1 IT management.
2 Finance management.
3 Users (and/or user management).

In practice, the IT budget for a particular department or user will be negotiated between the three parties. While different organizations have different management styles, when it comes to budgeted expenditure the user should have an appropriate degree of influence on level of spending. Line managers should be responsible for their own use or stewardship of those resources, i.e. their performance. Consequently they should have an input into and an influence on the resources that they need, and be answerable for the effective and efficient use of those resources. The IT Department should supply costings/prices and be responsible for the infrastructural budget. The IT Department is not responsible for the performance of the Sales Department and should not therefore set the Sales Department's IT budget. The IT Department should advise on technical matters and provide cost figures as requested. The role of the Finance Department is to ensure, with IT management and users, that proposed expenditure is cost effective and value for money.

It follows that preparation of the IT budget is not a stand-alone exercise. IT budgets must relate to the operations and plans of the organization as a whole. Coordination is essential and there must be allowance for the allocation of shared costs. Alas, it is not uncommon for all three of these principles to be ignored. The following are examples of bad IT budgeting practice.

- Budgets are prepared by the IT Department with minimal reference to user needs. Users then compete for the resources available.

- At the other extreme, IT budgets are prepared by user departments without reference to central IT management.
- IT budgets are determined by senior management with little reference to either the IT Department or the users.

To avoid these problems, it is necessary that all contributors to the budget process know and fulfil their proper roles and that good communications between all parties be maintained.

5.9 Building a budget

Given such complexity in the budget structure, the question is where to start? There are several ways of building up an IT budget. The following approach builds up the budget starting from the current base. It is a comprehensive framework and not all of the items and subheadings will be applicable in all organizations. It should therefore be used selectively.

There are four stages in the process. The budget is prepared for:

1 Committed expenditure.
2 Upgrades to existing systems.
3 Replacement of existing systems.
4 New projects.

This structure is designed to provide a clear and comprehensive procedure for IT budgeting. Each stage can be done at an enterprise, department or operating unit level. It can also be used for infrastructure. In what follows, it is assumed that a department budget is being prepared. The differences that arise in infrastructure budgeting are discussed later on.

5.9.1 Stage 1: Budgeting for committed expenditure

The first step in budget preparation is to compile a list of existing systems that have to be supported whether or not any further development, modification or enhancement of the system is planned. Much of the basic information for this stage of the process should be readily available, ideally from an asset database or at least from the previous year. However, it may be necessary to re-create it each year. Bearing in mind that we are referring to the current systems, the steps within this stage are as follows.

The first step is to compile a list of all hardware (if not already available). For each item identified prepare a budget for:

- depreciation (see below).
- Insurance (this may or may not be itemized).
- Service contracts (this may or may not be itemized).
- Other repair and maintenance costs (this may be grouped, e.g. all printers).
- Lease or rental costs.
- Interest costs. This is only applicable if borrowing is specifically related to hardware items. This is generally only the case for large items.
- Operating software licence(s).
- Network management software licence(s).
- Communications software.
- Internal hardware maintenance. This is the cost of internal staffing etc. (see below).
- Losses and write-off provision (only if not insured).

Next compile a list of all software costs (if not already available) to cover:

- Depreciation (see below).
- Licence fees.
- Anticipated upgrade fees (if not included in the licence).
- External support cost.
- Internal support costs (see below).
- External maintenance costs.
- Internal maintenance costs (see below).

Depreciation needs some thought. Smaller items of software, including all PC software, will generally be written-off on acquisition, i.e. they will be treated as a routine expense. Large packages and custom built software may be depreciated over a number of years. See Section 5.17 for a more detailed discussion of this.

Internal support and maintenance will be mostly made up of people or people-related costs (such as office rent, heat, etc.). If there is a group of staff dedicated to this task, it is only necessary to compute the cost of these staff and allocate the full charge to current software support. Alternatively some, but not all, staff time may be taken up with this activity. If this is the case, staff costs will have to be allocated to different activities. This is done as follows. For each staff member:

- Calculate all his/her costs, including:
  - salary
  - benefit in kind costs
  - overtime
  - social welfare costs
  - pension costs
  - office overhead (if applicable).
- Calculate staff available time. This is:
  - standard working hours for the year
  - less personal and statutory leave
  - less training time
  - less any provisions for illness.

The result should be expressed in hours. Next:
- Compute the costs per available hour.
- Estimate the time spent on each system/area of work.
- Calculate the cost of support for each system.
- Any unused time can be put down as an overhead or allocated pro rata over the other activities.

Example 5.3 illustrates this procedure.

Example 5.3: Cost of system support

Company D employs one systems support person (John). John is paid a salary of £18 000 per annum. Pension, social insurance and other costs add a further £3000 bring the total cost to £21 000. Officially he works 2000 hours a year. After allowing for leave, training and illness he works a net 1400 hours per year. Thus his cost per delivered hour is £15. It is estimated that during the year John spends half his time doing maintenance work on the company's general ledger, a quarter of his time on the payroll and the remainder in helping other staff out with their PC software. His allocated costs are therefore:

Ledger maintenance = 50% × 1400 hours × £15 = £10 500
Payroll maintenance = 25% × 1400 hours × £15 = £5250
User support   = 25% × 1400 hours × £15 = £5250

Total   £21 000

Of course, the final figures in Example 5.3 can be derived without computing cost per available hour but, from a budgeting perspective, computing this number often gives a degree of realism to discussions.

5.9.2 Other IT budget heading costs checklist

The following is a checklist of other costs.

Infrastructure

- cabling maintenance
- network management software
- information centre costs
- user support costs.

Bought in services

- outsourced systems or functions (contracted costs)
- contract staff
- recruitment services
- retainers
- value added network costs
- telephone
- off site storage
- disaster recovery/contingency services
- keying services
- cleaning services
- other overhead costs
- escrow services
- consultancy costs
- security.

Consumables

- paper
- CDs/DVDs
- diskettes
- printer toner and ribbons
- screen cleaner
- tapes
- labels.

Training for

- IT administration staff
- IT operations staff
- support staff
- development staff
- users
- management.

Note that budgets are for the cash costs of these activities. The full cost of training is a broader issue and is discussed in Chapter 3.

Normally it is not part of the IT budgeting process to review committed costs. They should be reviewed periodically as part of the review and audit process (Chapter 4). In the absence of such a process, then there should be a periodic review of all committed costs to ensure that they are all still justified.

5.9.3 Stage 2: Preparing the upgrade budget

Having prepared the committed expenditure budget, the second stage is to budget for any planned upgrades to the system. It is useful, though not essential, to consider upgrades and replacements as separate stages. The term 'upgrade' is used in the limited sense of enhancement of existing hardware and packaged software. Replacement of hardware and modifications to custom software are covered elsewhere. The steps in the upgrade budget are as follows.

Prepare a budget for all hardware upgrades including:

● addition of memory to host/server/client
● addition of disk to host/server/client
● CPU upgrades (possible with certain processors)
● communications hardware
● printer upgrades (addition of memory or fonts)
● operating software upgrade
● addition of boards to communications equipment.

For each of the above there will be the cost of the item. There may also be a depreciation charge, additional licence charges and insurance.

Software may be upgraded by moving up a version (or sometimes several versions) and/or by adding new modules. For software it is essential that all costs of the upgrade, including implementation, hardware, data conversion and training implications are both identified and budgeted. Upgrade costs may include additional module cost(s), deprecation charges and additional licence charges.

Any upgrade will incur an implementation cost. These will mostly be staff time which will include planning, installing, testing, training, additional user support and upgrading documentation. There may also be additional back-up costs.

Upgrades often involve data conversion costs. These can be substantial and may include raw data conversion, modification of code, re-compilation, re-testing and parallel running. Upgrades can vary from minor changes, such as adding a fax card to a modem or memory to a PC, to large projects such as a version upgrade of a database management system. The upgrade budget is consolidated into the main budget, but a separate copy is maintained.

5.9.4 Stage 3: Replacement budget

The third step is to decide which systems (if any) will be replaced, or are scheduled to be replaced, in the current year and prepare a replacement budget. This covers all equipment, software and systems. Replacement covers a spectrum from minor (e.g. a plan to replace a number of printers) to substantial projects (e.g. replacement of the accounting system). Replacement needs justification. This is discussed below.

Replacement can be divided into three distinct classes: hardware (including processors, peripheral and communications equipment), application software and the systems architecture. Each of these is covered in the following sections.

There are many possible reasons for replacing hardware, from unreliability and poor performance to inability to run new software, or simply incompatibility with a new architecture. The additional cost of replacing, as opposed to upgrading, hardware needs to be justified. Trade-ins (if any) on existing machines should be budgeted. It may also be possible to sell or auction old equipment. The budget must include:

- the capital cost of the new hardware
- leasing or other financing costs net of savings
- implementation costs
- switchover costs
- termination costs (if any) on existing hardware leases(s).

Allowing for the old hardware, a budget should be prepared for net changes in:

- depreciation
- insurance costs
- service contracts
- other repair and maintenance costs
- operating software licence(s)

- network management software licence(s)
- communications software
- internal hardware maintenance
- losses and write-off provisions.

This budget, like the upgrade budget, is consolidated into the overall budget, but a copy of the detail is retained.

Replacing application software can be a much more complex process than replacing hardware. Amongst the reasons for replacing applications software are that the current system is unreliable, lacks key business functions or is no longer supported. Less pressing problems, such as difficulties with current support, may also suggest pre-emptive replacement. Preparation of the budget here is similar to upgrade and committed budgeting.

The term architecture is used for changes to the structure of the system, for example from host to client server or from two level to three-level client/server. This type of upgrade may be driven by new business needs or technological obsolescence. Projects on this scale include strategies such as 'downsizing' and are best dealt with as new projects rather than replacements.

5.9.5 Stage 4: New projects

The fourth and final stage is new projects. New projects fall into a number of categories.

- Infrastructural (enabling) projects are generally initiated by the IT Department. Although occasionally they may come from senior business managers or users, this type of project is normally too specialized for users to initiate or manage. Such projects include, for example, replacement of the cabling/ network system, changes to the architecture (e.g. host to client server), operating system changes and pre-emptive software upgrades. Infrastructural changes are driven by current and anticipated future needs as well as by technology changes.
- Business need driven projects may include acquisition of new hardware or software or, more generally, of new 'solutions'.
- New projects may be separated out from the budget for planning, costing and cost justification reasons. New projects may not, for example, fall conveniently into a financial year. The impact of the project on the budget in terms of cash flow and profit and loss impact should be carried into the budget.

5.10 Project and expenditure justification

Unless a completely zero-based budgeting approach is being contemplated, committed expenditure does not usually require formal justification. All other expenditure does. Specific projects must be justified in financial and/or business benefit terms. The budget is not always the appropriate place to do this for a number of possible reasons. For example, a project may not fall completely within one budget year or it may span several years. A project may also be of sufficient scale to justify its own budgeting and control procedures independent of the normal day-to-day IT budgeting and control. The budget may, therefore, be like a 'window' on a project through which that part of the project expenditure that falls in the budget period in question is seen.

There are exceptions to this general rule. Organizations may budget to undertake a particular project as part of this year's budget. In these circumstances it is still appropriate to prepare a stand-alone justification for the project, but the actual expenditure and possibly the savings will be included as part of the normal budget package. However most IT projects are justified over a period of more than 12 months so a separate project justification will normally be necessary. Case history 5.3 is an example of this.

Case history 5.3: Database version upgrade

'. . . Part of the planned expenditure for next year is an upgrade of the current Relational Database System to the new version. The new version (Version 7) was released 18 months ago and is already at Version 7.2. Under the terms of its support and maintenance agreement, the company is entitled to the new software at no additional charge. However, there will be significant cash expense in installing the new version which we have estimated as follows:

Installation of the new system	£2500
Conversion of existing data	£10 000
Modification and recompilation of new code to take account of changes SQL syntax in the new version	£50 000
Re-testing of system	£15 000
Hardware upgrade	£30 000

Total external cash costs	£105 500
Estimated internal costs 400 workdays	£100 000
Total cost this year	£250 500
Estimated additional costs over three years	Nil
Estimated savings over three years	
Improvements in development software – displaced cost	£40 000
Estimated benefit to users of better features	£50 000
Administration savings	£30 000
Net three year cost	£130 500

Business benefits

In the view of IT management the Company has no option but to make this upgrade at some stage in the next 5 years. At the end of this time, support for the current version will be withdrawn and the company would then be in an unacceptably exposed position. We believe that now is the optimum time to make this change as there is plenty of expertise available in the market with experience of this transition. The net cost of making this change is likely to rise steeply with every year the decision is deferred.

The new version will provide a sound platform for future developments over the next 5 to 7 years.'

5.11 Charge-back budgeting

It is strongly recommended that charge-back be used in all IT systems. The rationale for this (and the methods that may be used) are described in Chapter 3. Charge-back can be handled in a budget like any other charge. The cost is charged to the user department and credited to the IT department. In certain circumstances, departments other than the IT Department may cross-charge each other.

The rationale for charge-back is that it makes users aware of the true cost of the resources they are using.

Charge-back is a form of internal transfer and should therefore balance. This is discussed in the next paragraph.

5.11.1 Internal transfers

In many larger organizations (and some smaller ones) departments, divisions and even functions may deal with each other at arm's length. Thus, for example, the temporary transfer of a member of staff from one department to another would be reflected in an internal charge. This can be applied to IT and can be cost effective. Internal transfer rules should be designed to encourage efficient behaviour in companies. Case history 5.4 illustrates how this can (and can fail to) work.

Case history 5.4: sending the right signals

The following is a simplified account of two real-life companies.

Company A had a large number of PCs of various vintages. The IT Department itself tended to use the most up-to-date, state of the art machines. These were continually replaced with new machines and the old machines could then be transferred to other Departments in the company.

The company had a policy of writing-off machines over 3 years. When a machine was transferred, the IT Department received a credit equal to the greater of £250 or the net book value of the machine, and this amount was charged to the receiving department. Thus if the IT department bought a machine for £1500 and passed it to the Personnel Department 2 years later, Personnel were charged £500 and the IT Department were credited with the same amount. If the machine was 3 years old, the figure was £250. Using this system, the company usually got 5 years use out of each machine.

Company B had a less enlightened attitude. It ran the same system except that it did not operate the £250 minimum. Thus when a machine was 3 years old, an internal transfer yielded nothing to the IT Department. However, staff in the IT Department were only too happy to buy the machines for themselves at a nominal cost of £100. From the IT Department's point of view, selling 3 year old machines to staff was perfectly logical: £100 credit was better than £0, which is what they received from an internal transfer. The

---

> result was that, without any incentive to re-deploy, more new machines were bought throughout the company and the average useful life of a machine was a little over 3 years.
>
> Naturally, over time, company B spent much more on PCs than company A.

It is essential that internal transfers in any budget balance. This means that if Department A budgets to pay Department B for certain services, Department B must budget to receive the same amount – otherwise the accounting will become totally confused. To ensure that the latter does not happen, where there is either charge-back or internal transfers, there must be a balancing matrix, i.e. a process in the budget whereby all inflows and outflows are matched. Many budgeting systems have such a process for other inter-department, inter-divisional or inter-company flows. If so, IT resource transfers can be included in this.

5.12 Phasing a budget

IT budgets are generally prepared for the year as a whole. Phasing is the process of spreading the budget across the year. Typically this is done by month or by accounting period. IT is a continuing cost. There therefore needs to be some mechanism for estimating the cost of IT over the reporting period. Phasing is also important for cash-flow management. Managers should be able to plan when expenditure will be incurred during the year. The budget should reflect this as it will enable management to check actual expenditure against expectations rather than receiving an unpleasant surprise at the end of the year. A good budget will give early warning of problems.

Phasing can be done many ways. A crude approach is to divide the total annual budget by the number of periods and allocate the same cost to each period. In many organizations this is perfectly adequate for control. A large proportion of IT costs may be staff salaries and equipment depreciation which are spread fairly evenly across the year. However, this method does not necessarily paint an accurate picture of performance against budget. For example, if a large expenditure is planned for the second half of the year, the organization will appear to be way behind budget for all of the first half. A better approach is to prepare a detailed expenditure plan. This is appropriate where it is anticipated that there will be large expenditures at certain times in the year.

5.13 Reporting against budget

Budgets are plans and only plans; and real-life does not always go according to plan. Circumstances change. Changes may vary from the trivial, such as a price rise in a minor piece of equipment, to major alterations such as a new business opportunity or an unexpected change in the regulatory environment. It is important to understand that just because expenditure is budgeted does not mean that the money must be spent (although some parts of the public sector do not always operate on this principle!). Equally, critical business operations or needs should not be held up just because they were not foreseen at the time the budget was prepared. For these reasons and a hundred others, actual outturns differ from budgets. It has been commented, semi-seriously, that an organization that always exactly meets its budget has a serious problem. Good organizations are flexible about budgets, but this flexibility is always fully controlled by management. Decisions to overspend on budget are conscious management actions, not something that happens by accident or default.

5.13.1 Principles underlying budget reporting

The are several principles underlying good reporting against budgets. First, budgets should be prepared to an appropriate level of detail. The key factors determining this are:

- Materiality. While most organizations would budget for, say, purchase of a new fault-tolerant database server, few are likely to budget for a box of CDs or a ream of paper. A practical approach is to have a 'miscellaneous' heading to cover the multitude of incidental expenditures that occur during the year. This is the budget equivalent of the petty cash box.
- Measurability. There is no point in budgeting for something if the actual expenditure cannot be measured. For example, there is no point in budgeting the allocation of staff time to different activities or departments if the procedures are not in place for measuring the actual time used in each area.
- Controllability. IT budgets should be either knowable or controllable expenditures (the same may not be entirely true

of other types of budget which can be more aspirational in character, for example, sales volumes). If they are not controllable by IT or user management, then they should be in the budgets of those who do control them.

Once the year starts and actual expenditure is incurred, the reporting of actual performance against budget requires that actual expenditure is captured. This is a key point. Some organizations prepare budgets with great care, but are then unable to identify all of the corresponding expenditure. There can be various reasons for this. The most common reasons are that the IT expenditure is buried under other headings or that the expenditure is deliberately or inadvertently classified as something else (such as office equipment or telephone costs). It is also important that actual expenditure can be analysed into the headings used in the budget. This is another surprisingly common mistake and source of problems. Budgets are sometimes prepared without due regard to the ability of the financial reporting systems to analyse the actual data in the same format. The result can be a mish-mash of budget and actual comparisons which do not quite match and which can be difficult to interpret.

5.13.2 Variances and how to analyse them

The basic principle of reporting is to show:

- budgeted amount
- actual amount
- the difference (or variance) between budget and actual
- commentary on the variance

for the current period (e.g. month) and the year to date. For predominantly expenditure budgets (such as IT) variance is normally defined as:

$$\text{Variance} = \text{Budget} - \text{Actual}$$

This definition causes confusion if the budget is for an income amount because if income is above budget, it will show a negative figure. A simple rule is always to show favourable variances as positive numbers and unfavourable variances as negatives. It is amazing how many financial reporting systems do not do this, leaving the reader to interpret the sign of a variance according to the context.

There are a number of further developments and refinements of these basic figures, including volume and rate (price) variances.

Volume and rate variance give information about how a variance has arisen. They are used when a budget is defined for a volume of goods at a budgeted price. Variances are then defined as follows:

$$\text{Volume variance} = (\text{Budgeted volume} - \text{Actual volume}) \times \text{Budgeted price}$$

$$\text{Price/Rate variance} = (\text{Budgeted price} - \text{Actual price}) \times \text{Actual volume}$$

$$\text{Total variance} = \text{Budgeted price} \times \text{Budgeted volume} - \text{Actual price by Actual volume}$$

A simple calculation shows that:

$$\text{Total variance} = \text{Volume variance} + \text{Price variance}.$$

This can be seen in Example 5.4.

Example 5.4: Variance analysis

A department budgets to buy 20 new laptops during the year at a price of £1000 each.

At the end of the year, the expenditure report shows the following (negative numbers are shown in parenthesis):

	Budget	Actual	Variance
PCs purchased	£20 000	£21 600	(£1 600)

This says that the department overspent by £1600 on its portable PC budget. But this analysis hides the full picture. What actually happened was that:

- the average price paid for PCs was £900
- the department bought 24 PCs.

It calculates as follows:

Volume variance = (Budgeted volume – Actual volume) × Budgeted price
= (20 – 24) × £2000 = (£4000)

Price (or rate) variance = (Budgeted price – Actual price) × Budgeted volume
= (£1000 – £900) × 24 = £2400

Total variance = (£4000) + £2400 = (£1600)

5.14 Forecasting

Budgets are often finalized well in advance of the actual period covered by the budget. It is common, for example, for companies to agree final budgets in November, October or even as early as September for the following year. By March or April of that year, the business or organizational needs could have changed significantly and parts of the budget may have become wholly inappropriate. In these circumstances, is it sensible to prepare a revised budget or forecast. Forecasts are sometime called flexed budgets.

There are three basic types of forecast:

1 Simple. This re-computes the budget from the next period to year end. While it takes into account the changes implied by the actuals, it does not take into account consequential effects. For example, if a large additional piece of equipment has been purchased, a simple forecast might not reflect the additional depreciation charge for the remainder of the year. A simple forecast would, however, allow for the fact that it is now known that a project is going to overrun or take longer to complete. Simple forecasts are quite limited, but can be useful as a management tool provided their limitations are understood.

2 Flexed budget. This is the most common type of forecast. A flexed budget starts with the actuals to date and re-computes the budget to year end. Unlike the simple forecast, this takes into account knock-on effects.

3 Rolling. This is a sophisticated process whereby a new forecast is prepared every period. This gives a powerful management tool, but in all but the simplest organizations it requires sophisticated software and tight integration between the financial accounting and budgeting systems.

Preparing a forecast is a resource-hungry process. Most organizations who use forecasting tend to do one or two forecasts per year. If more frequent forecasting is required, a rolling forecast should be considered and the proper facilities to do a rolling forecast should be developed.

5.14.1 Reporting forecasts

When a forecast is produced, the number of reporting options increases. For example a report can show any of the following:

- original (or fixed) budget
- actual
- variance

or

- forecast (flexed budget)
- actual
- variance

or

- original (or fixed) budget
- forecast (flexed budget)
- analysis of differences.

With multiple forecasts, even more permutations are possible.

Forecasting is particularly useful in volatile environments. A budget which bears no relation to the current business reality is not only useless, it may be positively harmful. This can be seen by considering the reporting options.

- Reporting against fixed budget only is simple to do and provides good budgetary control. It does not give users the idea that they can always change their minds later. It therefore provides a very tight control mechanism. However, it discourages users from fresh thinking. 'Once the budget is done, we stick with it come what may' and, as noted above, it can become unrealistic as the year wears on.
- Reporting against forecast only is more realistic and ensures that users continually review the position. It also tells managers what the most likely outcome for the year is. On the down side, it can lead to a more casual attitude to the original budget and it involves a great deal more work as well as more effort to control. It is easy to lose sight of the original budget.

- A third way is to use a combination of budget and forecast reporting. This shows both the variance from the original budget and from the current forecast (and sometimes the analysis of variance between budget and forecast). It shows the full position, combining the advantages of the preceding two methods, but it is even more complex to track and report. It also requires interpretation – there is a risk of confusion as to what the actual control base is (see Example 5.5).

Example 5.5: Forecast reporting

A department budgets for development of a custom-built system to be developed by a software house. The original budget is £1 500 000. Shortly after the project commences, there is a major change in requirements. After some negotiation with the software house, the cost is re-estimated at £1 900 000. Due to good project management, the software house actually completes the work for £1 650 000. The report might look like this:

	Budget	Actual	Variance	Forecast over budget	Variance from forecast
New system	£1 500 000	£1 650 000	–£150 000	–£400 000	+£250 000

This report shows an overall negative variance from the original budget of £150 000 and a positive variance of £250 000 on the forecast figure.

5.15 Good monitoring and reporting practices

There are several additional issues in reporting. Four important ones are:

1 Compensating variances. Variances can be compensating, as seen in Example 5.5. On a simple report without a variance breakdown, this may not be visible. For example, a company budgets to buy eight printers for £500 each, a total of £4000. However, before the budget period starts, the price of printers falls to £400 so they decide to buy ten. This will show up as a nil variance. However, good reporting should highlight the fact that rather than save £800 by buying the budgeted number of printers, the users elected to purchase two additional printers.

2 Supporting commentary. Reports should always be accompanied by a management commentary, even if that commentary is to the effect that everything is exactly in line with budget. Material variances, both positive and negative should be explained.

3 Exception reporting. Exception reports note major deviations from budget. The definition of 'major' and of materiality will depend on the organization. Financial management should set clear rules on this. For example:

> 'Where there is a deviation of more than 5% or £1000 from budget (in either direction), reports should include a commentary on the cause of the variance.'

4. Authorization procedures. There should always be clear rules on who can authorize spending in excess of the agreed budget. There may be different levels of authorization for differing levels of overspend. There should also be formal authorization levels for re-allocation of budgets, i.e. moving of money from one budget heading to another.

There is little point in controlling IT costs at a strategic level if day to day control is not effective. In all organizations there will be established financial budgeting, control and reporting procedures. However, in many organizations these will not include a proper IT budget and relatively few organizations can accurately budget, track and report all IT expenditure, wherever incurred. Proper budgetary planning and control take detailed planning and good procedures. The returns are well worth the effort.

5.16 Tracking hardware and software

In the days when everything was attached to the mainframe it was easy to maintain an inventory of hardware and software. In today's distributed system where every user has a CD or DVD drive on their PC and IT spending is often controlled by users rather than central IT management, keeping track of hardware and software owned or leased by the organization is hard work. To help manage this problem there are two types of software product now on the market.

1 Equipment databases. These are systems which are designed to hold all the requisite information about the systems in an organization. They are passive in the sense that the user has to

maintain all the information in them manually. An equipment database should be able to store and report the following information where applicable.

For hardware:
- purchase date
- name
- model number
- serial number
- purchase value
- depreciation charges/rates
- current value
- location
- user
- configuration details
- maintenance contract information
- maintenance history
- system software details (if appropriate).

This includes processors, peripherals and communications components.

For software:
- purchase date
- description
- version number
- licence terms
- configuration information
- licence number
- user name
- location
- maintenance agreement details.

2 Network management systems (which should be clearly distinguished from network operating systems) are now widely used as organizations seek to control diversified systems. Unlike equipment databases, network management systems (NMSs) are active tools that sit on the network server and monitor what is happening from minute to minute. A good NMS can prepare an inventory of all 'network aware' equipment connected to the network and will know, for example, if a PC is connected or removed. From a tracking perspective, the following are the important features to look for when purchasing a network management system:

- report on all hardware on the network
- report on all software on the network

- performance monitoring
- software licence control
- software distribution
- fault reporting
- activity monitoring.

There are several products of this type on the market today.

5.17 Accounting for IT

In understanding IT costs, the way in which costs are formally allocated and reported is important. Accounting policies affect decision making in IT as elsewhere. For example, if a manager can write a piece of equipment off over five years, it looks less expensive than if it has to be written off over three. Managers' and users' actions and attitudes are influenced by cost allocation and accounting policies. Good IT and financial management should send the correct signals to decision makers. For this reason, IT managers should understand the principles underlying accounting for IT. For the financial manager, accounting for IT raises a number of special issues which must be addressed. Good communication between IT and Finance requires mutual understanding of the other side's perspective.

The objective of accounting for IT, as elsewhere, is to provide an accurate picture of the different costs of IT, the nature of these costs and where they are incurred. Even where IT and IT-related costs are known to a high degree of accuracy, a number of decisions on how they are to be reported must be made, including:

- What items to include as IT expenditure?
- What to treat as current expenditure?
- What to treat as capital expenditure?
- What depreciation policies to use?
- Whether to absorb IT costs centrally or charge them out to user departments?
- If they are to be charged out, what basis should be used?

The latter two questions are purely internal management accounting issues and are discussed under the heading of charge-back (see Chapter 3). The first four, which may affect external reporting, are discussed in the following paragraphs.

5.17.1 Differences between capital and non-capital expenditure

As in other areas of company expenditure, IT expenditure can be divided into capital and current expenditure. This distinction is important and has implications beyond mere classification of costs. Capital and non-capital expenditure are reported in different ways in the company's accounts, will affect the company's profitability, and may affect its tax liability. In general, capital expenditure is not reported in the profit and loss. The profit and loss cost of capital expenditure is spread over several years in the form of depreciation or write-down. Capital expenditure can generally be at least partially set off against current taxable profits. The rules for this are complex and can change with each national budget.

By capitalizing costs, an organization can reduce the impact on current profits of major expenditures. If there is pressure on management to raise short-term profitability, there will be a strong temptation to defer and/or spread out costs for as long a period as possible to minimize their short-term impact. The danger of such policies is that they can give a misleading picture of the true cost of running the business, thus misleading shareholders, third parties and even management itself. To try to eliminate this type of manipulation, the Accounting Bodies have set up a number of Statements of Standard Accounting Practice or SSAPs. Two of direct relevance to IT expenditure are SSAP 12 (Accounting for Depreciation) and SSAP 13 (Accounting for Research & Development). SSAPs are statements of standards which auditors must apply when preparing financial statements. To these must be added the legal reporting requirements as set out in the various Companies Acts. The latter can be more stringent than the audit requirements.

Like many accounting standards, some aspects of these SSAPs are open to interpretation. This may give management a certain amount of flexibility in how it reports costs. Before considering this, it is worthwhile reviewing the advantages and disadvantages of capitalization.

5.17.2 Advantages and disadvantages of capitalization

The advantages of capitalizing IT expenditure are, firstly, that it spreads the cost over a number of years thus reducing the impact on the profit and loss in the year of acquisition or expenditure. Secondly, if the purchase has a reasonable useful life, it reflects the underlying business reality, i.e. that the equipment provides value over a period of time and that the cost of providing that value should be pro rated with it. There are some disadvantages to capitalization. If the asset actually loses value faster than it is written off, then the apparent value in the balance sheet will overstate the true value of the asset. This may have serious implications for decision making. Perhaps more importantly from a management perspective, for expenditure where capitalization is borderline, writing off expenditure over time may not send the best message to users. Under the accounting guidelines and the law, most company expenditure is readily classifiable as either capital in nature or not. However, when it comes to IT expenditure, some special problems can arise.

The reasons why capitalization and depreciation policy is a difficult one in IT are that for many organizations a considerable proportion (sometimes the bulk) of their IT expenditure falls into a grey area between straightforward capital asset acquisition and day-to-day running costs. For example, in certain circumstances, it can be argued that much of IT current expenditure is research and development which can be regarded as a capital cost. SSAP 13, which covers Research and Development, is couched in terms of companies developing products (including IT products) for future sale. Its interpretation for internal IT development is not clear. Furthermore, while the continual fall in the price of IT hardware suggests that fast write-downs are appropriate, this can lead to an incongruity between the market value of IT systems and both their useful and their physical lives. A state of the art PC bought today will have halved in (retail) price in 18 months to 2 years, be technologically obsolete in 3 to 4 years, but will work perfectly for 10 years or more. There is also a difficulty in assessing the useful life of software, and in particular custom-built software.

5.17.3 What can/should be capitalized?

The three key questions for managers are therefore:

- What *can* be capitalized?
- What *should* be capitalized?
- Over what period should I write off expenditure?

To answer these questions it is first necessary to consider what the rules state and where there is room for interpretation and then to take account of three sets of requirements, namely the company's interest, the accounting standards and legal requirements.

These three do not always coincide. The company's interest may include some or all of the following:

- optimizing profit
- minimizing taxation
- providing management with the most realistic information
- providing investors/shareholders with the most realistic information
- providing the market (and competitors) with a particular picture of the company.

Where a company has a high tax rate and taxable profits, it makes sense to use expenditure to reduce taxable profits as much as possible. Money today is worth more than money in the future. If a tax saving can be made now rather than later, it is more efficient to take it now. This can be done most effectively by simply writing off the cost against the profit and loss in the year of acquisition. However, with a large IT expenditure, this might cause unacceptable reduction in profits. By designating expenditure as capital, a company can gain the tax benefits without the corresponding impact on the profit and loss. Where a company does not pay tax (as in the public sector), leasing may be more attractive.

Accounting standards have a different perspective. The key rules are that a company may write off any item of routine expenditure in the year in which it is incurred, but large asset expenditure, where the assets concerned can be reasonably expected to have a useful life of over a year, should be written off over their expected useful lives. The period and rate of write-off should be commensurate with the value of the assets to the business. A number of ways of writing-down (depreciating) assets are permissible (see Example 5.6). The depreciation method should be appropriate to the product and should take into account the residual value of the asset (if any) and any revaluations (in either direction). Accounting rules permit companies to capitalize and then depreciate expenditure even where the expenditure involved is not a 'capital' item in the colloquial sense of the word. Important examples are research and development of a new IT product for sale to third parties and development of a new customized software package for internal use.

Example 5.6: Depreciation methods

There are several methods of depreciation, but three are commonly used.

Suppose that a company buys a high speed heavy duty line printer for £15 000 on 1 January and decides to write it off over 5 years. The following would be the depreciation calculations under the different depreciation methods.

The straight line method writes off an asset by equal amounts over a fixed period of years. This has the advantage of writing off the asset cleanly, but it may not reflect the fact that for many assets there is a greater loss in value in the early years. In this case the write-down will be:

	Year 1	Year 2	Year 3	Year 4	Year 5
Depreciation charge	£3000	£3000	£3000	£3000	£3000
Value of asset at year end	£12 000	£9000	£6000	£3000	£0

Declining balance writes off a percentage of the residual balance each year. This reflects the real position more realistically but it will never fully write off the asset, so the residual balance has be managed. As this method will not write the asset off over 5 years, the company has to decide an appropriate depreciation rate. Assume it chooses 33.3% and writes off the residual balance in year 5. The result is as follows:

	Year 1	Year 2	Year 3	Year 4	Year 5
Depreciation charge	£5000	£3333	£2222	£1481	£2963
Value of asset at year end	£10 000	£6667	£4444	£2963	£0

As can be seen, this gives rise to an anomaly whereby depreciation in year 5 is higher than that in years 3 and 4.

Sum of digits is a compromise designed to overcome problems with the straight line and declining balance methods. It both acts like a declining balance and writes-off the asset cleanly. It is computed by first adding up the values of all the years (1 + 2 + 3 + 4 + 5 = 15). The depreciation charge is then taken as 5/15 in year 1, 4/15 in year 2 and so on. This gives a declining depreciation charge each year and has the effect that the sum of the charges equals the initial asset value. In this case:

	Year 1	Year 2	Year 3	Year 4	Year 5
Depreciation fraction	5/15	4/15	3/15	2/15	1/15
Depreciation charge	£5000	£4000	£3000	£2000	£1000
Value of asset at year end	£10 000	£6000	£3000	£1000	£0

Legal requirements are given by the Companies Act 1985 (or in Northern Ireland, the Companies (Northern Ireland) Order 1986). These require that assets be shown in the companies' balance sheets as either intangible assets, tangible assets or investments. The values of the assets shown must be either their purchase price or production cost. It is permissible to revalue assets (up or down), but details of all revaluations and any consequences for depreciation must be disclosed in the accounts.

5.17.4 How fast can or should capital items be depreciated?

When it comes to accounting, some issues are clear. In general non-capital expenditure such as wages and salaries, power, heat, light, etc., consumables and insurance are all written off in the year they occur, thus reducing the tax bill for that year. Expenditures such as host computers, large servers, cabling, buildings and other large scale infrastructure are both sizeable and have long term value to the business so they are clearly capital though, within certain limits, some may be written off in the year in which they occur.

The difficulty arises in the so-called grey areas such as PCs, packaged software and custom-software. A major custom-software development can, under current accounting rules, be capitalized, but what defines 'major' is a moot point. The rules here leave scope for interpretation. Auditors tend to be conservative. They normally prefer IT assets to be written-down over a relatively short period such as 3 years. As noted above, this may not always suit the company. While the application of these rules is technically a matter for the company's auditors, in practice the company can argue for a particular policy and auditors will generally take a pragmatic view.

Guidelines for the main borderline cases are shown in Table 5.1.

Table 5.1 Guideline write-down times

Item	Practical life	Write-down
PCs	2–4 years	3 years
Most other hardware	3–5 years	3 years
System software	3–5 years	3 years
PC software	2–4 years	Expense
Major packaged software	5–7 years	4 years
Personal software	2–4 years	Expense
Custom software	5–10 years	5 years
Physical infrastructure	5–7 years	5 years

Factors which may affect the length of the write-down include the speed at which technology forces the business to change. For example, changes in PC technology may require a business to update its PCs faster than its printers even though printer technology is also changing just as quickly. The nature of the business also affects policy. Companies which depend on cutting edge technology for their competitiveness should write off IT assets faster than companies where IT plays only a background role. Finally, sudden large shifts in the technology or the market can lead to revaluations. For example, a decision by a vendor to withdraw his product from the market or end a product line may cause a sudden drop in the value of an asset.

If an organization's current accounting policies are conservative, it is likely that the value of IT assets in the balance sheet will be far short of their actual value when measured in terms of their importance to the company. This is particularly true of custom-ized software where 'intellectual property' of enormous commercial value may be embedded in the software. In these circumstances, management will have to negotiate with the auditors to reflect the inherent value of the software.

With all IT assets there should be regular review of their projected economic and/or technological life. While the value of IT assets are normally seen as something that falls fairly quickly, it is possible that, in unusual circumstances, the value of an IT asset could rise (for example, a customized piece of software might become saleable thus giving it a value it would not have had as a purely internal system).

5.17.5 Accounting for software development costs

Internal software development costs may be capitalized subject to certain conditions. These are governed by SSAP 13 'Accounting for Research and Development'. This entitles a company to accrue (capitalize) for:

> 'design of product, service, process or systems involving new technology or substantially improving those already produced or installed'.

Strictly interpreted, this applies to products that the company makes. However, auditors will generally permit major software and systems development to be capitalized, even where all the costs are internal and the benefits are not in terms of revenue but in terms of savings or other value to the business. SSAP 13 also states that in order to be capitalized, the following conditions must apply:

- There must be a clearly defined development project.
- The related expenditure must be clearly identifiable.
- The value/outcome of the project must be assessed with reasonable certainty (i.e. the company must be able to show that this system will work and will have value).
- The expenditure incurred must be matched by projected income or cost savings. This is critical as it implies that, for example, projects where the benefits are 'soft' or not easily quantified may not be capitalized.
- Where expenditure goes over more than one accounting period, there is reasonable expectation that the project will be completed.

The above rules are common sense and permit that in these circumstances, development expenditure may be deferred (i.e. written-off over future periods) where recovery of the expenditure can be reasonably regarded as being assured. Finally, the various companies acts referred to above add some further stipulations. The key points are that research costs may not be regarded as an asset in the company's balance sheet and that the company accounts must show the period over which any capitalized expenditure is being written-off. The reasons for capitalizing the expenditure must be stated and be clear.

5.17.6 Management accounting account code structure

Within the accounting system itself, coding of IT expenditure is important. The account code structure may have to permit analysis of any of the following:

- Expenditure type:
  - hardware
  - software
  - service
  - etc.
- Project for current projects in hand.
- Nature for charge-back purposes:
  - infrastructural
  - application
  - direct user.
- User department:
  - accounts
  - production
  - sales
  - etc.

Proper design of the account coding structure is essential for suitable cost analysis and IT cost control.

5.18 A final checklist

The following is a summary of actions points for control of IT costs.

- Develop a full understanding of IT costs.
- Develop an awareness of hidden costs.
- Analyse and understand all semi-visible costs such as maintenance.
- Ensure that the knock-on effect of all purchase decisions are understood before purchases are made.
- Implement proper purchasing procedures.
- Develop and implement approved products and suppliers list.
- Develop an asset view of IT. Do not regard IT simply as an overhead.
- Prepare an IT asset statement.
- Understand the benefits of IT.
- Implement proper IT expenditure appraisal and evaluation procedures.

- Prepare a proper IT budget which is realistic and against which performance is measurable.
- Ensure that controls are firm without being inflexible.
- Implement proper budget responsibilities and ownership.
- Ensure that all IT costs are being captured.
- Implement an IT cost reporting system.
- If necessary change the finance systems to generate the necessary data for reporting.
- Be practical, do not waste valuable resources managing or tracking small amounts.
- Implement a charge-back system.
- Consider use of selective outsourcing for specialist tasks.
- Consider use of total outsourcing, but do so with caution.

6 Specifying hardware and systems software

6.1 Introduction

To start with the obvious, before purchasing any computer system or component it is important to know what it is required to do. The more significant the purchase, the more precise this specification of requirements needs to be. Despite these self-evident statements, a common problem in much purchasing, including IT, is buying based on the features of the product rather than on the ability of that product to meet the real business need. This is, in turn, often the result of this need with not being clear, or at least not being clearly stated at the time of purchase.

Good IT purchasing presents potential suppliers with a clear statement of what is wanted. This may be expressed in the form of a shopping list of components or a description of the business functionality to be met. No reputable supplier will be willing to quote for hardware without a reasonably sound understanding on both its part and the purchaser's of what is required. The more professional the supplier, the more detailed the information it is likely to seek.

Despite, or possibly because of, the growth in standardization and the development of Open Systems, modern computer hardware purchasing has become increasingly complex. An old-fashioned host computer system would have had a single central processor, a few printers, some disk packs, tape drives and lots of dumb terminals. Modern distributed systems have many dozens of diverse components, more often than not from several different manufacturers.

Specifying hardware requirements is not difficult, even for non technical users, once a number of basic principles are understood. This chapter sets out these principles and provides guidelines and templates on how to specify the hardware and the system software components that they need to operate.

6.2 Two approaches to specification

There are two approaches to IT specification. The first is a *technical* or *prescriptive* approach. A technical approach to specification tells the supplier precisely what is required in technical terms. For example, a technical specification for a laser printer might be:

'The printer must have a resolution of at least 1200×1200 dots per inch and a minimum speed of 16 pages per minute. It must support Postscript level 2, Truetype, and PCL level 6. It should have USB, EIO and infra red ports. It should have 16 Megabytes of on-board memory with expansion capacity up to a minimum of 64 MB. It should have a standby facility. It must be capable of supporting paper of up to 150 grams/m^2 and be able to print standard letter-sized envelopes. It should have two paper trays and a manual feed capability. At least one of the paper trays must have a capacity of 500 pages or greater and the output tray should have a capacity of 200 pages or greater.'

This is a pretty thorough statement of requirements which leaves little room for deviation. Either the supplier has a printer that meets this specification or it does not.

There are three advantages of this approach. Firstly it is clear. There is no ambiguity and no grey areas which could lead to arguments afterwards. Secondly, it simplifies evaluation. It should be quite clear whether a product meets the requirements or not. Thirdly, suppliers can respond quickly. They are given all the information required to put forward a solution.

There are, however, several drawbacks in this approach. The first, and most significant, is that the purchaser assumes all the risk. If the product meets the specification, but does not do the job, then the purchaser has no comeback against the supplier. Secondly, the buyer needs to know how to assess the technical performance required. Purchasers sometimes over-estimate their own technical expertise and may not specify a component correctly. Thirdly, this approach may close off other options, if only because the buyer may not be aware of them. For example, there may be new printer features available. Suppliers operating on low margins and under pressure may respond to exactly what is requested and may not point out other product options.

The alternative is a *business* or *functional* approach. Here the specification states the requirement in terms of the business need rather than the technical features of the product. A functional statement of requirements for a similar printer might read:

> 'The laser printer will be used for printing of routine documents (letters, reports, etc.) and the internal company newsletter which includes text, diagrams and photographs. The quality of the print must be suitable for this. A variety of fonts are used in typesetting the newsletter. The printer will be shared by a group of six users and must be capable of handling their daily printing requirements.'

By comparison with the preceding specification, this statement is very loose. The supplier is given minimal technical information and the purchaser is dependent on the supplier's experience and judgment to suggest a suitable product.

The advantages of this approach are that it expresses the requirement in terms that the buyer and user (who may be different people) can understand. It gives the supplier an opportunity to ask questions and offer a number of possible products which might meet the need and it implicitly invites the supplier to talk to the user about the requirements (indeed, in the above example it would be a poor supplier who did not seek further information before proposing a suitable printer).

The disadvantages are that it can leave a large number of questions unanswered and can be ambiguous. The buyer may be presented with a wide range of options from the supplier or suppliers and may find it difficult to choose between them. Furthermore, because of the lack of clarity, the buyer may end up with an unsuitable machine which may, in turn, lead to arguments with the supplier.

Both approaches therefore have their strengths and weaknesses. In practice, both approaches can and should be mixed and the best specifications of requirements will have elements of each.

6.3 Important definitions

When specifying hardware in business or functional terms, simply stating the technical requirements is not always sufficient. Often it is essential to state the performance requirements as well. This is particularly important with host computers and servers or, if so-called 'total solutions' are being purchased, with the system as a whole. Even where a system is being replaced (for example, a host system is being replaced with a distributed system), it is important that target performance levels be set. Merely stating that '. . . the new system should provide levels of performance comparable with or better than the current system . . .' is not sufficient unless there are agreed measurements of precisely what the current performance levels are.

In addressing hardware purchasing, the following definitions are therefore useful.

- Performance. This means the response, calculation processing and/or throughput times required.
- Sizing. This refers to the permanent storage capacity, memory required and traffic bandwidth on busses and networks.
- Volumes. This covers a number of headings including the total number of users the system must support, the total amount of data to be stored, the number of transactions throughput and the number of enquiries.
- Transaction. This is defined as any action taken directly or indirectly by the user or the system that alters the data stored in the system. The three basic transactions are input/create, update/modify and delete/remove.
- Benchmark. This term has three possible meanings. It can mean a standard measurement of equipment or system performance. It can also mean a user performance test, or a comparison with other organizations in the same industry. In this chapter, the term benchmark is used for measures which assess processor or system performance.

While a modern system can contain many thousands of individual hardware components, these fall into a moderate number of categories:

- processors
- storage devices
- printers
- other output devices
- input devices
- communications devices and equipment
- cabling/communications
- system software
- other components.

System software is included here as it is normally part of a hardware specification. Each of these components has its own performance characteristics and is governed by certain standards (to which it may or may not comply). Each may also link to or work with other components in a variety of ways. For this reason, specification of hardware requirements requires specification of:

● all the components that are required
● the required performance characteristics of that component
● any legal regulations with which components must comply
● standards to which components must conform.

The remainder of this chapter describes how to specify all of the important components in the above list in a modern distributed or host system.

6.4 Specifying processors

Processors cover an enormous range of equipment from supercomputers to personal digital assistants. The general principles underlying the specification of requirements for processors are the same for all machines, but there are clearly going to be differences dependent on the uses to which they are put. The following are the important generic characteristics of a processor:

● the characteristics of the central processing unit (CPU)
● memory, including main and cache
● storage
● connectivity (number and types of ports)
● operating system(s) supported
● standards with which it complies
● expansion capacity.

Different types of processor will have special characteristics which are relevant only to them. For example, for a portable PC size and weight may be of interest. For a host minicomputer or server, the maximum number of simultaneous users supported will be important.

In the following sections, the possible features required on any hardware or system software component are listed in detail. Not all of these features will be important, or even relevant, in all circumstances. As well as providing a comprehensive checklist of features, each section includes a commentary on when it is appropriate to specify each type of feature.

6.4.1 Specifying host computers and servers

The traditional distinction between mainframes or mini-computers is today more-or-less archaic. In practice, there are two basic architectures: host and distributed. In theory, too, servers may be mainframes, minicomputers or microcomputers. In practice nearly all servers today are Intel or reduced instruction set (RISC) processors running some variant or derivative of either the Unix, Linux or Windows operating systems. From the point of view of specifying requirements, host computers and servers are broadly similar. It is therefore convenient to consider them together. There are differences in specifying each of these and these differences are highlighted where they occur. The following are characteristics of the host computer or server that should be specified.

- The number of users to be supported. The specification should allow for both the initial number of users as well as anticipated growth in user numbers.
- The user mix to be supported. One person running heavy and complex queries may have more impact on a host computer than 50 casual users. A useful way to consider users of a host system is to classify them according to an activity grid. Example 6.1 shows a simple grid. Analysis of activity levels can be more detailed. An example of a further refinement is given below. The user activity grid enables the supplier to gauge the level of demand on the processor.

Example 6.1: User activity grid

	Number of users by predominant activity			
	Query	Mixed	Transaction	Total
Active	37	23	112	172
Passive	40	74	–	114
Total	77	97	112	286

- The patterns and volumes of activity on the machine. To do this it is necessary to specify:
  - The transaction rate. The transaction rate is the number of transactions per day/hour/minute/second (as appropriate) which the processor will have to handle. This should be specified:
    - By size (i.e. by the amount of data of an average transaction). A simple approach is to divide this into:
      * small (say less than 100 bytes)
      * medium (say 100 bytes to 1 KB)
      * large (over 1 KB)
    - By level of complexity. This is done by dividing transactions into:
      * Simple. Transactions which only update one file or database table and have minimal processing.
      * Moderate. Transactions which update between two and five files or tables and may incorporate moderate processing.
      * Complex. Transactions which update more than five files or tables or involve complex validation and processing.
      * Highly complex. Transactions which update more than five files or tables and involve complex validation and processing.
    - By type. Transactions may be:
      * on-line
      * batch
      * keyed
      * machine-generated (e.g. by bar code readers).
  - The enquiry rate. This is the number of enquiries per day/ hour/minute/second (as appropriate) which the processor will have to handle. This should be specified:
    - By level of complexity. Queries may be:
      * Simple. Typically these involve a single look-up of an indexed file or table (e.g. 'What is John Smith's staff number?').
      * Moderate. These may involve a number of files or tables and some processing of the result (e.g. 'Get me the average age of all employees who have been with the company more than ten years').
      * Complex. These queries involve several files and possibly quite complex processing (e.g. 'List all personnel in the organization, showing their employment history and current salary, sorting by salary within grade and number of years' service.').

          * Highly complex. This type of query involves many files or tables, complex searches and sorts and/or large computations (e.g. 'List all orders, size of order and delay in weeks between order and delivery for the past 9 months, sorting by order size and delay. Show by sales representative and customer within sales representative.').

- Printing volumes. These should be specified as:
  - The number of reports or documents printed (this includes not just reports, but all documents produced by the system, for example invoices, payslips, etc.).
  - The volume (i.e. numbers) of each document printed.
  - The size of the document.
  - The frequency with which it is printed.

  Example 6.2 illustrates this.
- Processing requirements. Most host and server systems deal with a mixture of transaction, enquiry and personal computing needs. Some applications have a particularly heavy processing requirement and require the computer to do many calculations. Examples of heavy processing requirements include parts explosions in manufacturing systems, large

---

Example 6.2: Printing volumes

The following is an example taken from an accounts department estimate of its printing volumes.

The following are the major printing volumes that must be supported by the system:

Document	Average no. of characters	Average no. of lines	Number per month
Invoices	150	9	12 000
Statements	235	18	3000
Pay slips	100	7	5500
Letters	4 200	120	250
Reports	16 000	200	50
Other documents	2 000	100	50

computer models, computer-aided design and animation tasks such as ray tracing or rendering. If computation-intensive activities of this type are a major part of the processing, they should be specified carefully with an indication of the type of processing required.

- Back-up requirements. There should be an estimated size of the back-up to be taken, how frequently, and whether back-up is taken on- or off-line.
- Data volumes. These are covered under storage.
- Security and control features required. Multi-user archi-tectures, be they host- or server-based, generally have higher security risks than stand-alone personal machines. Amongst the security requirements which may need to be specified are physical security (locks, smart cards, etc.), password security, hardware encryption and, in extreme cases, biometric security features required. Purchasing of IT security is covered in Chapter 8.
- Resilience requirements. These specify the fault tolerance and recovery features required. They include:
  - Reliability. This is usually expressed by suppliers as 'mean time between failures' (MTBF). Other ways to express this requirement is to state percentage uptime required or the maximum expected number of hours or days per year of unscheduled shutdown.
  - Recovery. This is the time that the system takes to recover when it does fail. Requirement statements should cover roll-back procedures, back-up recovery time and the time required to switch to back-up machines.

Fault tolerance, resilience and disaster recovery are covered in more detail in Chapter 8.

6.4.2 Activity plan

A useful document when specifying major hardware systems is an activity plan This shows when the major demands on the processor or server take place. For example, a range of activities spread out over the week requires a much smaller machine than if they all take place on a Friday afternoon. Examples 6.3 and 6.4 are typical summary activity plans.

Example 6.3: Sample activity level summary

				Day of the Week		
Time		Monday	Tuesday	Wednesday	Thursday	Friday
08.00–11.00	Txns	High	High	High	High	High
	Enq.	High	High	High	High	High
	Batch	–	–	Payroll	–	–
11.00–14.00	Txns	High	High	High	High	High
	Enq.	High	High	High	Moderate	Moderate
	Batch	–	–	Payroll	–	–
14.00–16.30	Txns	High	High	High	High	High
	Enq.	High	High	High	High	High
	Batch	–	–	Payroll	–	–
16.30–18.00	Txns	High	High	Moderate	Moderate	Light
	Enq.	Light	Light	Light	Light	Light
	Batch	–	–	Payroll	–	–
18.00–19.00	Txns	–	–	–	–	–
	Enq.	Light	Light	Light	Light	–
	Batch	Daily Back-up	Daily Back-up	Daily Back-up	Daily Back-up	Weekly Back-up

Example 6.4: Detailed activity plan

Tuesdays	08.00–10.00	Invoice keying
		Purchase orders
		Overtime sheets
		User enquiries
		Sales order processing
	10.00–11.00	Invoice keying
		Overtime sheets
		User enquiries
		Sales order processing
	11.00–13.00	Printing of preliminary payroll report
		User enquiries
		Weekly management reports run
		Sales order processing

13.00–14.00	Stock listing report run
	Light user queries
14.00–16.00	Invoice printing
	Preparation of summary accounts file for transmission
	User enquiry
	Sales order processing
16.00–17.30	Stock updates keyed in
	User enquiry
	Sales order processing
17.30–18.15	System tidy up and administration tasks
	Daily/monthly back-up run

6.4.3 Specifying performance

For all processors, it is important to specify performance. However, this is much more crucial on servers and host machines than on desktops. Poor performance on a desktop affects just the user of the machine in question directly (although others may be indirectly affected). Poor server or host performance affects all users. Specifying performance is not simply a technical process. Performance needs to be specified in terms that can be measured by users and not in abstruse technical terms.

In the same way that hardware specifications can be prescriptive or functional, statements of performance can be specific or general. General statements of performance requirement are easier to make, but because of their imprecise nature, can lead to problems – particularly if they are to be put into a contract (see Chapter 11). General statements of performance requirement are often expressed in what seem to the user to be perfectly clear language but which to a supplier (or an independent observer or a judge) may be vague. The following are examples of this type of specification

- 'The system must provide a level of performance which will enable the department to avoid lengthy customer delays.'
- 'The system must be capable of meeting the transaction throughput requirements of the Company at peak periods.'
- 'Response times must be acceptable to users.'

187

These may all be meaningful to the purchaser. They may mean little or nothing to a supplier. While there is nothing wrong with these statements as such, they each contain words or phrases which are open to interpretation, such as 'lengthy . . . delay', 'the throughput requirements', and 'acceptable'. Few suppliers will undertake to meet such imprecise requirements, never mind write them into a contract. It is therefore in the interests of both purchaser and supplier to agree specific performance targets which the system must meet.

Specific performance requirements are precise and measurable and are defined from a number of perspectives. Performance requirements should be specified for three sets of circumstance:

1 Normal conditions.
2 Peak times.
3 Off-peak times.

For each of the above, performance requirements should be specified for each of the following:

- transactions
- processes
- enquiries
- back-up.

6.4.4 Specifying transaction performance

There are four categories of transaction that need to be considered. The first and most important of these is *on-line transactions* where data is input, modified or deleted inter-actively/directly by the user. This process may include reading tables or files, processing the data and then writing, modifying or deleting records. To protect the database or file system, a snapshot of the data to be changed may be taken first so that in the event of an error the transaction can be rolled back. In complex systems, such as distributed databases, a single transaction can give rise to this happening in a number of locations, so performance statements here are critical. On-line transaction performance requirements should be specified in terms of:

- No typing ahead delay. Typing ahead is where characters appear (or the cursor moves) a perceptible time after they have been typed on the keyboard (or the mouse has been moved).

- Field exit. In many transaction systems, when data is entered into a field on the screen, it is formatted (for example the decimal point is put in the right place or all letters are converted to capitals) and then validated by the system. Sometimes other fields are filled automatically (for example, on entry of a customer number, the customer name, address and credit limit appear). These events should happen more or less instantaneously.
- Commit (screen exit). This is the final step in a transaction when the data on the disk is changed. In a high-speed keying environment, this should also be more or less instantaneous. Even a complex change should happen within a couple of seconds at most.

The second class of transactions are *off-line* or *batch*. Most transactions are disk intensive. On-line transactions also tend to carry a high processor overhead. For large volumes, it is sometimes more efficient to use fast key-punching and to batch the transactions for later processing (see below). In a batch system, transactions are prepared in advance in the form of journals and then processed in background, usually during an off-peak period. Batch processing is used for long print or production runs (such as payroll cheques or customer invoices) and for accounting and banking systems which lend themselves to this type of processing. Batch processing is measured in throughput times, which are usually a matter of hours. However, batch processing can as easily be expressed in transactions per second, which may be more meaningful.

The third type of transaction is *high-speed data entry or keying*. Preparation of transaction journals is normally done using specialist key-punching staff. Punching is done on machines designed for handling this type of processing requirement. Performance is measured in keystrokes per hour. For normal mixed data, input rates of 10–12 000 keystrokes per hour are attainable and speeds of up to 20 000 keystrokes per hour are possible for numeric data.

In practice, large-scale key-punching has been steadily replaced by scanning as character-recognition technology has become more sophisticated and reliable. This is only a form of *machine transaction* input. Where mechanical or electronic devices generate data, then transaction performance requirements need to match the output speed of the devices concerned. It is important to specify either the type of machine input that the processor must handle or provide input rates. For example, barcode readers read moderately fast while scanning, but in computer terms, there are usually long delays between one reading and the next. Optical character-readers have similar characteristics. Scanners and machine sensors, on the other hand, can read large volumes quickly. High-speed scanners can read enormous volumes quickly and video and sound, even where sampling is used, both generate very high data input volumes.

If such input mechanisms are being used, then the transfer rates should be worked out carefully and specified if you do not want to put up with impatient users.

6.4.5 Specifying processor performance

Processes which are CPU-intensive can cause deterioration in the performance of all other activities on the system and should, where possible, be run at off-peak periods, although this is not always possible. Specifying major process performance require-ment must take into account all the activities on the system. For example, the following statements of requirements presents only part of the picture:

> *'The payroll starts at 12.00 a.m. on Thursday and final payslips must be ready for delivery to the bank by 4.30 p.m. that afternoon.'*

> *'The operational needs require on-line back-up be taken between 14.00 and 17.30 hours each working day.'*

For a supplier to interpret such statements, it must know what else is happening during these periods. This is done by preparing a system timetable. How to do this is shown above in Examples 6.3 and 6.4. A sample performance specification is shown in Example 6.5.

Specifying performance requirements for other components in the system is discussed in the appropriate sections below.

A further refinement of the above is to specify that the performance must be reached a certain percentage of the time. For example:

> *'The system must respond to queries in less than 1.5 seconds for 98% of all queries.'*

This is a less draconian performance criterion, but it is open to argument. For example, does the above mean 98% of all queries whatever they are, or are specific queries (i.e. the 2% of really

Example 6.5: Sample performance specification

The following is an example of a performance specification.

	System response time (seconds)			
	Simple	Moderate	Complex	Very complex
Transactions				
Normal				
Field exit	≤0.5	≤0.5	≤1.0	≤1.0
Screen exit (commit)	≤1.0	≤1.5	≤2.0	≤3.0
Peak				
Field exit	≤0.5	≤0.5	≤1.0	≤1.0
Screen exit (commit)	≤0.75	≤2.0	≤3.0	≤4.0
Enquiries				
Normal	≤1.5	≤2.5	≤4.0	≤6.0
Peak	≤3.0	≤5.0	≤10.0	≤15.0

Processes	Not longer than
Normal	
Payroll	2 hours
End of period reports	1 hour
MRP regeneration	8 hours
Full system back-up	Not applicable
Peak	
Payroll	3 hours
End of period reports	2 hours
MRP regeneration	Not applicable
Full system back-up	Not applicable
Overnight	
Payroll	3 hours
End of period reports	2 hours
MRP regeneration	5 hours
Full system backup	3 hours

difficult ones), excluded? Another problem is measuring 98%. To *prove* that the system is not performing to the required specification may require rigorous sampling or monitoring procedures.

Specifying 'percentage of the time' performance levels should be done with circumspection.

6.4.6 Specifying back-up performance

Traditionally, back-up was an off-line procedure carried out after the normal activity for the day was completed. One reason for this is that back-ups often require that nothing else is happening on the system at the time they are taken. Taking the back-up overnight or after the close of business facilitates this.

However, where there is 24/7 hour operation of the IT system or if, for personnel or security reasons, back-ups must be taken during the day, this must be clearly stated. Taking a back-up during live operations, where there may be continuing transactions on the file or database being backed-up, is feasible, but can be demanding on system resources.

6.4.7 Sizing

The objective of sizing a system is to assist in determining the:

- processing power
- memory
- on-line storage
- network bandwidth

required by the system and its components. Refined sizing will take into account other factors (such as cache sizes and channel widths), but for most normal commercial systems this level of sophistication is not needed.

Sizing each of these components is a reasonably skilled task. The best policy is for purchasers to give suppliers all the necessary facts to enable them to size the system. By specifying an exact size of machine or system, the purchaser implicitly assumes the responsibility for its subsequent performance.

6.4.8 Memory

The amount of memory required on a machine will vary with the machine and its function. Depending on the machine and the use to which it is being put, some or all of the following will impact on memory requirements of hosts and servers:

- the number of users
- the number of simultaneous users
- the operating system
- the application software being run

- the network or communications software
- swapping or paging
- memory reserved for print-spooling
- application work space
- the cache size.

Most operating systems support virtual memory, but this can be slow so it is important to get the amount of real memory correct.

Information on the memory requirement of each of the above will be available from suppliers and/or the software manuals. There should always be a safety margin. As memory comes in blocks of a minimum size which can vary with machine, this can often be done by rounding up to the next nearest memory size. When in doubt, always err on the side of too much memory. Memory shortage can lead to a rapid slowdown in performance and surplus memory can sometimes be used by a system to improve performance. For example, sizing a database service might involve allowing for:

- the operating system
- middleware
- communications software
- workspace for each user
- paging space
- a safety margin.

Most suppliers of such software will have configuration expert systems or models which do this job.

6.4.9 Benchmarks

Processor power is specified in terms of usage demand volumes and patterns. However, it is sometimes useful to use more generalized statements of power. This can be done using benchmarks. Great care must be take when specifying benchmarks. Specifying a required benchmark level effectively transfers the risk and responsibility for correct sizing from the supplier to the purchaser. This may be justified where the purchaser is confident of its ability to size correctly and/or where the purchaser feels its judgment in these matters is better than that of the supplier (not unknown!).

Unlike, say, memory, disk space and network capacity, there is no simple measure of processor power. The widely cited measure, millions of instructions per second (MIPS) is virtually meaningless except in limited comparisons (see below). To rank processing power therefore requires more sophisticated measurements. A number of these are available and, while they are valuable, they are also function- or operation-specific. Benchmarks measure specific functions of a machine or a system and do not necessarily reflect how a machine or system will operate under different operating conditions. For example, the TPC-C benchmark measures transaction efficiency. It would be a poor measure for the type of mathematical computation that occurs in, say, computer-aided design.

Benchmarks fall into four different classes.

1 Measures of processor performance. These benchmarks measure only the computing power of the central processor. They are often oriented towards computation-intensive operations such as engineering or scientific applications.
2 Measures of transaction performance. This type of benchmark measures the throughput in high transaction volume systems where disk access time is normally the most important component of performance.
3 Measures of system performance. This type of benchmark measures the overall performance of a system under a 'typical' workload (for example a mixture of an accounting system, a customer enquiry system and a personnel system).
4 Measures of application performance. These benchmarks are highly specific and measure the performance of a computer or system running a particular application or type of application.

The following are some commonly used (and misused) benchmarks:

- Millions of instruction per second (MIPS). MIPS tend to be machine- or at least architecture-specific. There are many definitions of MIPS and they are not all comparable. MIPS should be avoided except for specific comparisons between similar machines (for example machines in the same supplier range).
- Floating point operations per second (FLOPS). FLOPS are important in computing-intensive operations such as engineering, computer-aided design and computer modelling.
- Whetstones. Whetstones are one of the oldest benchmarks on the market. They measure raw computing power, particularly floating point operations.

- Drystones. This benchmark measure is a specialized tool of more interest to programmers than to users.
- System performance evaluation co-operative (SPEC). SPEC-marks are a widely used US measurement of processor performance. They are used for a variety of purposes, in particular measuring performance on multiprocessor machines.
- Transaction performance council (TPC). TPC benchmarks are amongst the most widely quoted and respected. They measure the performance of transaction processing systems. There are a number of sets of benchmarks (TPC-A, TPC-B, etc.) applicable to different types of application environment.

The above list, while it contains most of the major benchmarks currently in use, is by no means exhaustive. Information on TPCs and SPEC-marks is readily available on the world-wide web.

Succinct benchmarks, such as MIPS, which is just one number, are superficially attractive. However, system performance is a complicated subject and cannot be readily summed up in any one single measure. For this reason, single number bench marks should be avoided. More sophisticated and detailed bench-marks such as TPCs are much more meaningful and can, in some cases, run to several pages of detailed analyses for a single machine.

6.5 Specifying desktop machines

Desktop machines fall into three main categories.

1 Personal computers (PCs) based on Intel or look-alike processors and generally running some version of Windows or occasionally Unix/Linux or (rarely) other operating systems.
2 Workstations based on reduced instruction set computing (RISC) or Intel processors typically running Unix, Linux or Windows.
3 Apple Macintosh machines based on the PowerPC RISC processor and running Apple's proprietary operating system.

There are others, but they are mostly for games, home or highly specialized use. Modern PCs are standard and comparisons are straightforward. The typical contemporary PC advertisement blitzes the potential purchasers with a plethora of information. Of this, the key hardware-related features are:

- the processor
- the operating system

- the clock speed
- the disk capacity
- the cache memory size
- the ports available
- the type of screen
- what type of external drives it has (CD/DVD/zip/floppy)
- other features (in-built modem, Ethernet, sound card, etc.).

A specification should include each of the above. If the PC is stand-alone, there must be a method of taking a back-up of the data on the hard disk (back-ups for networked PCs can and ideally should be done over the network). There are three options for large-scale back-up on PCs:

1 Zip drives. These come in a variety of sizes and are fast and convenient.
2 Re-writable optical disks (CD/DVD). These have greater capacity than zip drives, but may be on the large side for users with little data to save.
3 Tape drives can store a great deal of information, but are relatively slow and are being displaced by optical technology.

The first two of these are options on most modern PCs, but for back-up on older machines a single moveable unit is sufficient.

A number of other features are worth considering including the so-called 'footprint' of the machine and the number of spare bays. Some of the features advertised for PCs are of marginal interest to the business user, although they matter to the hobbyist or specialist user.

One way of wasting money on PCs is to purchase machines that are far more powerful than is needed. Another is to purchase underpowered ones. Avoiding both errors is important. A couple of hundred pounds too much on one PC may not matter that much, but buy a hundred of them and that is a different story. It is therefore useful to categorize users into:

- Power users. These are technical specialists such as pro-grammers, engineers, and designers as well as users of hungry applications like desktop publishing, computer-aided design, high-powered computer models, graphics designers and so on. These users will want as much power on their desk as can be afforded.
- Heavy conventional users. These are staff who typically use end user products such as word processors, spreadsheets or

slide presentation packages, as well as using PCs for transactions and enquiries in client/server transaction systems continuously during the day. They include many clerical and secretarial staff as well as some junior and (occasionally) middle and senior management. These users need good mid-range machines.

- Light conventional users. These are users who would use their machines occasionally during the day, but would not use them in a sustained way. Often these users will be perfectly satisfied with low-end-of-the-range models or even outdated models, provided they perform the basic functions required.
- Occasional users. These are users who use their machines infrequently and then for specific purposes. Often they are senior executives. Some infrequent users may place heavy demands on their machines when they do use them. A common example would be a machine used to run an Executive Information System. These users need to be considered on a case-by-case basis.

It is important to classify users appropriately. Users should be given the type of machine that they need. Providing under-powered machines is inefficient and will cost far more than the additional cost of a better machine. Providing overpowered machines is expensive and wasteful. It is often feasible to pass on machines from one group to the next.

6.6 Specifying portable PCs

Portable PCs have most of the same characteristics as desktops. In addition, for portables the following should be specified:

- Weight. Beware: some portables are really 'luggables'. It may be appropriate to specify a maximum weight. Anything over 7 lbs/3 kgs is fairly heavy.
- Robustness. It is possible to specify robustness required in terms of the shock/force which a machine must be able to survive. This is important if the machine is going to be used in rough conditions.
- Size. Most machines now fit into an A4 area but there are significant size differences. If it is important, size should be stated. As most briefcases are a little over A3 in internal area, a larger-than-A4 machine will not leave much room for other papers.
- Battery life. Battery life requirements will be driven by the use to which the portable is to be put. If it is an occasional

portable, battery life is not that critical. However, if most of its time is spend away from a convenient power outlet, then minimum required battery life should be specified.

- Screen type. When buying portables, always make a point of looking at the screen in a variety of lighting conditions (particularly in bright, indoor daylight) and from a number of angles. Screen size and readability vary widely on portables.
- Energy-saving features. All portables have battery-saving techniques. These include automatic shut-down of the hard disk when it has not been used for a period, as well as automatic screen-fade and a sleep or standby mode. Features such as sleep mode should be user controllable.
- What's on board. Portables offer a trade-off between size and weight on the one hand and the number of extra bits you have to carry around on the other. So-called 'ultra-lite' portables often have nothing but the processor, hard disk, screen and keyboard. If you want to use anything else, from a floppy to a modem, you need to clip on a port board or insert a card. On the other hand, a portable that has everything will give your arm and shoulder muscles a good work-out.
- Docking. If a docking system is required it should be specified. All portables should be connectable to a full keyboard and standard screen. Some come with docking stations, which should be simple to use.
- Removable drives. These can be useful for security and other reasons.
- Interchangeable batteries. Most, but not all, portables allow you to switch in a spare battery and some allow you to change batteries without shutting down the computer.

Portables tend to be less powerful than desktops – in part because they often use special low energy usage versions of processors which tend to be slower. They are also considerably more expensive in terms of 'bang for your buck'. Only purchase portables for those who really need to move their machine around with them.

6.7 Specifying on-line storage

6.7.1 Disk storage

Modern storage comes in a wide variety of technical forms, but the basic mechanics are still disk and tape. Specifying disk storage requirement involves specifying four things:

1 Capacity.
2 Performance.
3 Resilience.
4 Number of drives.

Disk has become so inexpensive that the solution to a space problem is often to buy more. Tempting though this approach is, magnetic and optical disks should be properly sized and managed. Disk space is needed for:

- the operating system
- work space for the operating system
- virtual memory (if in use)
- the network operating system
- sorting space
- the application program code (executables)
- source files
- development tools
- user work areas/scratch space
- user application data.

Many applications programs, particularly databases, require their own work and sorting space. There should always be of the order of 20% (or more) free disk space on any machine, be it host, server or PC. This will vary with circumstances. On devices which are used by many users, i.e. servers and host machines, the safety margin needs to be higher. Factors to take into account when specifying disk safety margin include:

- The characteristics of the operating system. Some operating systems can cope with tight disk space better than others. Operating systems may require differing amounts of swap space.
- The nature of the operations. If the nature of the operations is such that new data is being added at a high rate then there needs to be plenty of spare disk capacity to allow for build-up of log files and transactions during busy input periods.
- The number of users. This impacts in two ways. Firstly, each user carries an overhead. Secondly, the greater the number of users, the less easy it is to control the rate of growth in disk usage.
- Systems administration procedures. If system administration is rigorous (for example, there are strictly applied rules on deletion of old files), then smaller margins of error can be tolerated. The user has to trade-off the cost of the additional disk against the cost of the additional administrative effort.

- The nature of the applications. Some applications use logging for recovery and rollback purposes which means that during the day large files can be built up. Although such files are deleted at regular intervals, it is important to know their size at peak. If sophisticated technologies such as on-line database replication are being used, this needs to be calculated with particular care.

As noted above, disk is so cheap that a simple solution is just to buy far more than is necessary. However, this only encourages sloppy use of storage. Good discipline is important.

Disk performance is measured by *access time*, the average amount of time it takes to locate the start of the required data (there are several sub-measurements here, but they can be ignored) and *transfer time*, i.e. the amount of time required to transfer a given amount of data to and from a disk. Transfer times matter where there is a large number of reads and writes occurring. Transfer times are affected by the disk's inherent speed and the ability of the system to write to more than one drive simultaneously.

Times measured in nano- or pica-seconds and megabits per second are generally not that useful for specification purposes. A better strategy is to specify needs in business terms, for example:

> *'Transfer of the files from the departmental server to main server must be completed within 3 minutes.'*

It is important to be careful when specifying disk performance that the real bottleneck is not elsewhere. A common error is to specify disks to certain performance levels and then overlook the limitations on network traffic. DVDs have much greater capacity per unit area, but are considerably slower than conventional hard disks and are not yet practical for high speed transaction processing. If juke boxes are involved, there will also be a delay in mechanically moving the DVD/CD to the reader.

Because they are moving parts, disks are the most vulnerable components in computer systems. Although modern disk technology is remarkably reliable, disks do fail from time to time. The system can be protected against this by a number of techniques, but there is a three-way trade-off between:

- reliability/recovery
- performance
- cost.

Specification of resilience is covered in Chapter 8.

6.7.2 Tape storage

Specifying tape storage is similar to specifying disk storage, although issues such as speed will be less prominent. Notwithstanding developments in DVD/CD technology, tape is still the preferred back-up medium for many corporate IT users. Tape is relatively slow, but it is easy to handle, robust, reusable many times and can store enormous amounts of information. For tape back-up, it is necessary to specify:

- back-up time/transfer speed
- whether compression is required
- capacity (normal and compressed)
- interfaces if the drive is external
- tape life (number of cycles per tape).

There are various different types of tape technology, from streamers to reel tapes. Most tape storage is now done using cartridge-based digital tapes either in single units or in arrays.

6.7.3 Storage networks

There are several network storage technologies. Storage networks are expensive, but offer considerable benefits in terms of speed, ease of maintenance and ease of administration. The specification of network storage systems uses the same criteria used for other storage. It is better for the purchaser to specify its need in terms of business rather than technical requirements. Again, the same basic criteria matter: capacity, speed, reliability and ease of maintenance. It is important when purchasing storage networks to be clear on the benefits over conventional storage. In some circumstances, it can be an expensive way of gaining marginal business benefits.

6.8 Specifying printers

While printers are relatively easy to specify, there are many features that can be specified and it is useful to be aware of the full list of possibilities. There is no point is purchasing a printer that is too sophisticated for the business need. The following paragraphs give a list of features for each type of printer. As elsewhere, not all of these will be relevant all of the time, but each should be considered.

201

6.8.1 Line printers

Line printers are appropriate for heavy duty and multi-part printing. High-speed line printers are expensive so careful specification of performance is justified. For line printers the following should be specified:

- capacity to print on different paper types including multi-part (number and weight), fanfold, card stock and labels
- number of parts it must print (and paper weight)
- ability to print variable column widths
- minimum number of characters per line required
- minimum number of lines printed per minute required
- reliability (mean time between failures)
- quality and definition of print
- acceptable noise level as measured in decibels (dB)
- jam-sensing power stackers
- ability to support different interfaces such as SCSI and USB
- colour printing (a rare requirement with this type of printer).

6.8.2 Dot matrix printers

Dot matrix printers have the advantage of simultaneously being robust and small and are therefore well suited to certain applications and environments. For dot matrix printers the following should be specified:

- capacity to print on different paper types including multi-part (number and weight), fanfold, card stock and labels
- number of parts it must print (and paper weight)
- resolution in dots per inch
- ability to print at a variety of column widths up to a specified number of characters in normal (non-compressed) mode and in compressed mode
- required print densities in characters per inch
- required speed in characters per second in draft and near-letter-quality modes
- reliability (mean time between failures)
- ability to print in draft and near-letter-quality modes
- acceptable noise level as measured in decibels (dB)
- ability to support necessary interfaces, e.g. serial, parallel, SCSI, USB, infra-red, etc.
- network connectability (i.e. have a network card on board)
- ability to work directly off the network without a PC to drive it (or have minimal impact on the PC to which it is attached)
- colour printing (a rare requirement with this type of printer).

6.8.3 Laser printers

For lasers the following should be specified if required:

- colour or monochrome
- level of resolution in dots per inch (vertical and horizontal)
- fonts and protocols supported (e.g. PCL 6, Truetype, Post-script level 2, etc.)
- sustained speed in pages per minute
- ability to support necessary interfaces including USB, SCSI, serial, parallel and infra-red
- number of paper trays and minimum required capacity
- manual paper feed capability
- ability to print on various paper types including papers of various density and surface characteristics, labels, envelopes and card
- reliability
- network connectability
- on-board memory
- memory expansion capability
- preloaded fonts.

6.8.4 Inkjet printers

Inkjet printers are an inexpensive alternative to lasers. There are also many portable inkjets. For inkjet printers the following should be specified:

- colour or monochrome
- level of resolution in dots per inch (vertical and horizontal)
- fonts and protocols supported (e.g. PCL 6, Truetype, Post-script level 2, etc.)
- preloaded fonts
- sustained speed in pages per minute
- ability to support different interfaces, e.g. USB, SCSI, serial, parallel and infra-red
- tray capacity
- manual feed capability
- ability to print on various paper types including papers of various density and surface characteristics, labels, envelopes, card and glossy paper
- photographic quality print capability (and non-fade printing if required)
- reliability
- network capability (i.e. have a network card on board).

Some inkjets are portable. If portability is a requirement, then size and weight specifications should also be stated.

6.9 Specifying communications requirements

With the growth in networks, sizing of networks has become another specification requirement. As the type of data (e.g. images) being sent over networks becomes larger, network capacity needs to be able to handle it. This means both accurate sizing and the capacity to grow – upgrading networks can be expensive and time-consuming and is something to be avoided if possible. While specifying communications requirements is becoming a more frequent requirement for IT management, as a general rule, unless purchasers are expert in data and tele-communications, it is best to state requirements in terms of business needs. As with memory, processing power and disk space, specifying communications requirements needs to include:

- quality of service
- volume estimation
- sizing
- performance specification.

This is quite complicated to do and a systematic approach is essential if a clear statement of needs is to be prepared. The following steps can be used for specifying communications needs.

- Draw up a communications matrix showing all locations on the network in a $n \times n$ grid.
- Classify all traffic by business category. Examples of this include:
  - electronic mail
  - file transfer
  - web access and nature of that access
  - electronic data interchange
  - client server transaction information
  - batch file transfer
  - on-line enquiries
  - replication data between databases
  - images
  - voice
  - teleconferencing
  - office documents (text, spreadsheet, graphics).

- Classify each business category by traffic type, i.e. batch transfer or on-line/interactive
- Classify each business category by volume. For example:
  - High – this might be over 100 MB per hour or more.
  - Medium – In the range 1–100 MB per hour.
  - Low – This might be ≤ 1 MB per hour.

The definition of high, medium and low is relative. The above might be typical of a moderate-sized business transferring business data. It would not be appropriate for a media company transferring video.

- Specify the quality of service required. This might be categorized as follows:
  - Critical – downtime is unacceptable. It must be kept to a minimum.
  - High – Downtime of up to 30 minutes is acceptable.
  - Medium – Downtime of 30 minutes to 2 hours is acceptable.
  - Low – Downtime of 2–6 hours is acceptable.
- Specify the response times required. Response requirements on a network vary with application and business need. For example, for accessing a webpage, a sub-second response time is unusually fast (even on an intranet), 5 seconds is slowish but quite common, and after about 8 seconds or so, most people lose interest. It is therefore necessary to specify for each type of web access what rates are required. Again this should be done in business rather than technical terms.
- Specify the priorities. This should show which traffic should get priority in the event of a limited bandwidth being available. The system should be able to react to the priorities.
- Specify security measures required, including any resilience or encryption requirements.

Computation of traffic volumes is a complex and specialized skill and should be left to the supplier. The above information should be sufficient for a supplier to size a network.

Where the purchaser has the necessary expertise, it may be appropriate to specify the requirements for individual components. These include:

- routers
- bridges
- modems
- multiplexers
- hubs/concentrators
- communications/gateway servers
- wiring.

However, specification of these is best left to specialists. Purchasers should stick to their business needs.

6.10 System software

The evolution of systems software has made life simpler in some ways whilst making it more difficult in others. In the desktop and server market, nearly all operating systems are either in the Microsoft Windows family or part of the Unix/Linux world. Realistically, the mainframe market is dominated by IBM operating systems. The demise of proprietary operations systems has decoupled most hardware and application software purchasing decisions. It has also eliminated the problems of customers being locked into their hardware suppliers for long periods because the cost of change was too high. The bad news is that the past couple of decades has seen the emergence of a growing range of middleware, systems software that sits between the operating system and the application software. Numerous integration suites, data management systems, communications protocols and so on vie for the customer's attention.

Specifying requirements for systems software is relatively unusual. It is also a highly technical issue and well beyond the scope of this book. In any case, for many acquisitions systems software is predetermined by organizational IT policy. However, if, for whatever reason, you have to specify operating software there are some basic issues which should be considered.

- Single or multiple operating systems? All operating systems have strong and weak points. Some may be strong on ease of administration, but poor on security. Others may support a larger number of users, but require more disk space or maintenance. As a general rule, a small organization, or one with a small internal IT department, is better off with as few operating systems as is practical. Larger organizations, with more support resources, may have the luxury of choosing horses for courses and be able to run a variety of different systems.
- Application support. A key decision factor in choosing an operating system is how well the business applications run on it and how widespread this particular combination is. Always try to avoid being only one of three users world-wide of the Unix version of package X.
- Ease of administration. All operating systems are complex, but some are more so than others (even within the one family).

- Stability. There is an old rule of thumb in the computer business that says never buy version 1.0 of anything, and nowhere is this more true than of systems software generally and operating systems in particular. Except in an emergency, never install new or major new releases of operating systems until they have had the time to settle down and the vendor has most of the bugs weeded out. Some operating system releases in the past decade have been followed by a positive rash of patches and bugs fixed in the months after they were launched.

- Standards. Operating systems should conform with industry standards such as POSIX. Most do, but some of the more eccentric flavours of Unix and other operating systems may not. With other system software, make sure that it conforms with widely used systems standards such as TCP/IP for communications or CORBA for object brokers. Communications software should support all appropriate protocols.

- Special features. Ensure that the operating system specification supports your hardware features. For example, if servers use symmetric multi-processing or have multiple processors, the operating system should support these.

One special type of software is *network management systems* (sometimes referred to as systems management systems, although the latter is a slightly wider concept). Such systems are used for managing and administering complex networks. Key capabilities to look for in such systems include:

- file/storage management
- network load management
- performance tuning
- security
- software distribution
- hardware and software inventory control
- software licence checking
- recovery and resilience.

Finally, a brief word about *real time systems*. Real time systems have highly specific response times. While an abnormal delay of a few seconds on a customer deposit transaction in a bank may not be material, delays of a fraction of a second may matter in a control system in a nuclear power plant. Every operation in a real time system must, therefore, be specified to extremely tight limits. Specifying such requirements is a job for specialists.

6.11 Specifying ergonomics

Poorly designed hardware and software costs money. Poor ergonomics causes a number of problems, including:

- inefficient use of people's time
- fatigue
- frustration
- injuries, including repetitive strain injury (RSI)
- eyestrain
- illness.

Having good hardware ergonomics is not just a matter of complying with EU and government health and safety regulations, it is good economic sense. It is important to understand this as ergonomic factors are sometimes dismissed by management as frivolous or faddish.

The following is a list of features that should be specified in hardware. These may be mandatory for public sector bodies.

- Keyboards should be detachable, have responsive keys (i.e. a clear click) and be adjustable for flat and angled use.
- Screens should be of a reasonable size (at least 15″ apart from portables). They should also be flicker-free and be able to be tilted and swiveled. They should be adjustable for brightness and contrast and have non-interlaced graphics resolutions of at least 800×600 and 1024×768 or better operating at a 72 Hz refresh rate. By law, they must meet the health and safety standards set out in EC Council Directive 90/270/EEC.
- Mouses should be ergonomically designed. Tracker balls should be considered for some users.

All mechanical IT equipment in an office environment should have a noise level of less than 53 dB.

7 Specification of application software

7.1 Introduction

The majority of large IT purchases are application software driven. In such purchases, the features offered by the software are often deemed to be more important than hardware, architecture or operating environment considerations. Purchasing of technology for its own sake or for non-core business benefits rarely makes good business sense. A system that is reliable, but dull, is preferable to one that is flashy, but prone to collapse.

Nowhere is this more true that in the purchase of application software. For many organizations, application software is not only the single largest element of their IT investment, it will be the component which most determines how cost-effective the IT system will be. Problems with application software are one of the major sources of unproductive IT costs. These problems can include project overruns, mismatches to requirements, software bugs, lack of flexibility, inadequate performance and inability to adapt to business change. Several examples of spectacular software problems and catastrophic failures (particularly in the public sector) have been widely publicized over the years. But while high-profile software failures are visibly expensive, poor application software can give rise to a steady unproductive overhead that, over time, can cost a large amount of money. On a daily basis many organizations that use custom software or modified package software have to handle a variety of problems with such software, all of which incur additional direct and indirect costs. Many of these costs can be avoided by buying the right product at the outset.

Purchasing of application software can be conveniently divided into purchasing of:

1 Multi-user packaged software supporting a function, department or the entire organization.
2 Custom software.
3 End user software.

Formal specification of end user software is rarely required today so this chapter focuses on the first two of the above list. For each of these, specification of requirements will have several common elements, but there are some important points of difference which are discussed in Section 7.5. Before considering how this type of purchase should be approached, it is useful to review some important principles.

7.2 The importance of good software specification

Many organizations, even those which do prepare specifications, tend to underestimate the importance of *good* software specification. The cost of inadequate specification is a large multiple of the cost of the specification itself. Time invested in specification has a high return. This is illustrated in Figure 7.1.

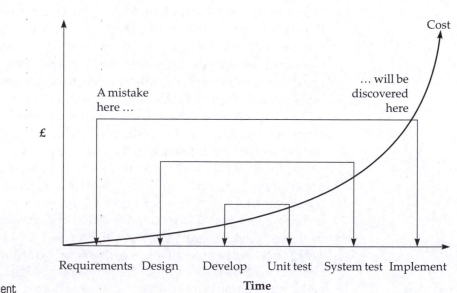

Figure 7.1
Cost of errors in
software development

Despite this, organizations constantly come up with a variety of reasons for not specifying requirements properly. The following are common justifications for skimping on specification.

- 'I don't need a written specification, I know what I am looking for.' This is one of the most common reasons given for not preparing an adequate specification. It may be true in the case of a user who is not only completely on top of the organization's needs, but is also familiar with all the technical possibilities. This description fits only a very small minority of users. Even when it is true, there remains the problem of communicating needs to others clearly and comprehensively.
- 'This is a standard application. Why waste time with a specification?' On rare occasions this may be true, but few applications of any size are so standard that they can be met by a totally unmodified standard package. Even applications as basic as payroll often need minor changes or enhancements to meet the special needs of different organizations.
- 'Our supplier has a package that it assures us will meet our needs.' If an organization is small and its business or operations are straightforward, it is possible that all their IT requirements can be met by one supplier, but relying on the current supplier's products can mean tailoring the organiza-tion's requirements to what the supplier's software can do. This may be an expensive option and, in certain circum-stances, may even harm the business.
- 'We can rely on the presentation. We will ask the tough questions then.' Relying on presentations is dangerous (see Chapter 9). Computer sales professionals are skilled at presenting the best features of their products and equally adept at hiding the less attractive aspects.
- 'We can check off the features from a brochure.' Software brochures, like their holiday equivalents, can present a thoroughly misleading picture.

Poor software specification is one of the major, if not the single largest, causes of cost problems in IT systems. It is therefore worth expending a little effort to get it right.

7.2.1 The dangers in not having a proper specification

Even more so than for hardware, there are several dangers in not preparing a proper written specification for application software. The first problem is that users may not understand their needs as well as they think. One of the basic skills taught to analysts and consultants is to extract from users what their real needs are. Firstly, many users cannot express their needs fully and clearly, even though they may (and usually do) think the contrary. Secondly, needs have to be communicated to suppliers and there are few better ways of doing this than having a properly organized specification. One key reason for this is the different world views of the parties concerned. Users are business-orientated and think in terms of business needs and benefits. Suppliers are (unfortunately) sometimes technically minded and locked into the features of their product. The result can be a communication problem where it can be difficult to match features and needs. Thirdly, for complex multi-functional applications it can be difficult to remember all the needs of different groups. Fourthly, in the absence of a complete specification, it is easy for users to be seduced by attractive, but unimportant, features of the system. In particular, priorities may be distorted by stronger personalities or senior staff who, while they may outrank the users, do not actually have to use the software on a day-to-day basis. Buying on features is bad practice. Example 7.1 is a demonstration of this on a large scale.

Example 7.1: The EIS magic bullet that missed

An interesting example of buying on features is the executive information systems (EIS) fad of the late 1980s. The original EIS packages ran on mainframes and were very expensive. Starting prices were often of the order of £100 000 and prices well in excess of £250 000 for an installed system were not unheard of, even in relatively small organizations. Executive information systems were sold to Chief Executives (or at least senior executives) and promised to bring information they needed to their desk and fingertips in an intuitive, accessible and easy to use manner. For many executives, frustrated by their information systems, it was the ultimate magic bullet.

By the early 1990s it was obvious that EISs were not working. Various studies reported failure rates in EIS projects of 50% or more and one UK study estimated that 80% of EIS projects failed to meet their stated objectives. The question was why?

There were several reasons for these disasters, but two simple factors underlay most of the problems. First, an EIS on top of an inadequate underlying information system cannot make up information out of thin air. Many EIS installations' prime achievement was to highlight the gaps in the rest of the information systems (which in itself may not have been a bad thing, but was not what was intended). Second, most of the information used by senior executives does not come from the internal computer systems and at that time external information was not as readily available as it is today.

These are not obscure points so why did so many organizations become sucked in at such huge expense? The reason was that purchasers bought the product on features rather than needs. Also, because the EIS was wanted by the CEO, people down the line, who may have known better, were reluctant to argue. For many organizations it was an expensive lesson.

Finally, in the absence of a specification, the impact of compromises may be difficult to assess. With application software, purchasing decisions often involve a trade-off between the cost of modifying a package to meet the user's need and the cost of the user adapting to the way the package operates or the cost of having a bespoke system developed.

For all of these reasons, a proper specification of software needs is essential. The degree of formality and detail in the specification will depend on the importance of the application, the complexity of the requirements, the size of the investment and whether a packaged or custom-built solution is being considered. For custom software, the development will also depend on the approach being used.

7.2.2 Good software specifications

A software specification is primarily about *what* and only sometimes about *how*. A specification serves two key purposes. Firstly it states what the users want in a single document and provides a common reference point. Secondly it conveys this information to the supplier. Both of these are more difficult with application software than with other aspects of IT acquisition. With hardware, for example, the range of choices is relatively limited. With software there can be an infinite number of subtle variations.

With software requirement specifications, two distinct situations must be considered, specification of packaged and specification of custom software. Matters are complicated by different custom-building approaches, in particular whether one is using a traditional waterfall method of system development or a prototyping/rapid application development (RAD) methodology. Detailed discussion of this issue is way beyond the scope of this book, but briefly there are several formal methodologies for system development. Probably the best known of the traditional methodologies is structured systems and application development methodology (SSADM) which is widely used in the public sector. There are many others. Techniques such as SSADM are primarily aimed at large projects, particularly custom-built systems. Development standards for RAD-type development exist, but are still emerging at the time of writing. Some of these are discussed briefly in Section 7.5. The good news is that for packaged software specification, it is often possible to be quite clear without going to the lengths of drawing up a full formal document of the type required for a bespoke system.

There is a number of characteristics of a good specification. A good specification should:

- Be clear and unambiguous. A requirements' specification is the blueprint on which the software will be built, or using which a suitable packaged software product will be selected. Lack of clarity may lead to misinterpretation and the purchaser may almost certainly find that the product as delivered is not exactly what was required.
- Be complete. It should never be assumed that suppliers have second sight. Suppliers cannot be expected to anticipate gaps in a requirements' specification. Contractually a supplier may be bound to deliver only what the requirement document states.
- Be comprehensible to IT staff, users and potential suppliers. A key purpose of the specification is to provide a means of communication between purchaser/user and supplier. A document which is difficult for either party to understand will undermine this. Suppliers may know little about the purchaser's organization or business. Users may know little about the technology.
- Take into account potential longer-term developments. A common error in requirements' specifications is to state what is wanted today without giving sufficient (or sometimes any) thought to possible future developments.
- Be appropriately detailed. A specification should provide a potential supplier with sufficient information to quote for (or deliver) the required product. Too little detail will inevitably lead to lengthy discussions or a risk of an inappropriate solution. Too much detail may box the supplier (and by implication the purchaser) in to an undesirable extent and may forgo potentially better options or compromises.

7.3 Specifying requirements for packaged software

From a purchasing perspective, there are two purposes in having a specification of requirements for packaged application software. Firstly it provides a checklist of features which the package must provide. Secondly it provides a basis for determining any required modifications to the package.

Stating the requirements for application software involves specifying some or all of the following items:

- business overview
- technical environment
- functionality required
- data or process flows
- interfaces to and from other systems
- reports required
- query facilities required
- support requirements
- security requirements
- performance requirements
- standards.

Each of these is described below, apart from data/process flows which are not that common in packaged software specifications, and performance which is discussed in Chapter 6. Data and process flows are discussed briefly in Section 7.5. In what follows, it is assumed that the document being prepared is for external suppliers. Specifications of requirements for internal use may be different in a number of respects (for example, they will probably not need a business overview and the nature of support requirements may be quite different).

7.3.1 Business overview

The first step in a requirements' specification is to prepare a business or application overview. This is only necessary where the software is substantial and the supplier is not familiar with the organization. The objectives of the business/application overview are to give a succinct description of the nature and business of the organization, department or functional unit that will be using the software and outline, in high-level descriptive and business terms, the objectives and functions required of the software. Where a number of quotations or proposals are being sought, it will also save time in having to repeat the same information again and again.

The business overview should contain:

- A summary description of the organization as a whole. This needs to be informative, but a page is usually sufficient. Where it is available, it may be useful to include an annual report. It should include any important jargon and acronyms.
- A summary of the role and functions of the unit or department that is seeking the software. This may or may not be appropriate depending on the circumstances. It is important that suppliers understand the business function and the business context within which the software will operate. Many problems arise from suppliers and developers having tunnel vision, i.e. seeing the business through the lens of the technology rather than vice versa. Another problem can arise when suppliers assume that the prospective purchaser's operations are the same as those in other similar customers. This is not always true.
- A brief description of the current technology in use. If the software is to be developed using the current hardware and operating environment, this will need to be quite detailed and may merit a separate section of its own.

Example 7.2 is a highly abbreviated example.

Example 7.2: Business overview

Nestegg plc is a publicly quoted company which manufactures and sells a number of well-established snack food products including Supernuts, Tastikrisps and Crackerwhiz. Turnover last year was £250 million. The company employs 1800 staff at three plants in the north-east of England. The company sells its products in the UK and mainland European market and has achieved strong growth, particularly in France and Germany in the past 5 years.

The company has for many years operated a proprietary minicomputer system with a financial accounting system originally developed internally in 1991. This system has reached the end of its useful life and the company proposes to replace it with a modern distributed and web-based system.

The business overview should be brief. A half-page to a page is normally adequate, but where the business background is particularly relevant to the purchaser, an appropriate level of detail should be provided. Where the business is complicated and it is important for suppliers to understand it, a formal briefing should be considered. It is in the purchaser's interest that potential suppliers have as full an understanding as possible of how the user proposes to use their software.

7.3.2 Technical environment

The specification should make clear the technical environment within which the system must operate. Where the selection includes hardware, this may be quite broad or even open-ended. Otherwise the purchaser should be quite specific. The specification should state the systems architecture currently in use and how (or if) the software is expected to fit into this. There should also be a description of the hardware and systems software on which the proposed system will be expected to run, including operating systems and any interface requirements.

This section will normally be fairly brief (see Example 7.3), although there may be circumstances when a detailed technical overview, including systems schematics (diagrams), is necessary.

Example 7.3: Specification of technical environment

The company runs a client/server network based on the use of HP servers currently running Linux, and Intel-based desktops running a number of different versions of Microsoft Windows (it is planned to standardize these on the latest release later this year). The network is based on a gigabit Ethernet backbone with switched 10 Mbits to each desktop. The network protocol used is TCP/IP. Currently there are 170 users on the network.

7.4 Functional requirements

The two core elements of any package specification are the functional and reporting requirements. The functional requirements:

- list all the functions that the software must perform
- define each function clearly
- where functions are non-standard, define clearly the inputs, outputs, storage and processing requirement
- define any special features required
- state clearly which features are mandatory and which are optional.

With most packaged software for business applications, it may be assumed that basic features and facilities are available. These may be dealt with briefly. For example, where buying a general ledger, it is not necessary to specify that the package should be capable of producing a trial balance. Features of this type may be handled with phrases such as:

'The package must provide a full audit trail for all transactions.'

It is not necessary to be specific as to how the audit trail is provided. However, if in doubt, spell it out.

The functional specification states the requirements of the package in business and/or operational terms. These need to be:

- Clear and unambiguous. Clarity not only means stating the needs in good English, it also entails avoiding (or if necessary explaining) company terminology, jargon and acronyms. Failure to do this can be a source of misunderstanding and consequent problems.
- Complete. The specification should cover all aspects of the needs. Even where needs are regarded as standard package features they should always be mentioned.
- Consistent. There should be no contradictions within the specification. While this sounds self-evident, in a large specification consistency is by no means trivial to achieve. A common example is where different users specify calculations differently, use different data definitions or have different views on access rules.
- Prioritized. In any set of requirements there will be priorities. Requirements should be classified as:
  Mandatory – these are features that the package must provide.
  Desirable – these are features that the package should provide.
  Optional – these are features that are of interest, but not important.

Functional requirements are clearly application-specific. The level of detail required is, as a general rule, proportional to the 'non-standardness' of the needs.

7.4.1 Functional overview

The first part of this section should contain an overview of the requirements. It is a good idea to include a diagrammatic summary of the system. Nearly all modern packages of any complexity come in the form of suites of modules. Frequently, the purchaser will not want all of the modules in a package. Whether or not all the components are required, the summary should specify clearly which components are needed. The following example is from a statement of functional requirements for a group of hospitals.

Example 7.4: Hospital system requirements overview

The key requirements being sought in this tender is for:

- master patient index
- patient administration
- order communications system.

Other modules which may be required over the next three years are:

- accident and emergency
- laboratory
- community health
- outpatients.

The following diagram gives an overview of the target application architecture.

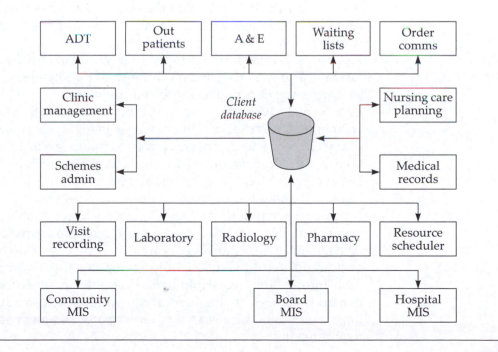

The objective of the overview is to provide the supplier with a frame of reference. Many users and even many IT managers tend to take their understanding of their own operations for granted and assume that others will immediately understand them.

7.4.2 Detailed functional specification

The overview is followed by a detailed specification of functional requirements, the contents of which are as follows.

- Data to be held in the system. It is not normally necessary to prepare a full data model for a packaged solution unless it is useful for the user to do so. (This is, however, an advisable step when specifying custom software, see below.) Where there are special data requirements, these must be stated. Special data requirements include:
    - Additional data storage or processing requirements. Storage of, or processing needs for, information that is not part of the standard package (or which cannot be reasonably expected to be in a standard package) should be stated.
    - Access data field requirements. It should not be assumed that because information is stored in a package it can always be extracted in the form the user needs.
    - Access security. It may be that the organization has its own rules on data access. The standard package may not support these rules.
    - Field sizes. It is important to specify any unusual field sizes for data. The field sizes in an off-the-shelf package may not be large enough for specialized requirements.
    - Data formats. A simple example of this is a system that may be required to hold customer names using a specialized character set. For example, if the company sells to the French market it may need to store characters such as 'ç'.
    - Data types. Modern user requirements often demand storage of data such as image and sound. These may not be features of a standard package. Many packages enable the user to put 'non-standard' information into free format text fields. Such fields however, cannot always be searched or manipulated in a sufficiently flexible manner. To make such information accessible in the required manner, may demand changes in the underlying data structure. It is important that the supplier be aware of any such requirements.

- Describe all transactions. It is not necessary to specify all transactions in detail. For example, in a financial system it is not usually necessary to state the information that must be input in order to generate an invoice. However, where there is any risk that a package may not meet even fairly standard processing requirements specification can be detailed.
- Describe any major processes or calculations. Some companies have special requirements for calculations in 'standard' areas. These may include processes that are unique to the organisation, for example a bank might have special financial instruments, a manufacturing company unusual overtime computation methods, or a food company a particular way of costing product recipes.

Case history 7.1 is a short extract from a highly complex payroll system requirement in an company which, over the years, had developed some pretty convoluted agreements with its unions on pay rates.

Case history 7.1: Payroll calculations

The package must be able to handle the different classes of overtime used in the organization. Specifically it should be possible to:

- define up to 20 overtime categories
- each overtime rate to have a distinct code (alpha or alpha numeric)
- define a rate for each overtime category, which is a multiple of:
  - Basic pay and/or
  - shift pay and/or
  - night shift pay and/or
  - bank holiday pay.

The system must enable the user to express a pay rate by addition, subtraction or multiplication of any of the above four basic components.

For example, a rate might be defined as:

Rate 3 = Basic × 1.5
Rate 5 = Basic + Shift × 0.25
Rate 17 = Night + Shift × 1.5 + Bank Holiday × 0.5

These calculations must be easy to set up and alter.

- Factors must be definable up to four decimal places.
- Overtime will be coded by the wages clerks as:
  - Hours overtime
  - Overtime code
- A member of staff may work at several overtime levels in a week. The package must enable the clerk to code up to five rates for any employee in a given week.

- Case history 7.1 illustrates several points:
  - it does not make any assumptions about the overtime codes available in the software
  - it specifies the minimum number of codes that are required
  - it sets out the calculations required
  - it defines modes of operation in the company which may differ from standard approaches
  - it specifies the facilities required.
- Describe any special or unusual features required. Special features may vary from unusual calculations (see Case history 7.1, above) to screens that match a corporate colour scheme!

7.4.3 Interfaces to other systems

Few enterprise software packages stand alone. Most pass information to and receive data from other systems. Often, although by no means always, these are systems from the same 'family' of products. Where such a suite is being purchased, it is not normally necessary to spell out interfaces. It can be assumed that the designers have already built these in. However, where there are interfaces to and from other third party or internal systems, be they packaged or custom built, these interfaces should be specified as follows.

- Data to be transferred in/out. This should state:
  - where the data is going to/coming from
  - fields to be transferred
  - format required, for example:
    - Sales volumes – 99999999999
    - Sales revenue – 999999V99 (or 8.2)
    - .GIF

- Volumes. This should specify the amount of data being transferred in terms of records or transactions required.
- Frequency. Data transfer may be batched or in real time (see next point). Where data is transferred by a batch process, the specification should indicate the frequency with which the transfer takes place.
- Triggers. These specify how the transfer is to occur. This might be:
  - Real time. Any change in one system is immediately reflected in the other. A good example of this is dynamic data linking.
  - Automatic. Automatic writing out or reading in of data can be built into the software (for example, on start-up each morning, the software reads in data created overnight by another system).
  - Time driven. This type of transfer is initiated by either the sending or receiving computer at a particular time. Time-driven transactions often occur overnight or at off-peak times, but can be done at regular intervals during normal operations.
  - User initiated. Data is only transferred when the user initiates it (for example, by selecting an option on a menu).
- Conversion required. When being exchanged between systems, data may need to be converted for a number of reasons, including different field formats, data type and field sizes. Typically, different systems interface by writing out an interface file from one system which is picked up by the other. Interface files may be required to comply with certain standards (for example, for electronic data interchange), or more sophisticated interfacing such as objects passing messages via extensible mark-up language (XML) and similar tools may be required. All interface formatting requirements should be thought through and incorporated into the specification.

7.4.4 Reports required

The second key component of many package requirement statements are the reporting requirements. Reports may come via a variety of media and formats including on-screen, on paper, textual, graphical or as a mixture. Reports are simple to specify, but report specifications are often poorly done. The following should be specified:

- all reports required
- for each report:
  - medium (screen and/or printed)
  - content by line
  - content by column
  - on-report calculations (i.e. computation of results at report-ing time)
  - layouts
  - frequency
  - other features required (for example special fonts)
  - sorting and sequencing required
  - subtotalling required

Cross-reporting is particularly important to specify. This is where reports may contain information sorted in special ways or from different parts of the system. For example, a sales report might be required:

- by product
- by customer
- by sales representative
- by region
- by brand
- by brand within region
- quarterly by product within customer

and so on. The simple, if somewhat long-winded, way to ensure that the report specification is comprehensive is to produce a book of reports. Specifying a generic report set is more concise, but requires care.

7.4.5 Queries

Application packages normally provide a range of enquiry screens. Many also provide an ad hoc reporting facility and most allow use of add-on/third party enquiry tools to interrogate the underlying data system directly. It is impossible to anticipate all the potential queries that users may make of a complex system. The specification should, however, identify all routine or regular queries, all fields and combinations of fields on which ad hoc queries are required, and generic query types. Example 7.5 is from the specification of a debtors' system.

Example 7.5: Queries required

The system should provide the following queries as standard:

1 Details of amounts owed (order details, date, amount, salesperson) by customer. Enquiry to be on:
   - customer number
   - customer name
   - sales representative
   - wild card search on customer or representative name.
2 Total value of current debtors.
3 All debtors who have debts outstanding from before a user input date.
4 All customers who have debts outstanding over a user input amount.
5 All customers who have debts outstanding over a user input amount and after a user input date.
6 Total balances outstanding by sales representative.
7 Total balances outstanding by weeks for a user input number of weeks from user input date.

The system should also enable the user to query individual fields using the standard comparison operators ($=$, $\neq$, $<$, $>$, $\leq$, $\geq$).

Where it is a requirement that an add-on enquiry tool be able to access the underlying data, this should be stated.

7.4.6 Security in packaged software

Security has several meanings. The primary meanings in the present context are access-related and recovery. Most enterprise software packages come with some levels of security. In sensitive environments, there may be special security requirements. Security specification should include requirements for:

- password protection
- access control by
  - function
  - screen
  - report/queries
- data access controls:
  - file level
  - table level
  - record level

- recovery mechanisms:
  - transaction logging
  - rollback.

Specification of security requirements should be in terms of capabilities, not of specifics. For example:

> *'The system should permit the administrator to specify access at record level'*

is better than:

> *'The following users should have access to the employee salary records'.*

Security in the sense of resilience and recovery from problems is covered in Chapter 9.

7.4.7 Support and maintenance requirements

The degree of support required for packaged software will depend on a number of factors including the number of users, the complexity of the application, the stability of the package, and the extent of the modifications (if any) made to the package. Formally *support* is defined as assistance in the operation of the package, *maintenance* is the correction of errors in the software. The term 'maintenance' is also used to include rights to software upgrades although these are sometimes the subject of a separate agreement. In practice, this distinction is not always made by either users or vendors and it is often convenient to consider them as one.

A number of things need to be specified for support. First it is important to specify what *level of support depth* is required. It is useful to ask how many supplier or vendor staff are in customer support and where such people are located. It is also useful to find out how many other sites are they covering. A general statement of the form:

> *'Suppliers must demonstrate that they have adequate resources for supporting the operation of the software'*

may be adequate. However, where the system is mission-critical, it may be necessary to be more specific, for example:

> *'It is a requirement of the company that any supplier bidding for this contract have a minimum of three staff qualified to support the soft-ware within 2 hours' travelling time of the company's head office.'*

The second aspect of support is *response times*. These need to be specified in terms of both nature and time. Support may be via telephone, modem, inter/extranet or call to site. Modem- or network based support is normally the front line. Suppliers claim that this is more efficient. It eliminates travel time and, by working from their own premises, they have access to all technical support staff, manuals and their own system (if, for example, they want to try to replicate a problem). Nevertheless response times should be clearly specified. Options may be:

- standard response, typically 4 hours during the normal working day (say 9:00 a.m. to 6:00 p.m.)
- fast response, i.e. response times of an hour or less may be needed for critical applications
- support person permanently on site
- weekend/bank holiday cover
- 24 hour cover
- 365 days per year cover.

Naturally, the more extensive and faster the cover, the higher the cost. The purchaser has to evaluate this cost against the cost of lost time or business when a problem occurs, and the probability of problems occurring. This can be done using the methods described in Chapter 10. As a package settles down (or user confidence in it builds up) over time, the level of support required may drop. For this reason, careful consideration should be given before entering into long term software maintenance contracts.

Thirdly, expected *escalation* procedures should be specified. Escalation occurs when the problem is not resolved by the current support level within a specified time. In this case, the next level of support is called in. Some suppliers operate a 'traffic light' system whereby when a customer reports a problem the site is marked as being on alert. If the problem is not resolved within a specified period this becomes an orange alert, and if still not resolved, a red alert. It is important that this is driven by customer/business needs, not by supplier protocols.

A final consideration is *access to support staff*. Some suppliers have rigid rules about who may speak to whom. Thus the user can find him or herself in the frustrating position of having to use a junior technician or some minion with a grand title like 'customer support liaison executive' as an intermediary with the real experts. If it is of benefit to talk directly to the specialist (i.e. if the purchaser has the technical expertise to use such a line of communication) so it can be worth specifying it as requirement.

7.4.8 Performance

The performance of any system is affected by many factors, including the hardware speed, network bandwidth, level of usage and the way the software has been designed and built. With packaged software, the latter two are unlikely to be changed just because one particular customer has specified a particular level of performance. Specification of performance for packaged software in isolation is therefore only appropriate where the hardware is a given.

Specification of performance generally is described in Chapter 6.

7.5 Specifying custom software requirements

Custom software requirements need to be specified to a greater degree of detail and with more precision than packaged software. This section contains a brief outline of some of the key issues in this process. For further detail, the reader is referred to one of the many excellent books on software specification and design.

A statement of requirements for custom software should contain some or all of the following:

- business overview
- technical environment
- functionality required
- data or process flow diagrams
- conceptual data model
- interfaces to and from other systems
- reports required
- query facilities required
- support requirements
- security requirements
- performance requirements
- development environment and methodology.

These are similar to the requirements for packaged software. However, for the technical environment and the functionality required, greater detail is necessary. Custom specifications generally need data models or their equivalent. The differences, therefore, between a packaged software and a custom software specification are in the:

- payment/contract structure
- technical environment
- level of specification.

Each of these is discussed below.

7.5.1 Payment/contract structure

A fundamental difference between buying custom software and most other types of IT procurement in that a price *estimate* is required. All IT purchases may be open to some degree of negotiation, but a supplier quoting a price for a custom software system cannot work from a price list and has to prepare an estimate. This creates both opportunities and risks for the buyer.

There are three basic approaches to purchasing custom software:

1 The first is to go for a *fixed price contract* covering everything from design to documentation. The advantages of this approach are certainty and stability. In particular, suppliers have no incentive to add on 'extras' or accept ad hoc modifications to the requirements (unless they reduce the work to be done). There are, however, some drawbacks. The first may be cost (this will depend on how competitive the situation is). A supplier may include a generous margin of error in its quotation. In the event of their original estimates being accurate, they are unlikely to hand this risk margin back to the customer. The purchaser can therefore end up paying more than the real cost of the job. A second disadvantage is the preparation effort. Professional suppliers will insist on a rigorous specification against which to quote. This must be prepared in advance. Sometimes this is not easy, especially if the technology is new and the purchaser has not yet got a good feel for what can or cannot be done. Some suppliers may be unwilling to quote for a complete development unless the specification is comprehensive. Another problem is lack of flexibility. Once the contract is signed, changes will be expensive. Suppliers may insist on delivering exactly what was specified, even though the user may have had second thoughts or circumstances may have changed. The cost of change may discourage the user from asking for important alterations to the system. Finally, there is always a small risk of panic! Where a fixed price project starts to seriously

overrun, suppliers may become desperate and start to cut corners. With fixed price contracts, it is important to be sure that the supplier is both reputable and has the financial strength to finish the job. Smaller software suppliers can be bankrupted by one large project which turns bad. If this happens, having a fixed price contract may be little consolation. Finally, fixed price contracts are only practical where a reasonably structured development approach is being used. For this reason, it does not usually work for evolutionary prototyping and rapid application development type projects (see below).

2 The second approach is *time and materials*. Under this system, the supplier charges a rate per workday to complete the job. The contract may be open-ended, i.e. 'whatever it takes to get the job done'. The advantages of this approach are simplicity and, potentially at least, cost effectiveness. If the supplier is honest and efficient, time and materials can work out cheaper than fixed cost because the customer does not have to pay for the supplier's safety margin or to recover the cost of preparing the quotation. Furthermore, changes are normally at the project rate so they tend to be less expensive. This approach is also flexible. Changes can be made as development progresses without constant re-negotiation of add-on costs. The disadvantages of this approach are fairly obvious. Cost control needs to be watertight if unpleasant surprises are to be avoided. This requires much more effort than with a fixed price contract. Furthermore, if there are any problems (including problems created by the supplier), the customer pays. A supplier who is dishonest and/or unscrupulous can exploit the arrangement to add on extras that may not be needed. Users may be encouraged to keep asking for more features and most users will happily do so provided someone else is paying the bill. This can lead to a deterioration in supplier–purchaser relationships. Time and materials can be convenient and cost-effective where the purchaser has good project management capability and the purchaser–supplier relationship is good and well-established, but should otherwise be avoided.

3 The third way is *fixed stage costs*. This is a compromise between the preceding two. Using this approach the supplier gives a fixed quote for the next stage of work to be done and a guideline quote for all remaining tasks. When the current stage is complete, the purchaser then has the option to terminate the work at that point, proceed to the next stage or

seek another supplier to undertake the next stage. The stages in this process might, for example, be:

- requirement specification
- logical design
- physical design
- system development, testing and implementation.

The above is only one possible set of stages. Other subdivisions are possible, including the preparation of the requirements specification. The latter may be useful if the purchaser does not have the necessary skills or resources to do this. The advantage of this approach is that costs are semi-controlled. At key stages the purchaser has charge of the situation. It also reduces the risk to both supplier and buyer. Because the stages are smaller and because of the work done to date, the supplier can quote with greater accuracy. On the down side, there is the risk of cost escalation. If costs escalate the purchaser can find itself in the difficult position of having spent a large amount of money already which can make it difficult to abandon the project. Another risk is loss leading. A supplier may quote low for the first stage on the assumption that it will be difficult for the purchaser to stop the project once it has started. Suppliers who inadvertently or deliberately under-quote for one stage may try to recover their profitability by deliberately overpricing a later stage, although this danger can be countered by opening later stages to competition. Finally, this process also requires several separate agreements which may require negotiation.

From a purchaser viewpoint, a confirmed, up-front fixed cost is always attractive. However there is much to recommend fixed stage costs – particularly if the relationship with the supplier is to be a long-term one. Starting on the right foot is always a good policy.

7.5.2 Technical issues

Where the technical environment for a custom development is predetermined, then the type of specification illustrated in Example 7.3 is perfectly adequate. With packaged software too, the hardware options may be limited or version considerations may dominate choice of operating environment. In other circumstances, certain technical options may be incompatible with some of the best software options. This is less of a constraint with custom software. When custom software is proposed it is common for there to be a number of possible ways of developing the system in the current environment. It is also common for a customized system to be developed using a different hardware and systems environment to that already in place.

In the latter case, three issues have to considered:

1 The hardware architecture. The issues here are discussed in Chapter 6.
2 The development environment.
3 The development approach.

7.5.3 Specifying development environments and methods

The development environment is made up of several components. A purchaser may or may not choose to specify some or all of these components. For example, a sophisticated purchaser may state that the database management system to be used must not only be Oracle or DB2 but even go so far as to specify the version and release number. For those who are not so technically skilled, the following are some broad guidelines.

- Data management. Most modern development is based on relational database technology. There are many other data storage paradigms including multidimensional databases, text database, object-orientated databases and so on. It is important the right data management tool (as opposed to brand) is chosen. For specialist applications such as On-Line Analytical Processing, a relational database is not very effective. Ensure that any data management product:
  - is widely used
  - can be adequately supported by the supplier
  - is not going to cause problems with recruiting staff.
  The latter is an important point. If the purchaser needs to hire a database administrator, it does not want to find that the skill set required is astronomically expensive or worse, impossible to find.
- Development tools. There is an enormous range of development tools now on the market, from traditional third generation languages such as COBOL and C through fourth-generation languages, Integrated Computer Aided System Engineering (ICASE) code generators, object-orientated languages such as C++ and Java, up to and including recent

developments in visual and web-based computing. There are also may hybrid products. In choosing a development environment, the following factors should be taken into account:

- Suitability for the application.
- Ease and cost effectiveness of ownership. This will impact on long term maintenance costs. If the purchase plans to develop an in-house support capability it is critical.
- Standards. When specifying software for development it is important to include any standards to be used. The need to specify standards is less than it used to be as the IT industry has moved steadily away from the world of proprietary computing. Nontheless there are standards for databases, development tools and development methodologies which are still not universal. The majority of the most common languages adhere to ANSI or other similar standards, but others such as Java and C++ come in a number of varieties.
- Technology independence. It is preferable that the tool run on a wide range of hardware and operating system platforms.
- Availability of skills internally (where relevant).
- Availability of skills in the marketplace for long term support.
- Middleware. Middleware has grown steadily in importance from the days where there was just the operating system, the compiler, the link-editor and the application code. Some areas of middleware, such as data management and communications, are relatively straightforward. However, others, particularly integration software, object brokers and so on, are highly technical and still evolving. If you need or wish to specify middleware requirements, it is best to seek professional advice from experts who are up to date in this field.
- Development approach. There are several development methodologies. In broad terms they divide into:
- Waterfall or systems development lifecycle (SDLC) models methodologies such as structured systems analysis and design methodology (SSADM). Variants include the incremental and spiral models as well as closely related approaches such as information engineering. Basically these work in a series of sequential (although sometimes overlapping) stages with each stage being signed off or approved before the next stage begins. Apart from SSADM, there are many commercial products supplied or used by companies such as IBM and Accenture.

The advantages of the waterfall method are that, in theory at least, they provide considerable control, enabling managers to plan and to understand how things are going and where the project is at any given time. This is crucial for large projects anyway, but especially when managing a supplier. Furthermore, because there is a formal design phase, the type of problems that can arise from the more ad hoc approach of prototyping methods are avoided. On the other hand, waterfall methods are long-winded, bureaucratic and generate vast volumes of paper. The term 'analysis paralysis' is sometimes applied to this technique as it can seem like an eternity before anything is actually delivered. It can also be inflexible. Once the design is set in place, changes are not encouraged as they can mean going back to the drawing-board. The result is that by the time the system is delivered, it no longer meets the requirements.

- The term rapid application development (RAD) is often taken to encompass a range of different techniques including evolutionary prototyping, extreme programming and object orientated development methods (of which there are a few). Strictly speaking, RAD consists of four phases (as opposed to the ten or more there can be in waterfall methods. SSADM has seven), namely requirements planning, user design, construction and cut-over. Rapid methods have the advantage of developing the system in front of the user's eyes, so to speak, so that requirements can be better defined because the user does not have to think things out on paper first. It can also deliver functionality quickly and there is less risk of not getting what you want at the end. On the down side, unless discipline is tight, rapid methods can lead to poorly designed and documented systems which may be difficult to change and, in some cases, be unreliable. These problems have, to some extent, been addressed by the development of methodologies such as the dynamic systems development methodology (DSDM).

- Unified methods have been proposed as a compromise solution and models are being developed by commercial suppliers. These seek to combine the best of both of the above worlds and include a diagrammatic language (the unified modelling language) which attempts to provide a common notation. It is quite possible to combine elements of both methods in a given development.

In a way, the arguments between proponents of waterfall and rapid methods are part theological and part cultural as well as technical. In general, if requirements are clear and stable and there is a need for tight control, waterfall methods are best. If there is uncertainly about requirements and the timescale is short, RAD type methods should be considered. When it comes to development environments and techniques, purchasers should also stick to the mainstream and assess carefully both the experience and competence of the supplier with the proposed technology and approach, and their ability to support the system afterwards. There may be circumstances when it is appropriate to risk using an exotic product or where a purchaser is willing to be first in the field with a new technique. Such adventurous approaches to development should only be considered where organizations either have a strong internal IT capability and/or there is a compelling business case. Where possible, avoid the bleeding edge.

7.5.4 Custom functional specifications

While the functional specification for much packaged software can be quite general, for some packaged software and for all custom software it is necessary to specify functional requirements to a considerable level of detail. For a waterfall approach (see above), this must be spelled out in advance. With prototyping methods, requirements can be developed alongside the system, but a broad initial statement of requirements is still required.

A key question is the importance of obtaining an accurate cost estimate. The more important a clear cost is (the extreme case being a fixed cost contract), the more precise the specification must be. In this case, precision matters. For example, when buying a general ledger package it is quite sufficient to state that the system must provide a full audit trail. However, custom building implies that processing is non-standard so the 'what' and sometimes the 'how' generally have to be stated in detail. This can mean a step-by-step description, rules, data formats, exact calculations to be carried out and so on. Example 7.6 shows an extract from a specification for posting to a general ledger (of course nobody would specify this nowadays, the purpose of the example is to show the level of detail involved in such specifications).

Example 7.6: Nominal ledger posting transaction specification

The nominal ledger must allow on-line input of:

1 Account numbers to which the transaction is to be posted (mandatory existence check against customer database). A facility to select a sub-account (from a list ex-customer database) is required.
2 Amount of transaction (minimum 9.2 digits).
3 Currency of transaction (selected from one of a pre-defined list and not editable. The default will be the default currency on the customer record). This must be validated against the ledger in use.
4 Transaction narrative (minimum 50 characters to include French and German character sets).
5 Journal total (minimum 11.2 digits).
6 Mandatory edit check field with full commit and rollback facility.
7 The system date and time must be posted from a non-editable display field.
8 A computer-generated terminal ID must be posted. This must show the user ID of the person making the transaction and the location from which the transaction was initiated.
9 A unique computer-generated journal number must be posted as a transaction identification. A unique computer-generated batch identification must be posted. Both of these are to be non-editable display fields (optional).

In addition the following are mandatory requirements:

1 All postings must comply with double-entry bookkeeping rules.
2 It must be possible to post both to current and previous periods.
3 Postings to any other period must be via a separate posting mechanism with specific controls as detailed in Section 4.
4 Cumulative value of postings-to-date within batch must *not* be shown on-screen.

In Example 7.6, the user spells out exactly how a transaction must work. Functional specifications of this type are time-consuming and expensive to prepare. In presenting a supplier with a functional specification, the purchaser reduces the risk of getting a solution that is not quite what is wanted, but in so doing takes on the risk of not getting the specification right. If the supplier provides what the user requests, the purchaser has no complaint if the software is not what was wanted.

7.5.5 Data flows

Two other common components of a custom software specification are data flow diagrams and data models. Data flows show the movement of data between the process and storage or holding points in the system. There is a number of data flow diagramming conventions including Gane and Sarson, De Marco and SSADM. Each of these uses a different symbol set, but they are in essence fairly similar. Data flow diagrams use the following components.

- External entities. These are things outside of the system that generate or receive data. Examples are:
  - customers
  - suppliers
  - other computer systems.
  An external entity may be shown more than once on the diagram if it helps readability. Note that these are items outside the system, not necessarily outside the organization. For example, from the viewpoint of the Order Processing Department, the Accounts Department might be an external entity.
- Processes. These are things that happen to data while they are inside the system. Examples of processes are:
  - process customer payment
  - take and confirm booking
  - register a hotel guest
  and so on. Processes can be stated at a high level and then broken down into lower levels (see below). Each process is given a number. The number is a label only and does not indicate the order of processing. Data flow diagrams do not necessarily show procedural logic.
- Data stores. These are points in the system where data is held, temporarily or permanently. Data stores may be any medium at all from the magnetic disks on the organization's computers to filing cabinets, cardexes or even in-trays. For ease of reading, data stores may be shown more than once on the same diagram. Data stores are labelled.
- Data flows. These are items of data flowing between processes, stores and external entities. Data may be computer traffic, forms, documents, e-mail or any other transmission by manual or electronic means.

Figure 7.2 shows the SSADM symbols for the above items.

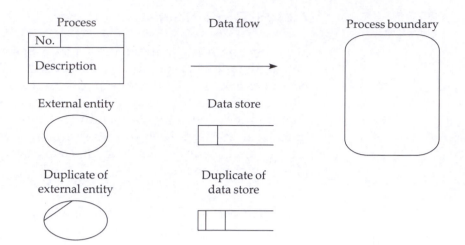

Figure 7.2
Data flow diagram
symbols

Processes may be 'exploded' down a level. For example, the process 'Process customer payment' above might be made up of five separate sub-processes, thus:

- the amount received is noted in a day book
- a receipt is issued
- the customer account is updated
- the cheque is lodged
- the lodgment slip and payment details are filed.

Example 7.7, which uses the SSADM notation, is a simplified version of a diagram taken from a real order processing department.

Data flow diagrams are a simple, but powerful, technique and are particularly good at communicating the operation of a system to potential suppliers. They are easy to master and should normally be included in custom specifications.

7.5.6 Conceptual data models

A data model is a graphical representation of the data used in the application being specified. While data models are an essential component of most custom software specifications, they are not always necessary or of particular value in a specification for a packaged solution. Data models are made up of a number of components.

Example 7.7: Example of data flow diagramming

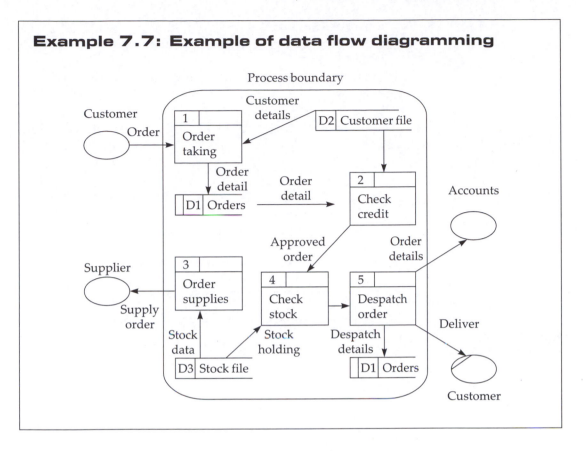

- Entities. These are things about which information is held. Examples are:
  - customers
  - products
  - departments.
  and so on.
- Relationships. These connect entities. For example, customers buy products, employees work in a department. These connections are called relationships. Relationships can be of three basic types:
  - One-to-one: for example, a piece of plant has a lease and each lease applies to one piece of plant. One-to-one relationships are relatively unusual in data models as they are often merged into a single entity.
  - One-to-many: for example, a department contains many employees, but an employee only works in one department.
  - Many-to-many: for example, a customer buys many products and a product is bought by many customers.

Relationships can also be:
- Optional: for example, a customer may or may not buy a product.
- Mandatory: for example, a patient must be assigned to a doctor.

Figure 7.3 shows the graphical representation of these symbols.

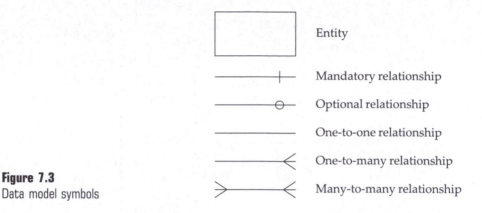

Figure 7.3
Data model symbols

Example 7.8 is an extract from an order processing system

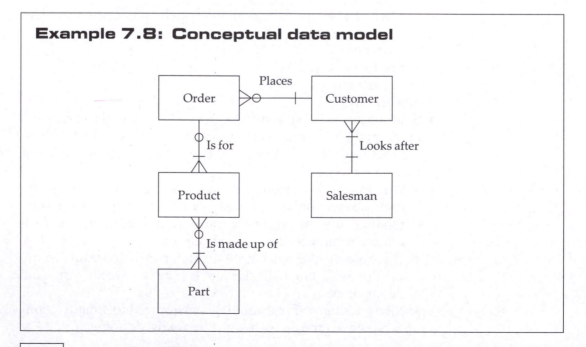

Example 7.8: Conceptual data model

and can be interpreted as follows: customers may place many orders. A customer must be assigned one and only one salesman. An order must be associated with a customer (i.e. there cannot be an order without a customer placing it) and is associated with one customer only. An order can be for many products and must be for at least one product. A product can be on many orders. There does not have to be an order for a product. A product is made up of many parts. A product must be made up of at least one part. A part may be in many products. A part does not have to be in any of the products. A salesman must look after at least one customer and may look after many customers.

Data models can be developed to a considerable degree of sophistication. This includes (amongst many other features) adding attributes (the information we hold about an entity) and normalization, a process whereby redundancy in the data is eliminated while data access and integrity are checked. These steps are essential for design, but are not necessary for a statement of requirements. There is no firm line which defines the exact point on the development of a data model where requirements' specification stops and design starts. Indeed the definition can vary with the methodology being used. In most methodologies, development of a full logical data structure is one of the first tasks in system development and is a task that the supplier will normally undertake as part of the project. The level defined above, the conceptual data model, should always be included with the requirements' specification.

7.6 Conclusion

Specification of software is a big subject and this chapter necessarily has to be confined to certain broad precepts and key techniques. The important message is that this is the highest risk area of IT purchasing and therefore needs the most attention. Writing a good software specification requires skill and experience, in particular judging the right level of detail. Specifications need to be accurate enough to ensure that purchaser and supplier are able to agree a fair cost for the development. On the other hand, a specification and development process should never become so rigid that users become totally frustrated. A certain degree of give and take is important. For this reason, always select a supplier that is not only expert, but which is flexible and with which your organization is comfortable.

8

Purchasing other IT products and services

8.1 Introduction

While hardware and software often make up the bulk of IT purchasing expenditure, IT purchasing covers a variety of other products and services. Where a company outsources its IT, most of its expenditure will fall under the heading of 'services'. When purchasing 'solutions' as opposed to simply hardware or application software, many other issues have to be taken into account. This chapter discusses these issues from a purchasing perspective, including the factors of which to be aware and the actions that should be taken.

There are organizations which can meet all of their IT services requirements using internal resources and there are organizations that choose to outsource all IT services to the extent of not employing any IT staff at all. The majority of organizations fall in between these two extremes, providing some level of service from their internal resources and buying in specialist or one-off resources as needed. Services which are frequently bought in, even by large organizations, include:

- software development services
- hardware maintenance
- consultancy
- systems integration
- contract programmers and other staff
- contingency planning/disaster recovery services
- security
- external communications services
- web-related services.

The first of these is discussed in the previous chapter. The remainder are covered in this chapter.

8.2 Purchasing hardware maintenance

Few organizations do their own hardware maintenance except for the most simple and routine tasks. Nearly all hardware maintenance is therefore provided by either the hardware supplier or by third party maintenance companies. The latter are commonly used for smaller equipment, particularly PCs, smaller servers and printers which manufacturers are not always well geared to support.

With either source of maintenance, purchasers normally have a choice of two options, namely a maintenance contract or buy-as-you-need. A typical hardware supplier *maintenance contract* costs between 7% and 15% of the initial purchase cost of the equipment per annum. The percentage will vary with the nature of the equipment and the type of response level required (see below). The advantages of hardware maintenance contracts are threefold:

1 Response time is guaranteed.
2 The cost is predetermined (or is at least substantially predetermined).
3 Where appropriate, it will normally include pre-emptive maintenance (necessary for high-performance mechanical devices like heavy duty printers or scanners).

The disadvantage is that, like insurance, the customer pays whether there is a problem or not. This type of maintenance is most suitable for mission-critical systems and large and complex machinery, such as host mainframes or large servers, heavy duty printers and other specialized equipment. Most suppliers offer various levels of service (usually with metallic names like platinum, gold and silver). The higher the level the faster the response time, the more cover and the higher the price.

The alternative is to *buy-as-you-need*. Hardware suppliers tend not to be enthusiastic about this arrangement (not surprisingly, as hardware maintenance contracts are a profitable business), but most will provide it if requested. This is akin to self-insurance: if there are no problems, there are no costs. As a result, even where there is an occasional problem it can be a lot less expensive if the equipment is reasonably reliable. On the down side, if there is a major problem, it can be very expensive indeed to get it fixed. Daily charge-out rates of well over a thousand pounds per day are not unknown. Suppliers may charge a premium for a first visit. Much more critically, there is no guaranteed response time. Customers with contract agreements will get priority. The purchaser must decide the risk of having a long wait for an engineer to come. This option is more attractive for peripheral devices and PCs.

The decision as to which of the above policies is better value involves estimating the costs and risks involved. The relative merits of each of these approaches can be assessed using the risk management techniques described in Chapter 10.

8.2.1 Types of support

With smaller items of equipment, such as PCs, modems, laser printers and so on, there are further variations on the above:

- Call-to-site. Under this type of contract the maintenance company will send out someone to the site to undertake the necessary repairs. An alternative, with networked processors at least, may be remote support, but this is of limited use for hardware faults (and obviously no use at all if the machine is dead!).
- Return to workshop. This type of maintenance service is much less expensive as the user is not paying (or at least not directly paying) for the engineer's travelling time or the risk that, having examined the machine on site, the engineer decides that it will need to go back to the workshop for repairs anyway. With some suppliers, this may be the only option offered.

There are several disadvantages of this latter policy. Firstly, it is inconvenient for the user who has to organize getting the faulty device back to the supplier/maintenance contractor. Secondly, and probably most important, in the case of PCs and servers, there may sensitive information or systems on the internal disk drives. Users may not be happy for such a machine to be out of the office on some unknown person's workbench. Thirdly, if the problem is a simple one to repair, it will take longer because the machine has to travel there and back. Finally, as it takes longer, there is the hidden cost in staff time and loss of facilities.

If a return to workshop policy is preferred, IT management should ensure that they have a back-up or re-deployment plan to cover the gap while the faulty device is being repaired. Generally for PCs in a moderate or large network, it is possible to find a spare machine which is temporarily unused and which can be re-deployed to replace a machine that has been sent out for repair. For larger organizations, it is worthwhile having one or more spare PCs available which can be deployed if one breaks down. However, while in theory re-deploying a machine from a less critical area is straightforward, in practice it can be at best awkward and at worst impractical – particularly where the users make extensive use of the local hard disk for software and/or data. In mission-critical systems, the above precautions may be needed even where there is a call-to-site agreement.

8.2.2 Specifying maintenance requirements

Hardware maintenance specifications should state:

- the exact equipment covered by the maintenance agreement
- the extent of the maintenance required (the purchaser may be able to carry out certain basic maintenance internally)
- response times
- escalation procedures
- maintenance policy, i.e. call-to-site or return to supplier. If necessary this may be specified by equipment category.

The supplier for its part should state:

- the charging basis
- what (if any) spares will need to be held on site
- where spares are kept by the supplier. For example, it is important to know if parts have to be sourced from outside the country. This may have implications for the time repairs will take
- for machines or models that are no longer manufactured, what the spares position is and the long-term policy and cost implications.

The specification of equipment covered may be general. For example, an agreement might cover all PCs in the organization or at a particular location. Ideally the supplier should have a list of equipment including the serial number of each item. Apart from anything else, this avoids the problem of users sending their personal machines (or their children's!) in for repair under the cover of the organization's maintenance contract.

Response times and escalation strategy must be specified clearly and fully understood. Where there is a call-to-site maintenance contract, the key variables are cost, response time and repair time. The standard guaranteed maximum response time to call-out tends to be 4 hours or same day. In the past, when a user 'phoned in with a problem, an engineer would be sent out by the supplier as soon as possible. Today, assuming the system has not failed completely, most suppliers use a modem- or extranet-based diagnostic system to try to find out as much as they can about the problem before they arrive on site. Where a problem is with software, the repair can often be done remotely. Even experienced users can sometimes find it difficult to differentiate between a serious and a minor problem. Response times (as with software) can range through:

- standard response. This is typically 4 hours during the normal working day (say 9:00 a.m. to 6:00 p.m.)
- fast response. Response times of an hour or less may be needed for critical applications
- support person permanently on site
- weekend/Bank Holiday cover
- 24 hour cover
- 365 days per year cover.

The latter two are typically referred to as 24/7. Faster response times and wide cover are naturally more expensive. For example a user might expect to pay premiums as follows:

Type of cover	% Cost over standard
Guaranteed same-day response	5–10%
Weekend/Bank Holiday cover	15–20%
365 days a year cover	40–70%

On the other side, maintenance costs can often be reduced if the customer is willing to wait longer, for example until the next day. Next-day response tends to be 20–40% cheaper than standard.

The second critical issue is the *escalation procedure*, which comes down to how long a problem takes to fix. Modern hardware systems are modular. When a component fails, the entire board is usually replaced rather than the single component on the board that is the source of the problem. With larger components (such as disk drives) suppliers may not have spares to hand and may be reluctant to replace them until it is clear that there is no other course of action open. Despite such wholesale replacement strategies, there can still be elusive hardware problems and the time required to fix a problem can become critical. It is therefore important that there is a clear escalation procedure. This defines the time period within which a problem is raised to the next level of action. This might be:

- replacement of an entire component
- provision of another machine
- replacement of the machine.

This is closely tied into the organization's contingency plan and should be considered in that context. One leading hardware company defines three escalation levels as follows:

1 Minor problem with only a few non-critical users affected.
2 Major problem with a large number of users affected.
3 System completely down.

Selecting the appropriate level of response requires an assessment of risk against cost. There is no point in paying a high premium for extensive cover where systems are not critical.

8.2.3 Security issues in hardware maintenance

Some users and organizations are concerned about the possible security risks arising from remote support. Any non-controlled remote access to the system is a potential security hole and care must be taken to ensure that support logins to the system are genuine. Where remote support (via modem or network) is in place, the systems administrator should monitor the situation at all times and periodically check on what the supplier engineers are doing. Suppliers should not be left unattended with the machine. Furthermore, external diagnostic lines or ports in the firewall should only be opened when there is a problem. It should never be possible to dial in without active action by the systems administrator.

When using dial-in support in highly sensitive environments the following additional precautions should be considered:

- Permit dial-out only. This means that only the user can initiate the connection by dialing the supplier's modem.
- Use an answer-back modem. This is a modem which, on receiving a call from an incoming modem, automatically hangs up and dials back a pre-programmed number.
- Keep a log of all commands issued during the session.

- Use a keypad/coding security system.
- Use a secure extranet.
- If using the internet, use a firewall where a port can be opened temporarily for the use of support.

Users have to place a certain level of trust in all of their suppliers. However, it is always wise to be cautious.

8.2.4 Summary

Call-to-site maintenance contracts are preferable for all larger and mission-critical hardware items, notably host mainframe and minicomputers, servers, specialist heavy duty peripherals and all mission-critical hardware. Contracted return-to-workshop arrangements are most suitable for smaller peripherals, non-critical PCs and mobile communications devices. Pay-as-you-need contracts are most suitable for non-mission critical, inherently reliable components which do not need planned maintenance including smaller servers, and solid-state peripherals such as modems and PCs. Organizations should choose the mix of strategy that best suits their needs.

8.3 Purchasing consultancy services

Most organizations use IT consultants at some time and some organizations have one or more consultancy firms seemingly permanently on site. Consultancy firms vary from broadly based firms offering a wide range of IT services to smaller organizations offering specialized services such as recruitment or security planning. In the consultancy business, demarcation lines are not always clear. Many software houses describe themselves as consultants and many consultancy firms earn a substantial part of their income from selling software services. Some 'consultancy' firms are even hardware re-sellers. Many large, traditional hardware firms have reinvented themselves as consultancy services who will happily (so they say) recommend that you install their competitors' hardware. It can all be pretty confusing for the purchaser.

When purchasing consultancy it is important for the purchaser to be clear on the nature of the service being sought. Key types of service include:

- Independent advice. This can be valuable for such issues as strategic IT/IS planning, when making evaluation and selection decisions or when assessing system and/or supplier performance. Independence is also an important quality in a systems integrator. There are some consultancy firms which are genuinely independent. However, some of the major IT consultancies today have alliances with various vendors and several of the traditionally independent firms have been swallowed up by product suppliers. There may also be formal or semi-formal arrangements that may not always have been publicly announced. Despite this, many will still claim to offer an independent advisory service. The more reputable consultancies may be able to do this by using a so-called Chinese wall. Where independent advice is important, then it is essential to select a consultancy that has no vested interest in the outcome and no relationship with any of the other parties involved.

● A specific service where independence is not a key issue. Important consultancy services include:
  • IT strategic planning
  • business process re-engineering (which comes under a variety of names)
  • systems integration
  • system specification, design and development
  • project management
  • evaluation and selection
  • software and system implementation
  • methodologies
  • training
  • recruitment
  • performance review and evaluation
  • security reviews.

In addition, some consultancies offer packaged software solutions, outsourcing and even hardware. When purchasing such services, it is important to be aware of the basic economics of the supplier. This enables a purchaser to negotiate more effectively.

8.3.1 Guidelines when buying consultancy

A purchaser buying consultancy is buying people. The key things to look for in a consultant are therefore:

● Expertise. Does the firm/individual have the necessary skills for the job? When buying consultancy, the purchaser is paying for specialist skills and experience that it does not have or cannot make available. It is important to ensure that those skills and experience are being provided.

- Personality. A good consultant must be able to get on with a wide variety of people. Is the consultant good with people?
- Culture. Different consultancies have different cultures. Some are aggressive and competitive organizations and will tend to suit an organization that is of the same mind. Others are 'softer' and more people-orientated and will tend to work better with organizations whose culture is similar to this. It is important that the cultures match. A consultant firm that continually makes the purchaser uncomfortable may not be the most suitable firm to deal with.
- Cost. Consultancy does not come cheap. Top IT consultants can cost in excess of £3000 per day and even middle-ranking consultants can run to £1500 per day or more. Controlling consultancy costs is therefore an important management issue.

All organizations whose principal product is people's time make their money from hours sold times rate per hour. Rates per hour are based on four factors:

1 Market demand.
2 Costs.
3 Recoveries (i.e. the percentages of the full charge recovered. If a fixed-price job overruns, the consultant will not recover 100% of the time incurred).
4 Hours charged as a percentage of hours available in the year.

The latter figure, known as the utilization, is a critical variable for all people-orientated IT service businesses. For example, a senior consultant at £150 per hour may have a theoretical income earning potential over a 1850-hour year of £255 500. In practice, allowing for leave, training, illness, administration and time when no work is available, a utilization of 60–65% is not untypical (although the figure may be much lower if trading conditions are poor). From the consultancy or software house's viewpoint, most costs are fixed and the marginal cost of additional income is to all intents and purposes zero. Additional hours above the break-even point are highly profitable.

A shrewd purchaser can take advantages of this. A consultancy or software firm might have an income target for the year for a consultant of say:

1300 hours @ £150 per hour @ 80% recovery = $1300 \times £150 \times 0.80$

$$= £146\,250$$

A supplier who is willing to offer 1600 hours guaranteed work could therefore argue that the rate for this should be £91.41 per hour (£91.41 × 1600 × 100%= £146 250), i.e. a 40% discount on the scale rate. In fact, a shrewd purchaser can do better because the budgeted figure is generally adjusted for some risk element, i.e. that the firm will be unable to sell 1300 hours of the consultant's time. By eliminating this risk, the purchaser can sometimes obtain an even more favourable rate.

Other points to be aware of when purchasing consultancy are:

- Always ask to meet the consultant(s) who will be assigned to the project. It is quite common for the people who sell the work to be different from the people who will do it.
- Beware of colonization. A key concept in consultancy is 'sell-on', i.e. selling further work to the client. This is not necessarily bad. Long-term relationships are valuable here as elsewhere. However, it can run out of control and an organization can find its IT operations and even the company itself virtually being run by consultants. See Case history 8.1
- Ask if they have a methodology. Some consultancies have advanced methodologies for all aspects of IT service. While not always publicly available, such methodologies are usually available to good clients and can be valuable in their own right. A good methodology is a sign of a structured approach.
- At all costs avoid time and materials charging. See Chapter 7.

Consultancy is a highly competitive market and this can be exploited by a purchaser. However, here, as elsewhere, long-term relationships are important and purchasers should never forget the hidden cost of changing suppliers.

8.1 Case history: A case of colonization

Some years ago, a medium-sized merchant bank employed a consultant from a leading firm to undertake a review of a problematic computer system. The consultant recommended further investigation, which in turn led to a number of projects to fix and enhanced even more systems. Within a matter of a few months no less than 60 consultants were beavering away on the site. Meanwhile, apart from the cost going through the roof, some users and departmental managers were starting to complain about the level of disruption to the day-to-day activities of the bank. As the situation slipped even further out of control, the IS manager took the easy option and quit.

His successor was a hard-headed lady who came from another financial institution which had a tradition of running a tight ship. After taking a few days to look around and see what was happening, she called in the lead consultant and told him that he had 3 days to make a tidy withdrawal and that she wanted a report on what they had delivered before any further bills would be paid. Furthermore future contracts would be fixed-price and delivery agreed in advance.

Unsurprisingly, the consultants were not too happy at being told to account for themselves in this manner and time-scale, but after some protest they complied – eventually leading to considerably better value for money.

8.4 Purchasing systems integration services

One of the advantages of purchasing a totally proprietary system is that one can (more or less) take it for granted that all the components will integrate properly and work together. With the widespread use of Open Systems and distributed computing this is not something one can necessarily assume and a variety of compatibility, migration and interface problems can ensue. This has led to the emergence and growth of system integration as an IT service. Systems integrators offer to put all the pieces of a system together and take the problems of a modern mixed system off a user's hands. It can be difficult for all but the largest organizations to maintain high levels of expertise in the range of technologies involved in a modern IT system. Systems integrators can fill this need for small to medium size and even large organizations.

Services provided by integrators may include:

- project planning
- specification of requirements
- preparation of invitations to tender or requests for proposal
- sourcing of hardware, software and other services
- selection and/or acquisition of equipment and services
- conflict resolution
- implementation management
- project management.

A systems integrator should be independent. Systems integrators are employed to bring the various diverse components of a system together. They cannot do this impartially when they are suppliers of a major component of the system themselves. It is important for purchasers to differentiate between systems integrators and lead suppliers. There are arguments for both approaches. The requirement for independence/neutrality has not stopped many suppliers whom one would not think of as naturally falling into the above categories from entering the systems integration business. The natural integrators are the larger consultancy firms and software houses. However, hardware suppliers such as IBM, Fujitsu, Hewlett Packard and others have made major investments in the systems integration business and have a significant market share.

A good systems integrator should have no conflicts of interest, be neutral and have the requisite skill set. When purchasing systems integration services, it should be made completely clear to the integrator that they will not be permitted to bid for or supply any part of the system.

8.5 Purchasing contract staff

The last decade has seen a major shift to contracting out a wide range of services including IT. However, contract IT staff, and in particular contract programmers, have been part of the IT scene since the earliest days of commercial computing. Some organizations employ contract programmers for years, often paying a multiple of what they would pay to an equivalent internal staff member.

The *advantages* of using contract programmers are:

- they are normally of good quality (if not, they can easily be removed)
- they can be bought in and disposed of as and when needed
- there are few, if any, overheads (such as pension contributions and social insurance payments)
- there is no long-term commitment
- the purchaser does not usually have to pay for periods of illness, holidays etc.

There is, of course, sometimes no choice about this matter (see below). The *disadvantages* of contractors are:

- they are expensive relative to internal staff
- they may leave at short notice

- they may have no loyalty to the organization (although this will vary with individuals and circumstance)
- they may be a higher security risk than internal staff
- they may leave to work for competitors
- over time they can acquire many of the legal rights of full-time employees, thus negating many of the advantages listed above.

Of course, some of the above risks exist with internal staff, but they tend to be less acute. Contractors may be individuals who are self-employed, supplied by an agency, or employed by a software house or consultancy firm.

Despite the high costs involved, it can make sense to use contract staff when any of the following conditions apply.

- There is a skill shortage and it is not possible to recruit someone permanent (or at least someone of sufficient calibre.
- Specific experience is required. When used for technology transfer, i.e. the transfer of these skills to internal staff, this can be cost-effective and enhance the value received.
- There is a short-term need.
- There is no other choice. This may arise for two reasons. It may be impossible to find suitable staff through normal recruitment or there may be a ban on recruitment (this is a particular possibility in the public sector).

Some organizations are prepared to pay substantially more for a contractor than an internal person would cost. This is generally because they are reluctant to employ an internal person due to the potential long-term costs. This may not make good economic sense. For example, a specialized database contract programmer may cost three to four times the salary cost of an internal COBOL programmer on an average industry salary. Even run-of-the-mill contract programmers tend to cost 175–200% of the cost of their internal equivalent. Contract prices vary widely with the market, both in terms of the general economy and specific skills.

When purchasing contract staff, the following should be borne in mind:

- Legal responsibilities. It is important to get the contract right from both a legal and a business viewpoint. Some of the legal aspects of hiring contract staff are discussed in Chapter 11.

- Completion. From a business viewpoint, it is important that contractors be given a clear incentive to finish the job. A simple way of doing this is to build in a substantial completion bonus.
- Confidentiality. Contractors must be made to sign non-disclosure agreements. In the public sector, they may need to sign the Official Secrets Act. Contractors in defence or other sensitive areas may need to be professionally vetted.

Purchasing contract staff is sometimes essential and often makes good sense. However, it is easy for an organization to slip into a pattern of long-term contractor use without thinking through the costs or the consequences. This can happen because there is a conscious policy of having minimal core staff which is applied automatically. It can also happen through sheer inertia. Where a firm has a large number of such staff, the alternatives of hiring permanent staff or outsourcing the entire operation or project should always be considered. Above all, the amount being paid to contract IT staff at all levels should be regularly reviewed.

8.6 Purchasing resilience and disaster recovery capability

Modern IT systems are reliable. However, where the cost of system downtime is measured in tens or even hundreds of thousands of pounds per hour, additional fault tolerance and resilience measures are justified. Naturally these come at a price and this price has to be measured against both the risk of and the impact of a failure. Computer failures vary from failure of a minor component to wholesale destruction of the system. Organizations can purchase protection against each of these and all intermediate possibilities. In such purchases, trade-offs must be made between risk and cost.

8.6.1 Purchasing fault-tolerant options

Fault tolerance is the ability of the system to cope with mechanical or software failures of system components themselves. Fault tolerance needs to be considered at several levels. A chain is as strong as its weakest link and there is little point in having a system which is highly resilient in one area while vulnerable in another. (An interesting example of this was early RAID (redundant arrays of inexpensive disks) systems which had only one communication channel to the processor. If the channel failed, all the resilience in the disk arrays was useless.)

Fault tolerance needs to be considered for:

● disk drives
● the central processors on the server or host machines
● the power supply
● communications
● key peripherals
● the overall architecture.

The latter three are matters of building spare, redundant or alternative options into the system design. For the first three, there is a number of specific technical choices which are considered below. Key resilience options are as follows.

● Disk mirroring/RAID. Disk mirroring is just one type of RAID technology, but is the most common technique currently in use for protection against disk failure.
● Redundant processors. This type of machine has one or more completely redundant central processing unit(s). Typically there is one spare processor. This technology should be distinguished from parallel processing machines (see next point).
● Parallel processors. As more and more servers and host machines are based on parallel processing, be it symmetric multiprocessing (SMP) or massively parallel processing (MPP), it has become possible for systems to adapt to the loss of a single processor. This requires the operating system to be able to recognize that a processor has failed and reallocate the processing tasks amongst the remaining processors.
● Failover. Back-to-back failover is the ability of a system to take advantage of whatever combination of components are still working. For example, in some mirrored systems if the disk fails on one machine and the CPU fails on the secondary machine the system stops despite the fact that there is still one CPU and one set of disks working.
● Heartbeat monitoring. With the most sophisticated fault-tolerant systems, users never know that there has been a component failure. A technique for this is so-called 'heartbeat' monitoring whereby each half of a duplicated system monitors the performance of the other half by a process of continually running diagnostics on its partner's performance.

8.6.2 Uninterrupted power supplies

An uninterrupted power supplier (UPS) provides continuing power for a short period after a failure in the mains electricity.

This gives the user sufficient time to close down the system in an orderly manner or for the standby generator to start up. The characteristics of a UPS are:

- Its ability to smooth out fluctuations in the mains supply. For organizations where spikes or dips in the power supply are a common feature, smoothing out the supply to the computer systems is important and can be even more important than continuity of supply. Computers are quite sensitive devices and can be damaged by a power surge. A power dip can also cause problems. All UPSs handle such fluctuations to some degree, but where mains supply is volatile (for example, in a plant where heavy machinery is switched on or off regularly), the UPS will need greater resilience to handle the variations. This may also be important if the organization uses a standby generator. Small generators cannot provide the same smooth output as the mains supply and may be affected by other devices in the building being switched on or off. In such circumstances, the UPS must be able to smooth out the supply to the IT systems.

- The duration of the supply. This is the amount of time that the UPS will provide power after the mains supply has failed. A minimum time of 10 minutes is common, but larger battery packs, which will provide power for 30 minutes or longer, are available. The duration of supply is specified for a given level of load and will be affected by the actual load applied.

- The level of output. It is important to determine not only for how long a UPS must provide power, but how many devices it will need to support during that period. At a minimum it must support the main server(s) and the console. It may be desirable that a number of other user devices (which should include a printer) are also supported.

- Ability to shut down machines automatically. Where a machine is left in unattended operation (for example over-night), it is important that, should the mains supply fail, the UPS is able to trigger an orderly shutdown. This can be done by the UPS (which detects the power failure) sending a message to the server/central processor which triggers an automatic shut-down sequence.

- Power cut-off. It is important that of the power fails entirely and the UPS runs out, that when the mains supply is restored the re-start be done in an orderly fashion. It is not unknown for a UPS to protect a machine against a power loss only for the machine to be damaged by the spike when the power is restored.

When buying a UPS it is important that the time required for an orderly shut down be carefully estimated and a safety margin allowed. For example, if a machine is constantly attended or there is an automatic shut down procedure, then the time to shut the machine down plus a safety margin of 5 minutes is sufficient. If, however, there is a possibility that the machine will be unattended and that time will be required for a suitably qualified person to get to the console, this should be provided for when specifying the required performance characteristics of the UPS.

If the organization has a standby generator, the duration will need to cover the time for the generator to start up and reach a stable supply of current.

8.6.3 Purchasing contingency planning

Contingency is closely related to, but a separate matter from, resilience. When it comes to a disaster, it should always be borne in mind that even where the probabilities of failure are minuscule, the expected cost of failure can be high. Using the techniques described in Chapter 10, if the chances of a disaster over a 5 year period are 1 in 10 000 but the cost of a disaster would be to put a company out of business at a cost of, say, £100 million, then the expected cost is:

$$£100\,000\,000 \times (1/10\,000) = £100\,000 \text{ or } £20\,000 \text{ per annum}$$

(see Chapter 10 for more on computing expected costs). Furthermore, the chances of a disaster are much higher than most people think. The principal causes of disasters are:

- fire
- flood
- earthquake
- other natural causes (wind, lightning)
- power failure or loss of other services
- human (such as negligence, terror attack, viruses, malicious damage, etc.).

Case history 8.2 is a brief description of a disaster that occurred in Sweden in 1988.

Case history 8.2: Flash flood

'Disaster struck with little warning. On the evening of Friday, 8 July, after a prolonged drought, a sudden and massive cloudburst deluged the city with 50 centimetres of rain in two hours. A stream near the office flooded and sent a torrent of water rushing down the hillside. With unbelievable force an estimated 200 cubic metres of rainwater, mud and stones entered the building lifting a 20 centimetre thick concrete floor 5 centimetres! The torrent tore down two steel doors, ripping off the door frames and wrecking the communications room and tape storage area.

In the computer room there was little sign of what was about to happen. Two operators were on duty. Suddenly a water detector near the second steel door was triggered alerting them. Almost immediately, the steel door caved in and a roaring wall of water pushed the door and several modem racks across the room towards the operators. The room was plunged into darkness as the water flooded over the standard power supply and the UPS in the area behind the machine room. As the water settled to fill the floor void and cover the false floor with a centimetre of muddy residue, the fire retardant system released its halon gas through the floor, spraying water and vapour into the air. From the beginning to the end, the incident took no more than 15 minutes.'

(From *Computer Disasters Contingency Planning*, The Amdahl Executive Institute.)

In the event of a fire or flood, an entire computer centre can be damaged or destroyed. Research has shown that most IT-dependent businesses without a recovery plan never recover from a disaster of this type. Various estimate of the chances of survival have been made. Table 8.1 summarizes this point.

It is therefore essential that every organization has a contingency plan. As with resilience, there is an escalating series of options to choose from. The more refined the option, the more expensive it will be. Contingency planning is based on a risk analysis of the possibilities of a disaster, an analysis of the potential impact of a disaster and a cost–benefit analysis of the options.

Table 8.1 Chance of a business surviving a total loss of IT services

Time system is down	Chance of survival
4 hours	100%
1 day	80%
2–3 days	50%
1–2 weeks	20%
1 month	10%

Given the risks, it is surprising how many organizations do not have an adequate disaster recovery plan.

8.6.4 Avoiding the issue

Companies which do not have adequate contingency plans give a variety of reasons for not having them, including:

- lack of time to prepare one
- lack of resources to do it
- too expensive
- too many possible hazards (the ostrich approach)
- lack of awareness of the hazards
- lack of awareness of the consequences of a disaster
- not knowing how to do it
- lack of clear lines of responsibility.

When unprepared organizations do have an IT disaster, they are invariably stunned by the fact that it happened to them. Case history 8.2 illustrated the effect of flood. Another problem is where management think that they have taken adequate precautions. Case history 8.3 is an example from a company that thought it was reasonably well prepared for a fire, but had an unpleasant surprise when catastrophe struck.

Case history 8.3: Safe as houses?

In the early 1980s a small regional supermarket chain had a major fire at its head office. The fire resulted in the almost total destruction of the company's computer systems as well as the entire office complex.

As part of their contingency planning, the company had purchased a fire-proof safe in which to store their back-up tapes. According to the manufacturers, this safe could withstand temperatures of over 2000 degrees centigrade.

Sifting through the wreckage the day after, the company was delighted to find the safe intact (although it had fallen through two floors during the course of the fire). However, when, after some effort, they got it open, their relief evaporated as they discovered that although their tapes had not burned, the fierce heat had reduced them to a congealed puddle of brown plastic on the floor of the safe.

The company survived, but needless to say today they have a more robust disaster recovery plan.

Expenditure on disaster recovery is like any other form of insurance. If the organization never has a disaster, a large amount of money is spent for what would seem to be no purpose. Nevertheless, in terms of risk and return, the investment may be one of the most important IT expenditures a company can make.

8.6.5 Options for disaster recovery

There are several approaches to disaster recovery/contingency planning. The following are the principal approaches and issues to consider when looking at possible investment in a plan.

- Fortress. This is where the organization chooses to have one highly resilient and well-defended site. Investment is put into waterproof rooms, fire-protection systems, bomb-proof structures and so on. The advantages of this is it is relatively low cost (although it is not cheap), and no additional staff or coordination with other centres is required so it is easy to manage. On the down side, everything is dependent on the one centre and management can never be certain that the defences are strong enough, as illustrated in Case history 8.2. The whole centre is vulnerable to failure in any one key component – even an external one such as the telephone lines or a local exchange. Many organizations place their faith in this type of arrangement as it is less complex to set up and manage than the alternatives. It is also relatively high risk when compared to other options.

- Mutual arrangement. Some organizations have a back-to-back arrangement with another nearby organization (or another part of their own organization) using the same type of equipment. Under such arrangements, if user A has a disaster, user B will allow it to run its systems, usually at night or off-peak, on B's hardware. The arrangement may vary from a few critical systems (such as the payroll or telesales systems) to all systems. The advantage of this are that it is relatively inexpensive. Typically, there will be an agreed fee if the service is ever invoked and some additional equipment may need to be purchased and put on the other machine, but other than this, costs tend to be minimal. This is the lowest cost option. However, it is, even when formalized, dependent on mutual goodwill. Furthermore, it is not very practical if there is likely to be a protracted delay in getting the systems back on line and it requires compatible systems in both locations. As hardware architectures become more complex, keeping both systems in harmony becomes more difficult. Both companies need to be in non-competitive businesses because it will be difficult to enforce privacy when a machine is being shared. Mutual trust is essential. Another drawback could be that restricted hours of operation may not be suitable (for example, a telesales system can hardly be run at night) and, if hours are not to be restricted, both systems must be large enough to run both company's operations at the same time. This means either having an average of 50% redundancy in both systems or both companies being willing to accept a deterioration in service. This can reduce the cost advantage.
- Supplier back-up. A variant on this is that the hardware supplier provides a back-up site. In an emergency the user transfers the software and data to a machine provided by the supplier. This is also a relatively inexpensive approach. Hardware support is to hand and suppliers can sometimes more easily tolerate daytime operations, and may be able to provide better facilities. The disadvantages are that supplier machines are often used for development purposes so performance can be erratic and, as with back-to-back, it requires compatible systems in both locations. As hardware architectures become more complex, keeping both systems in harmony becomes more difficult. Also, security risks are higher. Supplier machines may be used for development or experimental work and may not be as secure as the user's machine.
- Owned cold site. A cold site is an empty computer room. It has all the necessary infrastructure including power supply,

communications, environmental control, etc. and may have storage for back-up tapes and disks, but has no computing equipment installed other than (maybe) telephone lines. In an emergency, the system or a new system can be installed and brought on-line. The advantages of an owned cold site are that it can be relatively inexpensive, especially if a warehouse or a similar low-cost building can be used, it doesn't require staffing, it is easy to maintain and it can be used for as long as is needed. On the negative side, there is an ineluctable time delay in setting up the system. New equipment may have to be obtained and this may not always be possible to do quickly at short notice.

- Third party cold site. These come in two basic variants. The first is a fixed cold site. This is a system which is available for use at any time but the user has to provide all the equipment to be installed. It is sometimes possible to store back-up tapes at the site. The second is a mobile site. This is a complete computer room in a trailer or Portacabin which is literally driven up to the customer site, if necessary assembled, and operated *in situ*. The actual computer systems need to be installed, set up and loaded

There are several pluses and minuses of this approach. The advantages of the third party cold site are that it is always available (or at least it has a high availability), there is a low (but not a zero) probability of any conflict with any third party, and it can be rented so there are no capital costs involved. It may therefore be less expensive than an owned cold site. However, there are several disadvantages. For a start, it is still relatively expensive and although it is small, there is always a risk that the site may not be available (especially if it is a mobile site). In an emergency, it must be equipped, set up and brought on-line. This could take 24 hours or more. It may be necessary to share the resource with others. For example, if an area is flooded, several local organizations may be affected and a number of these may use the same back-up company. Finally, there is usually some time limit on usage. Within this time the purchaser has to find a more permanent home. This may be difficult.

When purchasing a cold site service from a supplier, the following should be taken into account:
- the availability cost
- the usage cost (there may be a separate charge if use of the site is invoked) – there may also be a schedule of charges depending on the length of time the facility is in use

263

- whether there are suitable back-up storage facilities on site
- the range of facilities provided
- what additional equipment it will be necessary to provide to get the centre up and running
- what security is in place
- the maximum usage period
- what the options are for finding a permanent (or more permanent) location during the usage period
- the options for getting replacement hardware and software.

Remember that if the organization has to leave the cold site after 6 weeks and has not found an alternative location, the real crisis will only have been postponed.

- Owned warm site. With a warm site, the user sets up a duplicate IT operation which is capable of running all the mission-critical operations. To be effective, this must include ancillary facilities such as furniture, security, communications lines and telephones. Often some of the routine processing is done on this site in order to get a better return on the investment. The primary advantages of an owned warm site are that it is always available and that it can be maintained with the exact configuration required. In addition, there is no conflict with, or dependence on, any third party and there should be minimal delay in restarting after a disaster. Warm sites are expensive. They require permanent staffing. In an emergency, it must be brought fully on-line.

Warm sites are suitable for organizations where loss of service for a moderate period of time (say up to a day) is acceptable. A warm site need not be a full replication of the main system. It need only be large enough for essential services. As noted above, such sites are typically used for non-critical day-to-day operations to get better value from the investment.

- Third party warm site. Some bureaux and specialist suppliers, including application service providers (ASPs) will offer a warm site service. The advantages of the third party warm site are similar to an owned site except that there is no additional staff cost. The disadvantages are similar to those of an owned site, but it is less expensive. On the other hand, such a site has to be kept in line with the purchaser's own systems.

The cost structures for this type of service are generally based on an insurance charge, i.e. the cost of having the facility available and a usage charge, i.e. a rate per day when the facility is in use. If the organization is carrying disaster insurance of its own, this may cover all or a substantial part of the cost of usage. If this is so, it may be in the purchaser's interest to minimize the insurance cost at the expense of the usage cost. Some suppliers are willing to negotiate on these. The techniques described in Chapter 10 can be used to evaluate alternatives.

- Owned hot site. A hot site is a system which is effectively shadowing the live computer system. Both systems are kept synchronized by use of tape or disk exchange, or more commonly via a high-speed link. This enables the organization to switch operations, usually within minutes or even instantaneously, to the back-up site. For safety, the back-up site needs to be some distance from the main site (20 kilometres or more). Hot sites are not for everybody. Their big advantage is immediate availability. This is the best form of protection against disaster and there is no delay in start-up. As the system is mirroring the live system, there is no risk (as on a cold site) that there may be start-up problems. The drawback is cost – this is the only significant drawback, but it is a big one. Hot sites are extremely expensive. Even where only critical systems are being mirrored, a whole duplicate system complete with staffing is required.

Hot sites are justifiable for organizations where even a few minutes of unavailability could be expensive or disastrous. Examples include air traffic control and commodity dealing systems.

Contingency plans do not come cheap. Even the least expensive options carry significant costs. When resources are tight, they can seem like a luxury. Before deciding to risk not having such a plan, every organization should undertake a proper risk and business impact analysis and assess the expected costs of these risks.

8.7 Purchasing security

The requirement for good systems security has been steadily moving up the agenda for many years, but has been given an enormous boost by the Internet and the growth of mobile computing. Other reasons for this growth include:

- the move away from mainframe to distributed computing, which means many more components and points of vulnerability, immature operating systems and multiple data locations

- the dispersion of IT responsibility
- outsourcing and application services provision
- use of public communications media, including wireless media and public switched networks
- the demand for staff to have remote access to systems
- skill levels of users and hackers.

All of the above need to be considered when purchasing IT security. A broadly accepted definition of security is that it contains three components.

1 Confidentiality. This covers the prevention of unauthorized read access to data.
2 Integrity. This includes ensuring that data is consistent and cannot be modified without authorization.
3 Availability. In the context of security, this term means prevention of unauthorized withholding of information or removal of key resources.

In addition to the above criteria, the following extensions to the definition of security are sometimes made:

- Utility. This encompasses the concept that information should be useful and that systems should not be cluttered up with useless data.
- Authenticity. As the title suggests, this aspect of security is concerned with ensuring that data is genuine and accurate and meant for the purpose for which it is intended.
- Possession. This aspect of security covers ownership and rights to and/or control of data.

The security risks associated with IT systems have increased dramatically over the past 10 years and are still growing. A

Table 8.2 Sources of security risk

Risk	% Mentioning
Internal accident	50%
Increasing number of access points	40%
External attack	35%
Immature technology	32%
Internal malice	8%

survey by a leading research firm found that the number of organizations identifying various principal risks to security were as shown in Table 8.2.

8.7.1 Buying security

When purchasing security advice and/or systems, be they hardware or software, the following features should be considered.

- Authentication. The first thing a security system must do is authenticate the person trying to access the system. This can be done by:
  - logon IDs
  - passwords, including password generators
  - pre-coded keypads. These are devices which, when a number is typed into them, generate another number. To access a system, the user first gives an ID number to the computer. The computer gives back a number which the user enters into the pad. The pad in turn gives the user a third number which the user enters into the computer. To access the computer, the user must have both his or her ID number and their own key pad
  - personal challenge calculators. These authenticate a user by asking a series of random personal questions (e.g. birthday, mother's maiden name, registration number of last car and so on)
  - biometric devices which check, for example, palm print, voice or retina pattern.
- Authorization. This process determines what resources the people may use, what data they may access and the nature of that access (read, write, create, delete, append, execute).
- Administration. A security system must be easy to administer. Administration facilities include setting up or deleting users and changing authorizations. There is a range of products on the market which provide these types of facilities and many others.
- Auditing and accountability. The system should also enable IT management to check patterns of access as well as alert management when there is anything unusual going on (such as an abnormally high number of failed logon attempts). It should also enable management to ensure that the current security policy is achieving the desired effect.

● Encryption. Encryption of data is now used routinely over public networks (often without the user being aware of the fact). Encryption comes at various levels from fairly primitive to highly secure. There are two costs involved in encryption, the front-end cost of the necessary software and the ongoing operating and administrative cost. Routine encryption of large volumes of information can be tedious, especially in large organizations. Secure encryption methods require every user to have a separate key for every other user, which leads to a large number of keys in all but the smallest organizations. The alternative single (public) key encryption is simpler to administer, but quite expensive to set up. Before investing heavily in any of these technologies, a careful cost–benefit analysis should be undertaken.

8.7.2 Protection against viruses

Viruses are a sufficiently large risk to justify special consideration. There are numerous PC virus-checking systems on the market and it is important, when purchasing such a system, to ensure that it is watertight, otherwise the expenditure may be wasted. Viruses come in two ways – via a network or via a diskette/CD/DVD. The latter is still a threat despite the higher risk posed by the Internet. A secure virus-checking regime will have an operating system-specific virus checker on each hard disk and a 'sheep dip' machine on which all external disks are checked before being put into any other machine on the system. This machine should be stand-alone and should contain a number of virus checkers all of which are fully up-to-date. Internet viruses should be stopped with a firewall (see below).

Virus checkers themselves should be automated as far as possible. For example, the boot sequence on the PC or log-on to the network should include a virus scan each morning and automatically check a diskette/CD/DVD for viruses when it is loaded. This is not always possible with older operating systems. A virus checker must have an update service. Only virus checkers which can provide a regular update should ever be considered. New viruses currently appear at a rate of around 4000 a year.

The cost of a virus outbreak can be a large multiple of the cost of the virus-checking system, even though no actual damage is done, as the following example illustrates.

Case history 8.4: Even a near thing can cost money

One August afternoon a virus was discovered on a portable PC in a professional services firm. The machine was a general purpose one which junior members of staff could take as and when required. The virus that turned up was one called 'the Ripper'. The Ripper virus is capable of severely damaging hard disks on PCs.

The firm had a sophisticated virus checking and control system and immediately an established emergency plan was invoked which involved checking all 350 PCs in the building over a period of 48 hours. Several IT staff worked through the night on the problem.

In the end, no further occurrences of the virus were found. The infection was limited to the one portable. However, the firm undertook a retrospective costing of the exercise and found that the opportunity cost of lost professional time alone (even without considering the time of the internal IT team working on the problem) was approximately £33 000 – a little under £10 per machine.

8.7.3 Firewalls

Any system which is connected to the outside world via a modem or, more commonly, the Internet is vulnerable to viruses, Trojan horses and other forms of hacker attack. There are various levels of defence against such an attack up to and including a so-called 'air wall' (i.e. having key machines physically separated from the network and accessible to other machines only by media transfer). The standard form of network defence is a firewall. This is a computer (real or virtual) that acts as gatekeeper to all who would send data into or out from an organization's internal network. Firewalls only allow messages from predetermined addresses through.

Originally firewalls were hardware devices only, although software firewalls are now often used for smaller systems and personal users. A firewall is not foolproof, but it can provide quite a good degree of protection. There are drawbacks, however, including making it awkward to establish communication with new contacts.

In general, a large installation will need a physical firewall, i.e. a specialized computer or router to provide protection. For smaller sites, software firewalls are a lot less expensive and do most of the same things. It should be borne in mind that, in theory, software security systems can never be as secure as hardware. Even with a firewall, you will still need virus protection and other security software. Key factors to take into account when purchasing firewalls are:

- the importance of the systems/data that need to be protected
- the level of external activity (i.e. external network traffic)
- the nature of that traffic
- the number of users
- administrative skills and resources.

Purchasing firewalls is a specialized business and needs expert advice.

8.7.4 How much to pay?

The cost of security is often not so much in the initial set-up as in the continuing overhead. Tight security is time consuming and the costs can add up.

Example 8.1: The cost of security

In an organization with 1000 users, the security system might take, say, 5 minutes per day of each user's time plus half the time of an administrator. The total cost of this, assuming:

an 8 hour day;
an average staff cost of £15 per hour;
200 work days per year;
an administrator cost of £30 000 per year

is, in rough terms:

$$(1000 \times 200 \times 10)/60 \times £15 + £15\,000 = £265\,000$$

This may be a necessary cost of doing business, but its scale should be borne in mind.

The cost identified in Example 8.1 needs to be set off against:

- the level of risk
- the nature of the risks faced by the organization
- the likely damage if there is a security breach.

Here, also, the techniques outlined in Chapter 10 can be applied. Case history 8.5, which is a simplified description of a real event, illustrates how this can be done.

Case history 8.5: Worth the risk?

Company A, which operated in the financial advice industry, was considering the cost of tightening its security. The company's host computer system currently used a standard login and password system. Passwords were changed every 3 months. However, there had recently been an unauthorized break-in into the system via a dial-in modem of which the company had several. As it happened, no damage had been done. The intruder had been spotted by a vigilant Systems Administrator and shut out before he or she could get very far. Nevertheless, it had given IT management a severe fright.

They investigated the option of replacing their existing modems with answer-back modems, i.e. modems that would call back a pre-coded telephone number once the external users who dialed-in identified themselves. As all the external users were at fixed locations, this was feasible. The cost of this was estimated as follows:

Replacement of existing modems	£7500
Annual write-off over 5 years	£1500
Cost of time lost per annum	£5000
Total annual cost	£6500

The company then had to estimate the risks. This was not easy, there were no guidelines available. After a lengthy discussion, they settled on the following assumptions:

Estimated risk of hacker break-in for any one year under present system	= 5%
Estimated risk of hacker break-in under proposed system	= 0.1%

Potential risk of successful hacker severely
damaging system $= 50\%$
Potential risk of hacker gaining and using
valuable information $= 25\%$
Cost of severe system damage $= £200\,000$
Cost of loss of confidential information $= £500\,000$

Expected annual cost of risk under present system:

$$(£200\,000 \times 50\% + £500\,000 \times 25\%) \times 5\% = £11\,250$$

Expected annual cost of risk under new system:

$$(£200\,000 \times 50\% + £500\,000 \times 25\%) \times 0.1\% + £6500 = £6625$$

The company decided to install the new system.

Purchasing security is a complex issue. Organizations where there are either high risks or high exposures and who are concerned about their security should consider having a security review carried out by suitably qualified specialists.

8.8 Conclusion

Security is a trade-off. While it is never possible for a system to be totally secure, it is possible for a commercial organization to achieve near-military levels of security if it is willing to pay for it. The cost will, in part, be in software and hardware, but the major costs are more likely to be in training, procedures, disciplines and administration. In other words, it is the overhead involved that needs to be assessed against the benefits obtained. Before purchasing security services it is, therefore, advisable to develop a good security policy. Otherwise there is a risk of over- or under-spending, no matter how wisely one makes individual buying decisions.

Evaluation and selection of IT

9.1 Introduction

Whether seeking informal bids, shopping around or going out to a full formal tender, purchasing of computer equipment frequently requires managers to make choices between different offerings. There are three fundamental types of acquisition decision.

1 Whether to proceed with a purchase or project at all?
2 Which of a number of potential investments should receive priority and/or funding if resources are limited?
3 Which proposed solution to buy?

The first two of these questions are addressed in Chapter 3. This chapter is concerned with the third question, i.e. given that a project or expenditure is to proceed, how does one go about selecting the best product or solution and obtaining the best value for money?

IT purchase decisions can be complicated. While it is possible for a given solution to be better than any of the alternatives on every decision criterion, this is a rare occurrence. The IT manager will nearly always find that he or she has to make trade-offs or compromises. These judgments can have long-term implications for the organization (and sometimes for the career of the IT manager concerned!). What is required is a method of arriving at the best decision, or failing that, at least at a good decision.

Case history 9.1: Too many cooks?

There are many factors that can complicate a purchasing decision. One organization classified the elements of a major purchase as follows:

5 sets of consultants (one for system design and development, one for acceptance testing, two for telecommunications and one for project control);
3 distinct user groups, each with slightly different perspectives;
5 main hardware suppliers (one for servers, one for PCs, one for specialist printers, one for communications equipment and one for the optical disk systems);
3 operating systems;
2 network protocols.

Making purchasing decisions in such a complex environment requires a clear and structured approach.

Figure 9.1 illustrates the purchasing process for major acquisitions.

IT purchasing can take a number of forms:

- opportunity, i.e. each purchase is made from whatever supplier one knows or is dealing with at the time
- preferred supplier or suppliers
- lowest price
- best of breed
- informal request for quotations
- formal invitations to tender
- formal requests for proposal.

A special case is outsourcing. Qualities that should be looked for in outsourcing suppliers are discussed in Chapter 2.

9.1.1 Advantages of formalizing evaluation procedures

There are many advantages in setting up proper evaluation procedures. These are:

- Communication. Evaluation procedures, if followed properly, provide a formal channel of communication between the

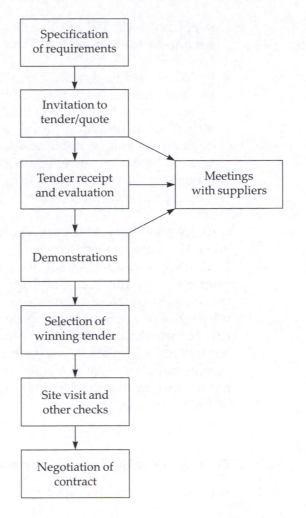

Figure 9.1
The major purchase
cycle

various parties in a decision. In a large expenditure decision this may include IT management, users, users' managers (not necessarily the same thing as users), the finance department, potential suppliers and senior management.

- Reduction in risk. Proper evaluation procedures reduce risk by obliging the purchaser to first identify risks and then to quantify them.
- Objectivity. Few management decisions are totally objective, but evaluation methods can provide a framework for objectivity. Even where total objectivity is impossible, good evaluation methods can reduce the subjective elements in a decision.
- Conflict resolution. Major IT decisions are sometimes controversial. There may be conflict between users regarding

suppliers, technical approaches, products, architectures and so on. Evaluation methods can be used to resolve such conflicts.

- Breaking deadlocks. In a similar way, formal evaluation methods can be used to break an impasse and force a decision in situations where there is deadlock.
- Structure. Evaluation procedures impose a structure on decision making. Sometimes decisions seem to take a long time to make (or in extreme cases are never made). This problem is avoided when formal evaluation and decision-making methods are used.

Clear evaluation and selection procedures are part and parcel of good IT management. However, it must be stressed that the level of sophistication and effort used in evaluation should be in proportion to the size and significance of the expenditure involved. Elaborate evaluation and selection procedures applied mindlessly to every purchasing decision waste valuable resources. Nonetheless, a simple statement of requirements and a request for a quotation is a better procedure than asking the current supplier what is available, and generally a great deal more cost effective than looking up catalogues or going to the nearest computer shop.

9.1.2 Preliminary steps

A good evaluation procedure has five components.

1 A clear statement of requirements. Meaningful evaluations can only be carried out where there is a clear understanding of the business need(s) and the product and product features which the buyer is seeking.
2 Clear evaluation criteria. These are the criteria on which the evaluation must be based. Evaluation criteria can be classified in various ways.
3 A clear evaluation and decision procedure. These must be simple and easy to follow.
4 A ranking and scoring method or methods. These are useful for evaluating complex options and bringing them to a common and comparable set of measurements.
5 Information. There must be sufficient information for the procedure to work and the decision to be made. There are methods for dealing with partial, absence of, and/or uncertain information, but hard facts are always best.

In summary, proper evaluation methods are an integral part of good IT management in general and good IT purchasing management in particular.

9.2 Overview of evaluation steps

Given that all of the above pre-requisites are met, the evaluation process proceeds in five steps.

1 The criteria for evaluation and selection are drawn up, classified and ranked.
2 The products/proposals on offer are assessed against each criterion.
3 The overall score of each product against all of the criteria is calculated.
4 The best product is selected.
5 Follow-up checks are undertaken to confirm the decision.

How to carry out each of these steps is described below. First, it is important to understand the nature of selection criteria and how to set them.

9.2.1 Ways of viewing criteria

Setting the correct criteria for any decision is fundamental to making the correct decision. Before considering the 'how' of setting criteria, it is important to be aware that criteria can take a number of different forms. Evaluation and selection must be based on clear criteria but, as will be seen, there is a number of ways of viewing criteria. All of these are useful in preparing a list of evaluation criteria.

The first, and most important classification is into:

● qualifying criteria
● award or selection criteria.

9.2.2 Qualifying criteria

Qualifying criteria, sometimes referred to as essential criteria, are criteria that the proposed equipment, software, system or solution *must* meet if it is to be considered for purchase at all. Qualifying criteria are important for eliminating irrelevant or spurious options. The fact that two products satisfy a qualifying criterion does not mean that they are equally good. For example, if a company was looking for a high-speed paper scanning system and specified a qualifying criterion to be that the system be able to handle up to 100 A4 pages a minute, then two machines, A and B running at 150 and 120 pages per minute respectively would both meet the criterion, but, all other things being equal, machine A would clearly be preferred.

There is a number of features of qualifying criteria:

- There may be one or several. In general there will be a number of these criteria.
- They must be binary. It must be easy to assess in an unambiguous way whether a proposed product or solution meets a criterion or not. Put crudely, the answer to a qualifying criterion is either yes or no.
- They must be clear. It follows that qualifying criteria must not include woolly or imprecise phrases such as 'the system must provide an acceptable level of performance . . .' or 'There must be ample expansion capacity. . .'.
- The order is not important. Unlike award criteria, qualifying criteria need not be ranked. It does not make sense to say that one essential criterion is more important than another essential criterion.
- They should be genuinely essential. Avoid making a criterion essential unless it really is (tempting though the thought may be on occasion). In the public sector, qualifying criteria must not only be essential, but be capable of being shown to be essential. Some sample qualifying criteria are given in Example 9.1.

Example 9.1: Sample qualifying criteria

'The proposed system must meet the performance levels specified in section 3.3 below.'

'The system must be capable of supporting the current software applications.'

'Suppliers must be able to demonstrate that they have a successful track record of developing systems of a similar nature and scale in the industry.'

'All printers proposed must support two-sided (duplex) printing.'

A useful device is to use the word 'must' when setting out qualifying criteria.

Having clear and correct qualifying criteria is useful for a variety of reasons. They discourage (or better still, deter) unqualified or inappropriate suppliers from proposing. This saves time and effort on both sides, but particularly for IT management. They thus enable IT managers to focus on the serious offerings/contenders and, in the public sector, they help avoid potential arguments from unsuccessful suppliers.

9.2.3 Exclusion criteria

A special type of qualifying criterion is an exclusion criterion. It can be useful to use criteria which exclude certain suppliers or products from the process entirely. This is often helpful in the public sector where there can be several dozen suppliers competing for a contract. Exclusion criteria are defensible, but wide-ranging criteria that eliminate certain classes of product, solution or supplier. The following are useful phrases in different contexts:

- 'The proposed solution must have wide existing installed base.'
- 'Suppliers must have a strong local presence.'
- 'Suppliers must be able to demonstrate no conflict of interest.'
- 'The proposed hardware/software must be scaleable.'
- 'Solutions must use the current hardware architecture.'

Care must be exercised, however. For a large public sector tender, the last of the above criteria would be risky under current EU law as under certain circumstances it could be construed as being anti-competitive.

9.2.4 Award criteria

Award criteria, sometimes known as desirable or selection criteria, are features that, while not essential, are required and differentiate one solution, proposal or product from another. In general, while failure to meet an award criterion may not rule out a proposal, the cumulative effect of not meeting several might rule it out.

Where there is a formal bidding process it is a good idea to make the criteria known to all potential suppliers in advance. In public sector tenders this is mandatory. In the public sector publicly stated criteria must be chosen with care (see next paragraph). If an organization states a set of criteria and then selects a supplier which clearly does not meet those criteria, its decision can be challenged in court.

If qualifying criteria include the word 'must', award criteria should use the word 'should'. Award criteria should be ranked in approximate order of importance (it is often impossible to be exact). It is important not to become boxed in by criteria, be they award or qualifying criteria. Public sector bodies have to list criteria in order of importance and must follow that ranking in any subsequent scoring. If the ranking is incorrect, it cannot subsequently be adjusted except by publication of the revised order and possibly extension of the bidding deadline.

Award criteria often start with a general catch-all criterion such as:

'The successful supplier will be the one who, in the opinion of management, offers the most economically advantageous proposal.'

The term 'economically advantageous' is open to a wide range of interpretations and is a useful covering phrase. It is a wider and more malleable phrase than 'cost effective', which is sometimes used. Award criteria must be testable and/or assessable, but are not usually binary in nature. Award criteria can be quite soft (indeed, it is often convenient to have a number of such soft criteria because they can help differentiate suppliers in a tight decision). Examples of common award criteria are:

- Price. Price is sometimes the only award criterion. In practice, price is rarely (or should rarely be) the deciding factor in IT purchase decisions. As a rule of thumb, price tends to be between the fifth and eighth positions in ranking of award criteria. Putting price in first place is a statement that the buyer is looking for the cheapest possible solution. This may not be the message that the purchaser wants to convey.
- Margin over qualifying criteria minima. Qualifying criteria often set minimum levels of functionality or performance. Much of the time products, systems or solutions will exceed this basic minimum. If exceeding the basic level is of value, this may become an award criterion.
- How well the solution meets the requirements. A system which meets the essential requirements may not meet all of the award requirements. In practice, and particularly with software, there may be features lacking, or the solution will meet the need, but not in the way the buyer wants.
- Ease of use. This can be an important criterion in its own right. It can also be a useful tie-breaker when, having applied

---

Example 9.2: Margin over qualifying criteria

A Local Authority is seeking a system to handle transactions. A qualifying criterion for the system is that it must be able to process a minimum of 5000 transactions per day.

Two suppliers, A and B put forward solutions. Supplier A's system can process 5500 transactions per day while B's can handle 7500 transactions per day.

In this case, both suppliers meet the basic needs of the purchaser and both provide a safety margin above the minimum. Whether this is valuable to the purchaser will depend on a number of factors, including anticipated growth. Clearly there is more scope for growth before an upgrade will be necessary with the offering from supplier B.

However, supplier B's proposal is more expensive. The purchaser has to balance this known additional cost against the probable or projected need for the additional capacity at some time in the future. In the case of a Local Authority, there may be policies with regard to price on tendering which may pre-empt this decision anyway.

---

all other criteria, there is still no clear distinction between the options available.

- Ease of installation. This may well be an important factor if a system has to be replaced or integrated into an existing system. It can be a difficult criterion to score.
- Running cost. This is often overlooked. Many decisions are made on the basis of up-front price without looking at the potential impact of running costs.

The above are classic general criteria. There are innumerable others which may be applied in specific circumstances.

9.2.5 Hard and soft criteria

A second useful way to view criteria is to divide them into hard and soft. Hard criteria are readily measurable and checkable. Examples of hard criteria are price, printing speed, disk capacity and number of support staff. Often suppliers will have brochures or reports which provide the necessary information. Soft criteria are less easily measured. They are frequently subjective and involve judgments by IT management and/or users. Examples of such criteria include ease of use, flexibility and closeness of fit to the requirements. Methods of scoring soft criteria are discussed below. In practice, most lists of criteria contain a mix of hard and soft criteria and both are important. Evaluation based purely on hard criteria is possible, but generally only applies in specific circumstances, like hardware component tenders.

9.2.6 Classification by type of criterion

A third useful way of considering criteria is to classify them by type. The following are useful categorizations:

- Core functions/features. These criteria are based on the features and functions that the product, system or solution must provide. As well as purely functional requirements, they may also include requirements such as security and resilience.
- Economic. Economic criteria cover price, running cost and cost effectiveness. To do this properly requires identifying the hidden and implicit costs of a proposal. The important point about economic criteria is that they should take into account all of the costs of the proposed solution.
- Performance. The system may be required to meet certain performance criteria. Performance criteria are best stated in a combination of business and technical terms. Benchmarks may also be used (see below).
- Standards. Standards may be driven by IT strategy, IT policy, Government and/or EU regulations. Public sector bodies have a growing list of standards with which their systems must comply. These include not only technical, but also health and safety standards. In addition, many organizations have their own corporate, house or even departmental standards.
- Flexibility. Criteria of this type cover the ability of the system to adapt to change. This will include not only growth, but also changes in the pattern or nature of the business or even the IT architecture.
- Supplier strength. These criteria are important when buying equipment, but vital when outsourcing critical functions or buying large, mission-critical software. Criteria here can include financial strength, number of staff, average level of experience of staff, staff turnover levels, quality certification and so on.
- Ergonomic and environmental. These type of criteria are becoming more important and, in some instances, may be legal requirements. Ergonomic criteria include noise levels

and screen resolution. Environmental criteria include energy usage and recyclability of components.

Finally the number of criteria applied to any one decision should not be excessive. There are two dangers in having too many criteria. Firstly, users may find it difficult to rank a large number of criteria meaningfully. Secondly, a large number of minor criteria can overwhelm a small number of important criteria. Where there is a large number of criteria, multi-stage evaluation methods should be used (see below).

9.2.7 A criterion checklist

IT management will use different evaluation and selection criteria at different times and in different situations. The following are checklists of useful criteria commonly used in evaluation and selection procedures. Not all of these will be applicable in every purchase and these lists are not exhaustive, but they provide a useful core set of criteria useful in many selections.

- Processors
  - features match needs
  - must be capable of running the key application software
  - must be capable of running standard software
  - must support certain operating software
  - minimum disk size required
  - number of disk drives
  - minimum memory size required
  - number of concurrent users supported
  - level of activity supported
  - potential expansion of memory, disk and users supported
  - location in machine range (i.e. top of the range, mid range etc.)
  - performance benchmarks
  - tape storage size and speed
  - mean time between failures (uptime)
  - ability to recover from failures
  - physical security
  - compliance with standards
  - upgradeability.
- Software
  - features match needs
  - portability
  - number of current users

- strength of local support
- modularity
- ease of interface with other systems
- use of windowing/browser technology
- easy to change
- ease of use
- flexibility
- extent of use in market
- standards to which it adheres
- underlying language
- underlying data management technology
- quality of documentation
- training available
- security and recovery features.
- Suppliers
  - local support capability
  - national support capacity
  - international support capability
  - track record
  - industry experience
  - market presence
  - relationship with own suppliers (for agents/vendors)
  - financial stability
  - Not working for competitors.
- Printers
  - type
  - speed
  - resolution
  - fonts available
  - types of paper handled
  - emulations
  - noise level.
- Storage (where separate from processors)
  - capacity
  - type (nature of media)
  - durability
  - expandability
  - number of drives
  - interface standards
  - speed of access for read/write
  - mean time between failures
  - resilience features (e.g. RAID level, mirrored, etc.).
- Networks
  - physical protocol required
  - transport/network protocols required

- bandwidth in G/M/kbits/second
- other standards required
- resilience
- ease of expansion.
- Economic
  - price
  - price/performance
  - front end cost
  - continuing cost
  - warranties
  - licence conditions
  - marginal cost of extras.
- Standards for
  - system software
  - data management systems (e.g. ANSI SQL compliant)
  - other middleware
  - quality generally.
- Ergonomic and environmental
  - noise level
  - screen resolution
  - screen refresh rate
  - screen adjustability
  - keyboard mobility, quality, layout and feel
  - mouse design
  - energy usage
  - recyclability of components
  - no pollutants on disposal (e.g. batteries in uninterrupted power supply, some circuit boards)
  - ability of printers to use recycled paper.

9.3 Supplier presentations

Where there is a reasonable deal in prospect, most suppliers are more than willing to demonstrate their products and/or to come in and tell the purchaser how suitable their product is. This can be useful provided that it is handled properly. It is important here, as in all dealings with suppliers, to understand the supplier's perspective. To maximize the benefit to the purchaser, this process must be controlled by the purchaser. The following are guidelines which will ensure a productive and informative presentation. For clarity, the guidelines have been divided into general guidelines for managing presentations and additional guidelines for solution/system orientated presentations.

Presentations are important and can make a worthwhile contribution to selection and evaluation decisions. Nevertheless, it should always be remembered that the objectives of the parties present will be quite different. The purchaser is seeking information. Most of this information will be factual, but he or she may also be seeking softer information and answers to questions such as 'can I work with these people?' or 'do they seem knowledgeable about my industry?'. On the other hand, the supplier will view this as an opportunity to convert a prospect into a sale and, if they are good, will have planned this session with the precision of a military operation.

When organizing a presentation, the following guidelines should be followed.

- Choose the venue carefully. As a general rule, it is better to have the supplier come to the purchaser rather than the other way around. There is a psychological benefit of being in one's own surroundings. However, this is not always practical. For example, if the presentation includes a demonstration, this may not always be possible on the purchaser's premises.
- Check the facilities in advance. Unless the presentation is taking place in the supplier's premises, the facilities should always be carefully checked. It is frustrating for all concerned if the overhead projector does not work or there are insufficient electrical outlets. This immediately puts the purchaser at a psychological disadvantage.
- Control the meeting. Suppliers like to take over meetings. Try not to let this happen.
- Try to match numbers. This can be tricky. At one level, if there are too many people present, the meeting can be unproductive for everyone. It is also important that all key staff from both sides be present. Given this, and all other things being equal, try to balance numbers. It is uncomfortable for a lone purchaser to find him or herself facing half-a-dozen sales staff.
- Adopt roles. One of the simplest and most effective stratagems in a meeting is to assign roles to your team. Such roles might include a chairperson who controls the meeting and acts as gatekeeper and time-keeper. Try to avoid the leading supplier salesman adopting this role. There should also be a note-taker whose job it is write down any key statements and/or commitments and to draw up a follow-up action list. These should be confirmed at the time and, if necessary, in writing afterwards. When important statements are made by suppliers, the note-taker should confirm these on the spot, for example:

'You said that the new version would be released in 2 months, is that correct?'

'You did say that this will run on the smaller server?'

Another useful role is the observer. The observer's job is to watch for signals or body language on the supplier team. See Case history 9.2

Case history 9.2: Reading the body language

A team of consultants were making a sales pitch to a financial services company. The purchaser had asked to meet the actual team that would be working on the project. As they went through their presentation, the consultants appeared confident of their proposal and the quality of their team.

One member of the purchaser's team noticed that a key member of the consultancy team, their lead technical consultant to the project, seemed, at times, to be quite detached from the proceedings, only showing an interest in the meeting when a question was addressed directly to him. He also noticed that the lead consultant started fiddling with his glasses every time the subject of project deadlines was mentioned.

Having observed this for some time, he eventually asked if all the team would be involved in the project and what guarantee the consultants would give that this team would be the one assigned to the job. After some hedging, it was admitted that the lead technical consultant had just handed in his notice and would be leaving the company in 8 weeks' time, long before the scheduled project completion.

Had the question not been asked, it is unlikely that the consultants would have volunteered this information until after the contract was signed.

The lead questioner should lead and manage the questions to the suppliers. It may be useful to have more than one questioner to deal with various aspects of the product or project. A two-man team gives a chance for each member to be preparing his or her next question while the other member of the team asks a question. Finally, the long-stop is there to pick up points that might be overlooked. The note-taker can double as long-stop, but a separate team member is better.

Remember that many statements and promises are made at such meetings. Where these are material, suppliers should be asked for confirmation in writing.

When it comes to a presentation, there is a number of special cases, particularly where any of the following are involved:

- package implementation
- systems implementation
- custom software development
- consultancy
- outsourcing.

In these cases, the purchaser should ensure that the presentation is attended by the actual team. It is known for suppliers (particularly software houses and smaller consultancies) to send the sales team and/or senior people to such presentations. These are frequently not the people who will be doing the actual work. The latter are the people you want to meet. In addition, try to form a view of the personalities as well as the products concerned. The company may have to work with these people for some time. Will they fit it? Are they easy to get along with? Do you trust them?

Role assignation is valuable and makes for a much more effective meeting. Afterwards, the information gathered from the presentation can be evaluated using the ranking methods described below.

9.4 Demonstrations

Demonstrations are mainly used for software. There are some hardware items that can be meaningfully demonstrated (for example, printers), but mostly there is little one can learn from looking at a processor or a router. Hardware evaluation centres on factors such as capacity, performance, reliability, expandability and so on, none of which are easy to demonstrate in a sales office. Throughout the remainder of this section, therefore, the term 'demonstration' refers to software demonstrations unless otherwise stated.

The first and most important rule about demonstrations is that they should be treated with great circumspection. Demonstrations are usually set up in controlled conditions and the product may not always behave in a real operation the same way that it does in the dealer's showroom. This is particularly true of new software which may just be emerging from beta testing to first general release. The old IT adage 'never buy version 1.0 of anything' has a certain wisdom.

Demonstrations can be passive or active (the latter are sometime called 'test drives'). Where possible, active demonstrations are preferable for reasons which are stated below.

It is important to have a clear idea of requirements before attending a demonstration and that both the supplier and the audience are aware of them. One of the commonest problems in purchasing is buying product features rather than user needs. The sales team will be geared to show off the best features of their product and the user who does not know his or her requirements can easily become carried away by the flashier features.

Case history 9.3: Features before foundations

A Local Authority was making a selection of a new financial accounting system. As local authority accounting has many special requirements, standard company financial packages were not suitable which ruled out most of the industry leading products.

After an invitation to tender and an evaluation, two packages were shortlisted. Both were roughly equivalent in price. One was a slightly old-fashioned, but well-proven product. It was host-based and used text screens. The package was comprehensive, possibly a little too comprehensive as it contained many features that the authority deemed were not needed. It was also difficult, though not impossible, to modify. It had good local support and was based on a leading database management system which the Authority used widely for other applications.

The second product was a state-of-the-art system which, rather than providing a fully functional accounts package, consisted of a blueprint or skeleton system plus a rule-based programming capability that enabled the user to

---

develop a system customized to their exact requirements. The suppliers claimed that this system could be used to develop an exact fit to these requirements very quickly. Unlike their competitors, they also promised a Windows based client/server version within 18 months. This package could also harness the Authority's database management system. The main weaknesses of the proposal was that it was new, the company that had developed it was still small and there were few sites where the product was installed. As a consequence, support was weak. There were also rumours that the product was not as easy to use as was claimed, although these were dismissed as malicious gossip by competitors.

Both suppliers were invited to demonstrate. The first product was what it was, it looked and felt like an early 1980's system – functional, but unspectacular. The second demonstration was impressive. Using the rule-based system the sales team were able to make modifications on the fly at the user's request. They won the contract. Unfortunately for the Local Authority, the rumours they had earlier dismissed turned out to be true. The system was not as easy to work with as it had appeared in the demonstration. Support was not adequate to the job and after nine frustrating and expensive months, the project had to be abandoned, leaving a lot of egg on various people's faces.

In a passive demonstration, the prospective purchaser watches while the supplier puts the product through a series of usually pre-planned demonstrations. The following are guidelines for finding out what you need to know in a demonstration.

- Ask if you can try the package. This will give you a feel for how easy the system is to work with. A skilled demonstrator can make a system look simple to work with and easy to learn. This can be deceptive. A good system is intuitive. One way to find out how intuitive a system is, is to sit down and try it.
- Ask to see features that are not demonstrated. Demonstrations often follow carefully planned routes through the menu system. By asking the demonstrator to try features or options that are not in the planned demonstration programme, it is possible to assess how confident they are that their product works well and is reliable (or how well the demonstrator knows it).

- If possible, ask to see how well it works under extreme conditions. This is not always easy to simulate, but in certain circumstances it is possible. Validation checks are a good example. For instance, suppose a there is a field on the screen designed to take a money amount. Try asking what happens if you put in a minus number, a number larger than the field size, alpha text into a numeric field and so on. There are some people who have a natural talent for crashing systems. This is the one circumstance in which this ability is valuable.
- Ask questions and pursue evasive answers. Don't accept bland assurances, ask to see how or ask for proof. Watch out for phrases such as:

  'That's too complicated to show here . . .'

  'That would take too much time. . . .'

  'That can be done, but I am not familiar enough with the system to demonstrate it . . .'

Always remember that demonstrations are just that. They are always set up in such a way as to show the product to best advantage, but they can be structured so as to hide serious problems, bugs or weakness in the system.

9.5 Benchmarking

Benchmarking (as opposed to commercial benchmarks, see Chapter 6) is the process of measuring the performance of a system under a number of user-defined test conditions. Benchmarking is hard work and requires considerable time and effort to do properly. Nevertheless, benchmarking can be a valuable exercise. If it is proposed to invest £1 000 000 or more on a new or replacement system, £10 000 spent on a benchmark could be money well spent.

Benchmarking is not always feasible. Benchmarks are usually simplest when replacing an existing system. For a brand new system, it may be too expensive or too time consuming and the purchaser will have to depend on demonstrations, site visits and/or commercial benchmarks. A particular problem is to test a machine's performance in a multi-user transaction operation. This may, for example, involve setting up a database, defining a set of transactions to be carried out, setting up the test with a number of users or simulation of a number of users, and measuring the result. For most organizations, benchmarking of this type is only practical when comparing a new system against an existing system where there is a base with which to compare.

To set up a benchmarking test requires:

- A test harness. This is a set of data and/or programs to be processed by the system. These will be run through the system and the performance in terms of response or run time measured. To put a modern machine to a serious test, a test harness has to be large and/or sophisticated.
- A test team. It is not normally practical to undertake a benchmark test with one user. While it is possible to simulate multiple users on a system, typically several real users will be needed if the test is to be effective. Simulated users cannot react to unexpected developments and do not always react as real users might when faced with a given set of circumstances.
- A suitable test environment. A key part of a benchmark is to try to test the system in as close an approximation of the real environment as is possible. In order that comparisons be valid, the same conditions must prevail in all tests.

A benchmark should test the system under normal conditions, peak conditions and extreme conditions. The latter simulates situations that will probably never occur in real life (such as a dozen users simultaneously launching massive, complex queries on the same major table in the database).

9.6 Weighted ranking methods

IT managers are constantly faced with having to make a choice between two or more options for purchase. There are a number of techniques which can be used to help in making such decisions. The most important and useful is a subset of multi-criteria, multi-objective decision making called *weighted ranking*. Weighted ranking can be used when information is complete and certain or when information is incomplete and/or uncertain. Both are useful and are discussed separately below. Weighted ranking is a simple and powerful technique, but it needs to be executed with care, especially if multi-level scoring and ranking is involved.

9.6.1 Simple weighted ranking

Simple weighted ranking is used when the following conditions apply:

- there is a small number of distinct options from which to choose
- each option is similar and comparable – this means comparing apples with apples

- information is complete
- information is certain
- there are clear, agreed and unambiguous criteria.

The latter is essential if the technique is to give meaningful results. It is particularly important where there are different priorities between different users or conflicting opinions within management.

The process is in four steps. For illustration purposes, the simple (and simplified) example of selecting a printer is used throughout what follows. Example 9.5 gives an example of a more complex ranking exercise.

The steps are as follows.

1 Each criterion is listed and weighted in order of importance. Each feature is given a 'weight' on a suitable scale (usually 1 to 10, or 1 to 20). The higher the weight the more important the feature. For example, features on a printer might be weighted as follows:

Feature	Weight	Comment
Low noise	8	The printer will be in an open office
Speed	7	Speed is important
Resolution	4	Not very important, this is for draft documents only
Character Set	2	Only basic characters and fonts are required

The value is given to each feature referred to as its *weight*.

2 Each offering is then scored on each criterion. This may require subjective judgment. This score should also be on a suitable scale (again 1 to 10 or 20 is usually adequate). This score is independent of the weighting. For example, this may yield:

		Score		
Feature	Weight	Printer A	Printer B	Printer C
Noise level	8	5	3	7
Speed	7	8	9	4
Resolution	4	5	5	6
Character Set	2	9	9	8

3 The weighting is then multiplied by the scores and the results totalled. This gives the following result:

Feature	Weight	Printer A	Printer B	Printer C	Maximum
Noise level	8	×5 = 40	×3 = 24	×7 = 56	80
Speed	7	×8 = 56	×9 = 63	×4 = 28	70
Resolution	4	×5 = 20	×5 = 20	×6 = 24	40
Character Set	2	×9 = 18	×9 = 18	×8 = 16	20
Score		134	125	124	210
% of maximum		64%	60%	59%	

The resulting score is referred to as the weighted ranking

4 The highest scoring option is selected. On the above ranking, printer A is best.

Weighted ranking is a useful tool, but it must be used with discrimination. In particular, if the highest scoring option scores particularly badly on a non-essential, but still important, feature, this should be taken into account. An option with a slightly lower overall score but a better balance across all the criteria may be preferable. Ideally, weighted ranking should never be applied mechanically, however, in the public sector formal tenders may have to be decided purely on the basis of the top score.

9.6.2 Tie-breaking

Weighted ranking is an efficient way of 'tie-breaking' in difficult decisions. This can be done by asking all involved to:

● Agree the criteria. Users should be asked to write down their criteria. The results are then consolidated into one list. It is good practice to obtain consensus on the final list.
● Divide the criteria into qualifying (essential) and award (desirable). Normally this is not difficult. The essential features of any system are fairly obvious to all users. Award/ desirable criteria can be more contentious as different parties can have quite different viewpoints. It is important that consensus be obtained on the weighting if at all possible (see below).
● Weight the criteria. Users must do this honestly. Two problems can occur. Firstly, some users cannot make up their minds and weight everything equally, thus invalidating the

whole process. The way round this is to give such users a 'pool' of marks (e.g. 100 marks) which they can distribute as they wish. Secondly, in extreme circumstances, where there are strongly held, but divergent, views users have been known to weight all of their preferences 10 and weight all others zero. A technique to handle this is to limit the number of criteria that can be give a certain score (e.g. at most five items can be scored 10 and so on).

- Take an average of the results. For example, if three users were involved in the selection of the printer in the above example, they might weight the criteria as follows:

	Score			
Feature	User 1	User 2	User 3	Average
Noise level	8	8	8	8
Speed	6	8	4	5
Resolution	9	4	2	5
Character Set	2	1	3	2

These techniques do not guarantee consensus, but they can help provide commitment to the decision-making process and ultimately to the decision itself.

9.6.3 Multistage weighted ranking

A further refinement of weighted ranking can be used when evaluating more complex decisions. For example, suppose a selection decision involved hardware, software and support services. Each of these might, in turn, have several features. For example, hardware criteria might include performance, price, expansion capability, capacity and so on.

Under simple weighted ranking, all the features from each heading would be compiled into one large table. The problem with this is that the uniform ranking system may mask, or at least make it difficult to weight, the relative importance of each heading.

For example, suppose that the really critical part of this decision is the software. Then each of the main headings might be assigned weights as follows:

- hardware = 7
- software = 10
- support services = 6.

The general weighting needs to be reflected in the detailed final evaluation. To clarify matters, weighting and scoring can therefore be split into steps:

- each major heading is weighted
- criteria within each heading are weighted and scored

Example 9.3: Double weighted ranking

Two consortia, A and B, have put forward proposals for a new departmental computer system. Both are proposing hardware, development software, packaged software, some customized software and project management and implementation.

The purchaser weights each of these as follows:

Category	Weight
Hardware	5
Packaged software	7
Development tools	8
Software development	9
Project management	6

On the individual weighted rankings, the suppliers scored as follows:

	Supplier A	Supplier B
Hardware	80%	80%
Packaged software	80%	70%
Development tools	75%	80%
Software development	80%	90%
Project management	70%	60%

These percentage scores are then weighted by the weightings for the corresponding categories:

	Weighting	Supplier A	Supplier B
Hardware	5.0	80% = 4.0	80% = 4.0
Packaged software	7.0	80% = 5.6	70% = 4.2
Development tools	8.0	75% = 6.0	80% = 6.4
Software development	9.0	80% = 7.2	90% = 8.1
Project management	6.0	70% = 4.2	60% = 3.6
Total	35.0	27.0	26.3
Percentage of total score		77%	75%

- total scores as percentage of the maximum possible are calculated
- the total scores are then weighted by the heading rankings.

Example 9.3 illustrates this method.

Multi-stage weighted ranking is useful in clarifying the decision-making process where decisions involve many different services such as consortia, lead contracting, systems integration and outsourcing.

9.6.4 Weighted ranking with uncertainty

Sometimes clear information is not available. For example, a delivery date is quoted by a supplier, but the supplier is unwilling to give a guarantee. The uncertainly can also be on the part of the purchaser. For example, expansion capability may be important if sales growth continues, but the latter is not certain. There may be various possibilities forecast.

In such circumstances weighted ranking must be adapted to take account of the probability of the various possible outcomes. The principles are no different from weighted ranking with certainty but this approach makes use of the concept of an expected score, which is here defined as:

$$\text{Expected score} = \text{Score} \times \text{Probability that this will happen.}$$

A further refinement is the use of negative scores which can be used for risk assessment. Example 9.4 illustrates this technique.

Example 9.4: Weighted scoring

Two suppliers, A and B, are quoting for development of customized software. Supplier A is quoting a guaranteed delivery of 9 months. Supplier B is quoting a delivery date of 6 months, but with a possibility that this will not be met, i.e. there is no guarantee on the delivery date. The purchaser needs the system urgently and would much prefer to have it in 6 rather than 9 months. The purchaser believes that there is only a 50% chance that supplier B can deliver in less than 9 months. He weights early delivery as follows:

6 months	10
9 months	6
Later than 9 months	−4

Note that 'later than 9 months' is listed as a negative value, representing a penalty cost to the purchaser of a late delivery.

He also rates supplier B's chances of delivery as follows:

6 months	50%
9 months	25%
Later than 9 months	25%

and supplier A is, logically:

6 months	0%
9 months	100%
Later than 9 months	0%

An expected score for the two suppliers is calculated as follows:

	Supplier A			Supplier B		
	Probability	Score	Expected score	Probability	Score	Expected score
6 months	0%	10	0.00	50%	10	5.00
9 months	100%	6	6.00	25%	6	1.25
Later than 9 months	0%	−4	0.00	25%	−1	−1.00
Total score			6.00			5.25

On balance, therefore, the purchaser should choose supplier A.

Chapter 10 on risk and risk management develops the ideas in this section further, and includes decision analysis and decision tree techniques which can also be used.

9.7 Reference sites and site visits

Reference sites are a useful back-up to the evaluation conclusions. Unless totally new technology is being purchased, most suppliers will have a number of sites already in operation where the proposed solution (or at least a component of the proposed solution) can be viewed. A buyer should be suspicious if a supplier is either unwilling or unable to provide a reference site (unless, of course, the technology is brand new).

Site visits, while valuable, should be kept in perspective. It is highly unlikely that the reference site will have exactly the same characteristics as the purchaser's site. Obviously, it makes sense to view a site as similar to the purchaser's operation as is possible. Unfortunately this is not always an option. Suppliers will always encourage a prospective customer to visit their 'tame' or flagship sites. No supplier is going to send a prospect to see a dissatisfied customer or a problem system. To circumvent this problem, the following techniques can be used:

- Ask for a (long) list of sites. Unless there is a good reason, suppliers should be willing to make such a list available.
- Use public directories. There are many publicly available sources of supplier information.
- Use professional advisers. Consultants, auditors and other independent advisers can be useful sources of reference sites. Often professional advisers may be able to comment on other sites with which they are familiar (provided that they can do so without breaking confidences).
- Use user groups or associations. Ask for the address of the user group or users' association. Most major IT products have user groups. They often have regular meetings and have an active and up-to-date awareness of the product.

The objective is to find as independent a view (or set of views) as possible. Try where possible to do your own research as well as using information from a supplier.

9.7.1 Visiting the site

When visiting the test site, the most important rule is to be prepared. Questions should be prepared in advance and, ideally, typed up with space for the answers underneath each question. Questions can be explicit and general. Try to ask open or open-ended questions which invite the respondent to give more than a single syllable answer. The following general questions are always helpful in eliciting information:

- What would you say are the strong/weak points of the system?
- Have you been happy with the system?
- What problems (if any) have there been?

- How has the supplier responded when there have been problems?
- How long have problems taken to resolve?
- How well does the system match your needs?
- How well did it match your expectations?
- Would you buy the same system again tomorrow?
- What would you do differently?
- Have there been any unpleasant surprises?
- Have there been any pleasant surprises?

Try to avoid questions that are critical of the customer's decision to buy the product or are likely to put the interviewee on the defensive in any other way. A common problem is a conspiracy by supplier and user to cover up problems. It may be in neither party's interest to reveal that things have not gone well. It is important to try and sense if this is the case.

9.7.2 Organizing the visit

It is neither sensible nor polite to send a large delegation on a site visit. The visiting team should be chosen with care. It should include representatives of IT management and key users. It should also include a technical member (if none of the other attendees fit this description). The team should have sufficient expertise to cover any questions that need to be asked.

Suppliers always want to be present on site visits. There are advantages to having them there. It helps if the discussion becomes technical and more of the questions that arise can be answered on the spot without having to go back to the supplier to check. Furthermore, the relationship between supplier and customer can be observed. For example, is the relationship comfortable, edgy/nervous, businesslike or a little too cosy? There are drawbacks as well. For a start, the customer may be inhibited from being totally candid and the supplier may try to divert the discussion away from awkward issues. The supplier may also start to answer the questions. On balance it is better if the supplier is not present. The customer is more likely to be open and frank in the absence of the supplier and the conversation will flow more freely.

During a site visit, various statements may be made on and off the record. For the former at least, it may be appropriate to check or confirm in writing. A simple, if somewhat devious, way of doing this is to write a thank you note with the key facts mentioned in the letter (see Example 9.5).

Example 9.5: Confirming the facts

Mr. J. Smith
Smith Industries
Highchester

Dear Mr. Smith,

On behalf of my colleagues and myself I would like to than you and Mr. Jones for taking the time to see us yesterday.

We found our visit most informative. In particular we were interested in the problems in installation of the package and the fact that the server had to be upgraded to obtain the level of performance required. We will take this into account when planning our own installation.

Yours sincerely

A. Woodely
IT Manager
Example Co. plc.

9.7.3 Company search

Many IT suppliers are not large public companies whose annual results are discussed at length in the *Financial Times*. When faced with a smaller supplier, it may be appropriate to undertake a company search, i.e. to look up the company results or to get a credit or other rating for them. This service is provided by a number of organizations.

9.8 Summary

Many buying decisions are made without clear criteria or evaluation procedures. Such decisions are more likely to be poor decisions and will be difficult to defend later if they turn out to be bad. It must be stressed that purchase decision making is a process. There should be a timescale and deadlines, otherwise decisions can be dragged out for months or even years. It is always possible to delay IT buying decisions on the (perfectly valid) grounds that the technology will be better next year. In the meantime, however, opportunities will be lost and time wasted. Good buying decisions are, in this sense, just another aspect of good management.

Risk and risk management

10.1 Introduction

Much IT expenditure involves risk. The level of risk can vary from low, for example that a non critical project will be late, to a 'bet the company' project that could have catastrophic consequences if it were to fail. Risks may be calculated or unconscious. Some IT dependent companies take enormous risks without even being aware of it by their failure to have an adequate disaster recovery plan. Good IT managers will be aware of all the risks inherent in IT including purchasing and acquisition risks.

IT risk comes in a variety of forms, not all of which are related to purchasing (for example, security risks). As elsewhere in life, IT risk generally has a cost trade-off and good decision making requires information about, and understanding of, both. This implies:

- understanding exactly what the risks in a given course of action are
- knowing the strategies available for managing these risks
- knowing the cost and effectiveness of each strategy.

With this information, management can decide on what level of risk it wants to accept and the implicit cost of that level of risk. Alternatively it can decide how much it wants to spend and determine the implied risk that will be taken on.

It is useful to consider risk under a number of headings, namely:

- suppliers
- hardware and IT architectures
- system software
- packaged software
- custom software
- consortia
- people
- major projects.

The risks arising in each of these areas and management strategies for handling them are described in the following paragraphs. Each risk is briefly described and a number of strategies for managing it are then suggested.

10.2 Supplier risks

10.2.1 Suppliers going out of business

The degree of exposure to the customer's business or operations from this risk will vary. If there is a replacement supplier or the product can be easily substituted there may be little or no risk. However, some suppliers, particularly suppliers of major application software packages or custom software, are not easily replaced. An organization may find itself dangerously exposed when the supplier of a key system ceases to trade (see Case history 10.1).

Strategies:

- Before entering in a business-critical relationship with any supplier, look at their financial statements. If they are a public company, these should be readily available from the supplier.
- If they are not a public company ask to see their financial statements. If they are unwilling to do this for reasons of commercial confidentiality, suggest that your auditors or an independent third party undertake the check. If they refuse it may be wiser not to do business with them.
- Check their financial status using publicly available credit worthiness services such as Dun and Bradstreet. Have they ever had any judgments registered against them? What is their credit rating?

303

> ## Case history 10.1: Checking things out
>
> A printing and publishing company was looking for a page make-up and typesetting system. They had been approached by a local distributor of a new state of the art system which looked good in a demonstration and which was already being used successfully by one of their competitors.
>
> As the manufacturer of the system was a small and newly formed organization about which the firm knew very little, the company asked its financial advisers to check them out. The advisers ran a check on the supplier through the *Financial Times* database and found several articles over the previous few months which mentioned the vendor concerned. This showed that the supplier was indeed recently formed as the result of the management buy-out of part of a larger organization that was in financial difficulties. While the bought-out company was solvent, it was not financially strong and would probably need considerable investment to stay competitive in its market. Furthermore, during the management buyout, a number of their key technical personnel, including the technical director, had left.
>
> On reviewing all the risks, the company decide not to purchase the system.

- Ensure that there is an escrow agreement in place. A properly drawn up agreement can guarantee access to software source code in the case of supplier failure. Escrow agreements must be carefully drawn up and must cover not only the purchaser's rights but also maintenance of the escrowed code (see Chapter 11)

10.2.2 Friendly takeover

In the wrong circumstance, this can have unfortunate consequences for customers of the supplier who is taken over – especially if the new owners decide to rationalize production by discontinuing a product on which the customer's current IT operations depend. Existing customers can find themselves under pressure to change to the new owner's products.

Strategies:

- Build legal protections into all contracts which will bind any predator company into protection of the customer's rights. In particular this should protect the right of the customer to terminate any contract without penalty in the event of a takeover.
- Ensure that any disclosure of information to third parties extends to prevention of disclosure of information to any new owners without the customer's permission.

10.2.3 Competitor takeover

This is rare, but not unknown. Where systems are sensitive or valuable, conflicts of interest can arise and there is a risk that commercially sensitive information could fall into the wrong hands.

Strategies:

- Where packaged software is involved, ensure that this possibility is covered by the escrow agreement, i.e. that, in the event of a takeover, the customer has a right to the source code of the package. Ensure that there is always an up-to-date copy of the source code of any critical software with the escrow agent.
- Have the supplier and/or its staff sign non disclosure agreements.
- Investigate fall-back suppliers. In extreme cases, it may be necessary to terminate all relationships with an IT supplier at short notice. In such cases, having an alternative supplier to whom one can immediately turn is essential.

10.2.4 Lack of supplier expertise

A supplier may lack the expertise necessary to support or implement the products it is selling. This is a common problem in the IT industry, particularly with smaller suppliers (and occasionally with large suppliers).

Strategies:

- Always vet the skills of supplier's support staff carefully before entering into any purchasing arrangement which will leave your organization dependent on their skills.

- Ensure that any contract gives you the right to seek support elsewhere in the event that the supplier cannot (or will not) provide adequate support. This requires a definition of 'adequate', but suitable wording can always be found.

10.2.5 Loss of key staff

This is another particular risk with small suppliers, but it can also apply to larger suppliers. The departure of a key expert can leave the customer exposed. Sometimes the customer may find that a trainee or inexperienced person is thrust into the gap, effectively learning at the customer's expense.

Strategies:

- Look at the length of service of supplier staff. Suppliers where many or most staff have many years service are likely to be less volatile.
- Look at the depth of support that the supplier has. How many technical staff does it have that can support its products and to what level?
- Ask what contingency plans the supplier has to cover customer needs if key staff leave. Insist that the supplier ensures that key staff always have an understudy.
- Establish good relations with key supplier staff where possible. Should they leave, it may be vital to have their goodwill during a transition period. Their new employer may be willing to tolerate an employee working for his or her former customers for a while.
- Use technology transfer. Designate suitable internal staff members to learn from supplier staff. Where and if possible, reduce supplier dependency.
- In certain circumstances, it may be desirable to ensure that the supplier cannot make key staff redundant without consulting its customers. This might be difficult to enforce legally, but it may be possible to put an effective 'agreement between gentlemen' in place.

10.2.6 Working for competitors

A common occurrence is where the supplier is also working for one or more of a customer's competitors. While all suppliers will claim to have 'Chinese walls' between staff working for competing customers, there is always the risk of leakage (see Case history 10.2).

Case history 10.2: Sleeping with the enemy

A leading supplier of enabling software (call it Company A) had a large number of system development houses among its customer base. These developers used the enabling software to deliver application solutions to their clients. The developers operated in a fiercely competitive market and were very protective of their client bases. Any new contract coming on the market would become the focus of aggressive and competitive bidding.

The supplier employed a liaison consultant whose job was to meet regularly with their software house customers, to keep them up-to-date with new product developments and generally assist them in marketing the product. Unfortunately, one day, she announced her engagement to the Managing Director of one of the largest of the software houses. The other developers immediately decided that, despite profuse promises of 'Chinese Walls', they could not be certain that matters raised in confidence with the liaison consultant would not be discussed over the cornflakes the following morning.

In this instance, a number of the developers approached Company A and quietly suggested some staff re-deployment. The consultant was moved to another part of the firm and the developers were happy.

Strategies:

- One way to manage this risk is to make it a contractual condition that the supplier does not work for any competing company (see Chapter 11). It may even be appropriate to have named companies for whom the supplier must not work, although this may not be a realistic option unless you are a major or dominant customer.
- Use non-disclosure agreements. Have these signed by all staff who work directly or indirectly on sensitive systems (see above).
- Where the risk is still unacceptable, change suppliers.

10.2.7 Failure to deliver on time/lack of reliability

Suppliers that consistently deliver late or deliver poor service or product quality should either be actively managed until the problem is resolved or should be replaced. Sometimes the former is not possible, at least in the short term. In the latter case it is necessary to take other precautions.

Strategies

- If the customer is in a position to do so, it should consider seconding a suitable member of its own IT management to the supplier on a part-time basis.
- Consider using a systems integrator and putting it between you and the supplier. It is usually easier for a systems integrator to be tougher with a supplier on the grounds that it has more relevant technical knowledge and is therefore less likely to be blinded by science.
- Work closely with the supplier. It may be that the customer's project management expertise can be transferred to the supplier.
- If possible, insist that the supplier have appropriate staff trained or that it put proper management procedures in place.

The best way of dealing with supplier problems is not to have them in the first place. The risks from supplier difficulties can be significantly reduced by only selecting good suppliers. How to do this and the qualities to look for in good suppliers are described in Chapter 2.

10.3 Hardware purchasing risks

Hardware risks tend to be low and are easy, if not always inexpensive, to fix. Hardware today is dependable, and with the growth of standards much hardware is interchangeable. However, the IT industry is still far from the position where hardware can be switched around at will and many problems remain. Similarly, while hardware reliability technologies such as fault tolerant processors, fault-tolerant operating systems and RAID/mirrored storage systems are improving rapidly, such security comes at a price.

10.3.1 Reliability

While modern IT hardware is extremely reliable, machines do occasionally break down. The cost of a machine failure at a critical point or time can be high. Components with moving parts such as printers, disk and tape drives are the most vulnerable.

Strategies:

- Consider fault-tolerant disk storage. Options here include mirroring, storage networks and redundant arrays of inexpensive disks (RAID).
- Consider fault-tolerant processors. Fault-tolerant machines come in a number of guises with various degrees of survival and recovery capabilities.
- Consider a fault-tolerant operating system. Some operating systems (including some variants of Unix) will provide fault tolerance on symmetric multiprocessing machines.
- Use fault-tolerant processors with switchover. This 'belt and braces' strategy effectively doubles up both disks and CPU. In the case of a failure of either CPU or either disk, the remaining disk and/or CPU will continue to operate normally.
- Use partial system duplication. This may provide limited operations for essential services while repairs are being carried out on the faulty system.
- Use full system duplication. There is a range of options here which are described in detail in chapter 8. There is a corresponding range of costs.

10.3.2 Performance

One of the commonest hardware risks is that a machine under-performs. This can happen because there are problems in the hardware design, the machine is under-specified or simply because the machine is not capable of handling the work mix.

Strategies:

- Specify performance requirements precisely. How to do this is described in Chapter 7.
- Build performance guarantees into the contract. This is a common sense safeguard which is overlooked in many hardware purchases. Much hardware purchasing is based on the standard contracts offered by suppliers which can limit the rights of the customer.
- Assess the machine using standard industry benchmarks (and ensure that the appropriate benchmarks are used). Benchmarks, especially the more refined benchmarks such as TPCs can be particularly useful. Benchmarks are described in more detail in Chapter 7.

- Look at similar sites. A good, if somewhat unscientific, test is to find a site as similar to the customer's as possible where the proposed configuration is running.
- Run a test of the workload on the machine. This is time consuming and can be expensive, but may be worth the investment where performance is critical.

10.3.3 Compatibility

As proprietary systems have declined and with the trend toward highly heterogeneous systems where many hardware, system software, application software and networking technologies are mixed and matched, compatibility problems inevitably arise. This problem is diminishing with time, but is still far from being a thing of the past.

Strategies:

- Before buying, ask suppliers for reference sites where this type of hardware (and operating software) combination is working in an operational environment.
- Never embark on a mission-critical or time-sensitive project which involves pioneering new technologies or architectures. If new technologies are to be employed, implement them in a small way in non-critical areas until expertise is built up and the problems and how to solve them are known and understood.
- Build a prototype system to check out key interfaces. This is an effective, if expensive tactic. It might not be economic in smaller organizations.
- Ensure that expertise is available to help should it be needed. This may be internal, from one of the suppliers, from a systems integrator or from a contractor.
- Employ a lead contractor, i.e. purchase only from one supplier and get it to purchase all other components. It then becomes the supplier's responsibility to make sure all the parts work together. It also avoids the situation where two suppliers blame each other for the problem and both use the other as an excuse for inaction.
- Ensure that there is a fall-back position, i.e. that there is another way of meeting the needs in the case of all else failing.

10.3.4 Running out of capacity

The demand for IT services continuously grows. As it does, the demands on the hardware increase and upgrades are required.

Where there is another larger machine in the range this process is normally straightforward. However, where it involves changing a machine range, it can be messy and expensive.

Strategies:

- Try to avoid buying any piece of hardware, but particularly a processor, that is near the top of the range.
- Where this is unavoidable, try to establish what new and larger machines are planned or are in the pipeline. Major suppliers are usually able to predict available dates for new models with reasonable accuracy.
- Have a fall-back plan. Ensure that, in the event of capacity on the existing configuration running out, further resources can be used albeit in a different way.
- If expansion means changing machine range (as opposed to moving to a larger machine in the same range), establish the feasibility of moving current systems to the new range.

10.3.5 Technology cul de sacs

A risk with some hardware is that insufficient development will be put into it or it will cease to be developed further and gradually fall into obsolescence. Many organizations today still rely on such 'legacy' systems.

Strategies:

- Think long and hard before buying non-mainstream products.
- Look at a product's market share. If this is shrinking and the product is non-standard, do not purchase it unless there are compelling reasons to do so.
- Look at the supplier's current expenditure on R&D and the trend in R&D expenditure. A decreasing spend on R&D is a sign that the product is mature and/or that there are no plans for its long-term future development.
- Establish with which standards (*de facto* or *de jure*) the proposed hardware complies.
- Establish to which standard-setting bodies or consortia the supplier belongs. If a supplier does not belong to any and neither complies with, nor has any plans to comply with, current and emerging standards, then there needs to be other compelling reasons to consider purchasing from that supplier.

10.4 System software risks

System software comprises:

- operating systems
- network management systems
- middleware
- communications software

plus miscellaneous utility and other software. Managing system software risks is not easy and the options for doing so can be limited. Risks in systems software tend to arise when new and innovative technologies are being used. The system software risk from, say, an IBM mainframe operating system is virtually non-existent because these (and other similar) systems are well-established and have been tested over many millions of machine hours of operation. However, the same cannot be said of all operating system software.

A draconian approach to this risk is to avoid it entirely by using a well-established minicomputer or mainframe technology and, if absolute reliability is paramount, this may be the best choice. However, most businesses today need to work with mixed and/or less mature technologies, so risk management strategies are needed.

10.4.1 Obsolescence

Over the past 15 years there has been a steady decline in the market presence of a wide range of proprietary operating and networking systems. In such circumstances, a supplier can go into a vicious circle where falling sales and a declining maintenance revenue base leads to a reduction in investment. As a result the product falls further and further behind its competitors and leaves its users/customers with ageing systems and limited options for their future development.

Strategies:

- Stick with mainstream suppliers. Avoid purchasing proprietary operating systems except where they have a substantial market presence (which in practice is limited to less than half-a-dozen such systems).
- Consider carefully before purchasing smaller niche market products. Be certain that the communications and compatibility problems are fully understood.

10.4.2 Immaturity

Like whiskey, operating systems tend to improve with age. A new operating system or network management system is generally (although not always) going to be less reliable than an older product – at least in the short term.

Strategies:

- Avoid buying new system software in the first year of release if possible. There is a number of reasons for this. First, new software is more likely to have bugs. Second, it pays to wait until a critical mass of support and experience with the product is available in the market. Last, and not least, it may be wise to see if the product succeeds in the marketplace before making a commitment to it.
- Defer upgrading to new releases for a couple of months unless there is a compelling reason for so doing (such as an important bug fix in the new release).

10.4.3 Compatibility problems

Distributed systems call for large numbers of components, more often than not from several suppliers, to work together. In such systems, numerous small compatibility and communications problems can occur at several levels.

Strategies:

- It is important to assess the risk that features may be lacking. For example, lack of memory protection may not be that important if it is planned to run a simple system using market-leading standard software. However, if use of complex or new software is being planned, it may be safer to stick with more proven or expensive products.
- Ensure that there is sufficient technical expertise to resolve the types of problem that might occur.
- As in other areas, the main risk reduction strategy is to stick to proven architectures.
- If there is a good business reason for innovation, pilot the system in a small area first. Establish basic skills in linking and getting components to work together before embarking on a large scale project. Case history 10.3 is a cautionary tale.

Case history 10.3: There is no substitute for reliability

Company X was a successful financial services company which operated in a global business where high technology was very much part of the industry. The IT department was given a large budget and a great deal of freedom to develop a state of the art information system.

For two years, the IT department invested heavily in leading edge equipment, software and architectures on a company-wide scale. The resulting company information system was pretty impressive – when it worked. Unfortunately this was not very often. System crashes several times a day were not unusual as the support team constantly struggled with immature applications, enabling and systems software and user demand. Eventually after a particularly bad run of problems, the users lost confidence. A new IT manager was brought in whose first action was to suspend all further development of the system, close down many of the 'star wars' projects and implement some bread-and-butter applications to give management useful information. By proper project management of the development team and steady building up of a core of reliable systems, the company was able to salvage many of the useful developments of the preceding years. Others were judged not to justify further investment because of the risk that they might never work.

Although systems development was now under control, the company still had to write off several million pounds worth of IT development expenditure. With proper risk management strategies, much of this write-off could have been avoided.

10.5 Packaged software risks

Packaged software varies from desktop systems costing under £100 to mainframe systems costing well over £1 000 000. Both types of software have associated risks. Unfortunately, quality control in the software industry is uneven and buggy products or new releases still find their way onto the market with depressing regularity. In this section, a distinction is made between risks which are specific to packaged software and general system or project implementation risks. The latter are covered later on in this chapter.

10.5.1 Failure to meet requirements

This is oldest risk of them all. The package may simply fail to meet the user needs.

Strategies:

There are four golden rules:

- Ensure that requirements are specified fully. Where requirements are volatile, the package will need to be flexible. Never, ever buy a package on features without a statement of requirements against which to compare it. This elementary rule is forever being broken by purchasers who, in many instances, should know better.
- Use thorough evaluation methods. Check that features that are stated to be present are present *and* that they work. Never take features for granted in an unfamiliar software package. Case history 10.4, which sounds unbelievable, is a true story.

Case history 10.4: Vapourware

A small but successful software house had grown and prospered on the back of an accounting system designed to run on IBM mid-range machines. This product was now beginning to show its age and the software house was faced with the prospect of an expensive redesign of their existing product or acquisition of a new offering to take advantages of advances in hardware and changes in customer expectations. While the management were considering this issue, they heard of a new US package which sounded as if it might meet their needs. The US developers were looking for a partner who could modify the package for the European market and sell and support it in that market.

Excited by the prospect, they contacted the Americans and, after a brief telephone discussion, a technical team was dispatched to Florida to meet the US company's management. At the meeting they were shown the user manuals

---

and documentation for the new product. It looked superb. It had all the features they were seeking and had a modern look and feel. They naturally asked if they could have a demonstration. To their astonishment, the Americans replied, with totally straight faces, that the product had not yet been built. Actually they had not yet started on the design. The 'manuals' were designed to test consumer reaction. If they received enough interest, they would then, and only then, develop the software. With luck, the product would be available in two years.

- Have the product test run on site with users. Users will often spot problems or issues that may escape IT management.
- Build an acceptance test into the contract. This will give you the right to ensure that the package meets requirements and that it will perform adequately (see Chapter 11).

10.5.2 Reliability

A package may be buggy. It may cause problems with other programs or, in extreme cases, even cause the system to crash or hang.

Strategies:

- Never buy new-to-the-market software where there will be a high commercial dependency on the system unless you are prepared to undertake exceptionally thorough acceptance testing.
- Where possible, wait at least 6 months before implementing new-to-the-market software. Never volunteer to be at the bleeding edge without sound commercial reasons.
- Talk to existing users of the software before purchasing. Find out if there is a local or national user group. It may be possible to attend one of their meetings and get a sense of how happy customers are with both product and supplier.
- If the investment is substantial, purchase a technical review. There are several companies that provide such information.
- Search the web for comments. It is surprising the type of (often quite uninhibited) information that can be found on the web. However this type of research needs to be done with care. There are many 'headbangers' on the web.

10.5.3 Performance

The software may perform too slowly for the user's need. This problem may be global, i.e. the whole package performs poorly, or it may be localized, i.e. certain functions perform poorly.

Strategies:

- Look for similar environments where the package is running and talk to users there. This is often the best and is certainly the least expensive way of assessing performance.
- Ensure that the hardware is adequate and that there are options to upgrade the hardware if needed. It is nearly always possible to buy one's way out of a performance problem with additional hardware. This may not be an attractive idea financially, but it may be better than losing customers or going out of business.
- Build performance guarantees into the contract.

10.5.4 Lack of support

There may be a shortage or absence of support for the package. This may be at the level of implementation support, training, post implementation user support or bug fixing.

Strategies:

- When purchasing, check out how many support staff the supplier employs and how many other customers they are supporting.
- Check out rights of access to deeper support levels. It can often be much more efficient to cut out the middle-man, especially when the customer has reasonable technical expertise.
- Consider developing an in-house support capability.

10.5.5 Inflexibility

The package may be unable to adapt to changes in the user organization's operations. Poor design and documentation may hamper modifications.

Strategies:

- Think outside the square when specifying. Many purchasers buy to meet today's needs rather than tomorrow's.
- Look at the development environment. Ensure that the package itself is built using tools that will make it easy to

maintain. Avoid packages which are built in old or specialized languages and use outdated file management systems. Products written in COBOL or C/C++ are preferable to relatively specialized languages such as FORTRAN or languages designed for other purposes, such as BASIC.

- Ask about the modification procedures. Suppliers may have a number of possible modification levels including modifications that the users can make themselves, changes which can be made by the local support person, and changes which must be made at the supplier's development centre.
- If you are really suspicious, ask to see the systems documentation. The state of the systems documentation is sometimes a good indicator of how well a system is written and how easy it will be to modify.

10.5.6 Hardware/operating software compatibility problems

This has become an increasing risk with the growth of distributed systems and the regular launch of new operating systems and operating system versions (e.g. Windows 3, NT, 95, 98, ME, 2000, XP to name but a few). Suppliers trying to maintain many versions of a product can find themselves unable to keep all products at the same level of development and often have insufficient resources to give the necessary attention to minority versions of the software.

Strategies:

- Where possible, avoid being a minority player. Think carefully before purchasing an unusual or small user-base version of any software, even popular products. Suppliers sometimes have version levels of their software. These are usually classified in various ways, such as:
  - Strategic, primary or lead platforms. These are the hardware platforms on which new versions are first released and which tend to have the best and least troublesome versions.
  - Secondary platforms. Versions for these machines come out only when the strategic versions have been completed and released. This can mean a delay of a year to eighteen months or more between the first new version release and a secondary version.
  - Tertiary platforms. These may be a number of years behind the primary version. Such versions should always be avoided.

- Check the number of versions of the product available. The more there are, the larger the supplier should be. Small suppliers supporting multiple versions of software can become overstretched.
- When a supplier offers to port its product to a new platform specially for the user, the long term implications should be thought out including maintenance, documentation, support and running costs.

10.5.7 Errors

It is useful to make a distinction between errors and bugs. Any problem with the software is a bug. An error is a particularly dangerous type of bug that could actively cause damage or loss to the organization, for example by calculating incorrect overtime pay or tax liabilities.

Strategies:

- Some packages are formally certified as complying with required regulations. Where this is applicable, ask to see the certification. Case history 10.5 is a strange, but true, example.
- Consider a full acceptance test. Acceptance testing is essential with custom software (see below) though something of a luxury for a package, but it may be well worth it.

Case history 10.5: Approved programs

The pharmaceutical industry is subject to extremely strict controls on its products and this control extends to some software systems used in the drug manufacturing and process control.

Because there is no other formal procedure for approving the quality of such software, the Federal Drugs Authority in the USA approves the software using the same system as it does for drugs. In effect the FDA deems the software to be an approved drug. The testing process is so rigorous that pharmaceutical companies have some of the oldest and most reliable software around. The cost of having a new system tested is so large that many are reluctant to incur the expense.

- Where a package is replacing an older system and has been heavily modified or tailored to the customer needs, parallel running can be used to check the software.

10.5.8 Usability

If users are unwilling to use the package or dislike it, the organization will either have to write it off or incur a potential ongoing morale problem (or worse).

Strategies:

- Invite users to try out the software. If this can be done on the user's own site so much the better. Try to avoid relying on supplier demonstrations where possible.
- Bring users on board. Users should be involved in the specification of the requirements, evaluation and testing. Users' expectations need to be managed. If expectations are built up to an unrealistic level, users will sometimes reject a perfectly good solution for poor business reasons.

10.6 Custom software risks

Custom software is the highest risk area of IT and there is plenty of research which suggests that as complexity increases, risk rises exponentially. There have been many examples of large-scale disasters where custom software projects have not delivered.

10.6.1 Time overruns

Only a tiny minority of IT custom software development projects of any size are completed on time. Even many of the most skilled and reputable professional IT firms have problems from time to time on major projects.

Strategies:

- Set realistic targets. Always allow for the natural optimism of software developers. It is sometimes useful for the customer to have a hidden (and less demanding) timetable behind the scenes.
- Freeze the core specification of requirements once design commences. Once the project starts, only absolutely essential changes in requirements should be allowed to interfere with the development.

- Put in place a clear change/enhancement request procedure. See Chapter 3 for more on this.
- Review progress regularly. Set up a steering group to monitor progress. Ensure that the supplier provides regular reports on progress and exception reports showing all delays as soon as they start to materialize.

10.6.2 Cost overruns

When a project overruns on time it may or may not overrun on budget. Likewise, a project may finish on time, but still run over budget.

Strategies:

- The key to risk management of costs is a solid contract. Contracts are discussed in Chapter 11.
- Freeze the core specification. It is common for suppliers, especially when they have won a contract after a competitive bid, to try to recoup some profit by charging over the odds for deviations from or additions to the specification.
- Put in place a clear change/enhancement request procedure for any changes that are going to cost money.
- Do not, under any circumstances, allow users to request chargeable extras or changes from the suppliers. Many suppliers are flexible enough to tolerate minor alterations and changes without reaching for the contract and asking for extra payment. However, even easy going suppliers will eventually get to a point where they will start charging for extras, even small ones.
- Make it absolutely clear in writing to the supplier that no extras will be paid for unless approved in advance by the internal project manager or the project owner. Consider use of formal purchase orders, but use them sensibly (see also next point).
- Use the organization's accounting system for management and tracking. Obtain written quotations for all changes or modifications to the original specification. Request itemized billing and reconcile all additional charges back to quotation. If the supplier cannot produce proof of a written quote and approval or purchase order, refuse to pay. After this happens a few time most suppliers will take the hint and comply with procedures.
- Review all additional costs regularly. Keep a clear running total and reconcile all work in progress invoices against agreed additional spending.

10.6.3 Failure to meet specification

There is always a risk in that a system will not match the specifications, i.e. that it will not provide the functions and features set down in the specification or the design.

Strategies:

- Ensure that the specification is clear and complete. How to do this is described in Chapter 7.
- Use standard specification techniques. There is a number of widely accepted industry standards for specification (such as structured system design and analysis method, SSADM, or dynamic systems development methodology, DSDM) which should be used where possible. See Chapter 7.
- Specify requirements in business as well as functional terms. Try to ensure that the development team understand the business need and are not just coding blindly.
- Ask the supplier to provide regular presentations on the design and development as they progress. Make sure that key users attend these sessions.
- Consider the use of prototyping. Prototyping is expensive, but can be cheap at the price if it highlights deficiencies in the written specification or helps to bring users aboard.
- Ensure that the supplier uses a modular development technique. Do not wait until the whole system is complete before looking at it for the first time. Regular demonstrations of work to date should be given by the supplier to users and to management.

10.6.4 Failure to meet user needs

This is not the same thing as failure to meet the specification. A system may perform fully to specification, but if the specification itself is incorrect, then the system will not meet the users' actual needs. One classic reason for this is where users do not know or fully understand their own needs (see Case history 10.6).

10.6.5 Total system failure

This occurs where a system has to be totally abandoned. This may happen at any stage of a custom development project, but in the nature of things it tends to happen later rather than sooner. A related risk here is the inability of those involved to bring themselves to abandon an obviously doomed project.

Case history 10.6: Blaming the messenger

A leading bank employed a specialist software firm to develop distributing trading profits amongst its client base. The latter was not a simple task as the organization managed funds for private clients, corporate entities and unitized funds.

The software house specialized in a particularly sophisticated system development language, but knew little about banking. There was no formal specification for the system as it was to be prototyped. The software house undertook the contract on the (verbal) understanding that its expertise was in the software only and that it had no part in specifying the system functionality.

Soon after the project started, the executive who had initiated the project left on promotion to another part of the organization. The prototype was developed and put into operation with seeming success.

Unfortunately there was a flaw in the way the users had specified the profit distribution method that tended to disadvantage certain client groups. This was only discovered after a couple of months when one of the senior managers noticed the rather unusual pattern in the distributions. Immediately the computer was blamed and several frantic late-night sessions with piles of print-out were spent trying to find out what was happening. Eventually it was discovered that the original specification was the problem. However, the users, in an attempt to exculpate themselves, blamed the software house for not pointing out the flaw, even though the software supplier never claimed to understand the intricacies of the allocation methods involved.

It took the management of the software house several months to prove to the bank's senior management that they were not at fault. However, by that time so much credibility had been lost on both sides that despite the fact that (ironically), once spotted, the problem had not been difficult to fix, the software house was eased out and it took them several years to obtain further work with the bank.

Strategies:

- Avoid very large projects where possible. Try to keep projects short. Long projects in dynamic or unstable environments are not sensible.
- Ensure that suppliers use a modular approach to development. This type of approach is made much easier by object and distributed system technology.
- Ensure that suppliers use suitable development tools and that development is in an easy to modify development language. In general, fourth generation languages are easier to modify quickly than third generation languages such as COBOL or C. CASE tools using code generation tools may also be too cumbersome for a highly dynamic environment. Fourth generation languages (4GLs) are easy to code, but 4GLs lack standardization and can cause performance problems. These drawbacks may outweigh their flexibility.
- Consider an object orientated approach. This is still a bit state of the art for many non-IT commercial organisations, but is becoming less risky as time progresses.
- If all else fails, request a competent outsider to review the system. This may be an internal staff member or an external consultant. Ideally this person should have had no prior involvement with the project. He or she should be of sufficient stature to kill the project or recommend to management that the project be killed should that prove necessary.

10.6.6 Insufficiently reliable/poor quality software

Even if none of the above arise, custom software can exhibit a variety of problems. It may simply be buggy, i.e. give errors or stop working if certain options are chosen. Bad software can also cause problems with other supposedly unrelated software.

Strategies:

- Assess the supplier's development standards. Does it have ISO 9000 or equivalent certification? However, it should be noted that although ISO 9000 and similar certification is a good sign, it is not a guarantee of good software.
- Review modules as they are developed. Break the project into stages with approval for later parts of the system being contingent on satisfactory performance in the earlier stages.

- Where new technology is being used, build a small part of the system or a pilot or prototype first. As noted elsewhere, this is expensive, but can be invaluable if developers learn useful lessons from a small-scale system first.
- Ensure that acceptance testing is thorough.

10.6.7 Difficult to maintain

Problems with maintenance can arise for several reasons including poor design, poor construction, the fact that the application is written in an obscure or difficult language or data management system, and/or poor documentation.

Strategies:

- Build ease of maintenance requirements into the specification of requirements and the contract.
- Insist on documentation being written as the system is built. Try to prevent suppliers leaving all documentation to the last minute (when it may never be written or where it may be skimped because the project is over budget).
- Review maintainability regularly. Potential sources of further trouble to watch out for in the design and development are:
  - absence of good development standards
  - hard coding of data
  - too much denormalization of the database
  - monolithic programs
  - lack of comments in the programs
  - poorly structured code
  - programming that is 'too clever', i.e. hard for others to understand
  - absence of clear and simple naming conventions
  - lack of proper version control
  - inadequate testing.

10.6.8 Performance problems

Even if the system works to specification and is reliable, it may be unusable if performance is not adequate.

Strategies:

- Ensure that suitably specified performance requirements are built into the contract (see Chapter 11).
- Where a hardware and software supplier are bidding as a consortium, ensure that there is one lead contractor.

- Avoid depending on top of the range hardware for the required performance. This will leave nowhere to go if the system does not perform adequately. Although software tuning may solve the problem, it can often take several months to complete. It is comforting to know that in a real emergency one can buy one's way out of the problem by upgrading the hardware.
- Test the performance of individual modules as the development proceeds. Be aware, however, that this may yield limited information. If the tests go poorly, it is informative. If the tests go well, they may not be indicative of how fast the live system will be.

10.6.9 User rejection

There is always a risk that users will not use the system once it is ready. This may be despite the fact that the system works to specification, is reliable and performs well. The root cause of this may, in fact, have little to do with the system per se, but rather be a reflection of broader organizational problems within the purchaser's organization.

Strategies:

- Involve users at all stages of the development. Consult with users and ensure that their views are taken into account.
- Have good user representation on any steering group.
- Insist on users signing off on all deliverables.
- Make users take ownership of the system. Ensure that users are aware that it is *their* system and that it will reflect on them, not IT management, if they reject it.

10.7 Consortium risks

As IT has become more complex, it has become common for major IT projects to be undertaken by consortia. A typical consortium may comprise:

- a main hardware supplier
- a supplier of peripheral or specialist hardware
- a package software supplier
- a systems integrator or project manager
- an enabling software (such as an RDBMS) supplier
- an integration (middleware) software supplier
- a communications technology supplier
- etc.

A large number of combinations and permutations of supplier types are possible. The specific risks when dealing with a consortium are discussed below.

10.7.1 Mutual blame

When there are problems with a consortium project, suppliers may blame each other rather than focusing on sorting the problems out. This has been described neatly (after an old television advertisement) as the 'It's a biscuit. It's a bar.' problem where suppliers argue over the cause of the problem rather than its solution. Common difficulties which give rise to consortium arguments include performance problems, budget overruns, compatibility problems and delivery delays.

Strategies:

- Only sign one contract with the lead supplier. Make that supplier subcontract all the other members of the consortium. Make it clear in the contract that the lead supplier is solely and totally responsible for the delivery of the required system.
- If adopting the above strategy, ensure that the lead supplier is sufficiently strong in both financial and size terms to meet its obligations. There is no point in making a small software house the lead supplier in a contract where, because they lack 'clout', they will be unable to force a large hardware supplier to contribute to the solution of a problem.
- Ensure that the contract stipulates that the solution of the problem and the delivery of the product is the lead supplier's main focus. Much of the benefit of having a lead supplier will be lost if the supplier takes an inordinate amount of time to resolve its own internal problems. Case history 10.7 illustrates the above points.
- Employ an experienced and reputable systems integrator. This can be an alternative or a supplement to the above strategies. A good systems integrator may be seen by all parties as an impartial arbitrator and may be able to resolve difficulties faster than might otherwise happen.

10.7.2 Poor project management structure

If the consortium is not well put together and thought out, their project management can be poor. Consortia are often put

Case history 10.7: High-risk management

A public sector body put out a tender for a series of systems including a financial system to manage its highly specialized accounting requirements. As it happened, there was only one software supplier in the market which had a suitable package and even this required considerable modification. Unsurprisingly, all four consortia shortlisted for the contract had included this supplier on their team.

The problem was that the software house was small and known to be in a tight financial position. The buyer was concerned about the risk of the software house going out of business and leaving no support for the modified package.

The organization therefore decided on a two pronged risk management strategy. Firstly, it offered only a lead contract to the hardware suppliers. This contract bound the suppliers into resolving the problems should the software house fail. As the contract was a large one with huge potential sell-on, the suppliers were happy to accept this as part of the deal.

Secondly, it insisted on an up-to-date escrow copy of the source code and up-to-date systems documentation being maintained at all times by an agreed third party (an independent law firm). The escrow agreement gave the organization rights to the source code for internal use only in the event of the software house going into receivership or failing to supply adequate support.

This strategy turned out to have been a wise manoeuvre. About nine months after the project started, the software house went into receivership and shortly afterwards into liquidation. The support team lost their jobs and were scattered. Under the contract, the hardware supplier had no choice but to sort out the mess. It did this by finding another specialist software house to come in, obtaining the source code from the escrow agent and thus enabling the new software house to learn how the package worked.

Although this was financially painful for the hardware supplier, it stuck by its agreement and the new software house eventually acquired sufficient expertise to first maintain and then modify the accounting system.

together as a one-off arrangement to undertake a particular project or to bid for a given contract. It may be that some or all of the members of the consortium have never worked together before.

Strategies:

- Install a proper management structure. A good structure (certainly for major projects) is described in Section 10.9.
- As implied in the structure, ensure that there is one project manager in overall charge of the project. This person should either be provided by the lead supplier or the systems integrator.
- Avoid taking on responsibility for sorting out consortium problems. For this reason, it is usually better if the project manager is not a user or a member of the customer's team. If an internal project manager is preferred, then the lines of communication must be clear. There is no point in having a lead supplier if the customer project manager can bypass that supplier to deal directly with subcontractors, thus undermining the whole structure.

10.7.3 Culture clash

Where consortium members have not worked together before there can be clashes between different corporate cultures, styles and standards. On occasions this can be aggravated by personality clashes. This can lead to poor internal relations within the consortium.

Strategies:

- Ensure that all members of the consortium are present at the sales presentation and try to assess the chemistry between them. This is not always easy to do, but certain signs can flag potential dangers. For example, where one supplier dominates the meeting or there is no obvious synergy between the members of the consortium there may be cause for concern.
- Try to avoid employing consortia where there are grounds to believe that they may not work well together. All other things being equal, it is better to have a well-motivated and well-integrated (but competent) team than one which, while it may be better technically, is likely to be fractious or difficult to work with.
- All other things being equal, try to use consortia that have a good track record of working together successfully.

10.7.4 Lack of communication

Poor lines of communication to the customer can also be a problem with consortia. This will happen when there is a lack of proper management structure and procedures.

Strategies:

- Establish clear reporting lines and procedures from day one.
- Try to avoid short-circuiting proper channels. This does not mean being inflexible or refusing to listen to people, but proper management can be undermined when informal back channels become the dominant form of communication.

10.8 People risks

Temporarily engaging people, be they contractors, consultants, systems integrators, etc. is normally a relatively low risk in that they can be disposed of fairly quickly if necessary. Nevertheless, there are some risks involved which need to be managed.

10.8.1 Security

If contractors are working on sensitive systems or with sensitive data, they may not have the same sense of company or organization loyalty as permanent staff. In addition, contractors may go on to work for competitors. Security risks may never be an issue for some organizations; others will have sensitive data and need to keep it under control.

Strategies:

- Where they are likely to be working with sensitive information, make all temporary staff sign non-disclosure agreements. This should cover not just while they are working for the customer, but afterwards.
- Where possible, avoid using temporary staff in sensitive areas. If this is unavoidable, consider the option of using them for development and test-pack testing only and having all testing with live data done by permanent staff.
- Make it a rule that temporary (or indeed all) staff are not allowed to take work out of the building.

10.8.2 Unexpected departure

At the wrong moment, this can be inconvenient and cause major problems. People who work on contract are always on the look-out for the next assignment as they do not want to find themselves out of job for a long period when their current contract ends. There is no way one can stop someone walking out the door. However, the probability of this happening can be reduced.

Strategies:

- Build a termination bonus into the contract. This guarantees the contractor a substantial sum of money on completion of the contract. This may have conditions attached (good work, proper attendance, etc.).
- An alternative (stick rather than carrot) is to build a penalty into the contract whereby the contractor has to reimburse the customer if he or she does not complete the contract. Apart from the negative attitude this implies, such a clause may be difficult to enforce. Often such people operate on a global basis and it may be difficult to get money out of someone who, for example, has gone to the Middle East or the west coast of the United States.
- Develop their loyalty to the organization. Contractors, even though temporary, should be made to feel part of the team. Always invite them to office social events. With long-term contractors, it may be cost effective and appropriate to include them on company training courses. A contractor who feels good about the organization is less likely to let it down.

10.8.3 Difficulty in getting rid of them

The converse problem is getting rid of temporary staff or consultants who are not satisfactory or who are no longer needed. With consultants, this is often not a problem. Many are on daily rates and it is unusual for there to be a formal contract which guarantees that the customer will pay even if the assignment is terminated early. With contractors, however, there can be a problem.

Strategies:

- The only effective risk management policy here is a watertight contract. Organizations which hire contract staff should be familiar with the law in this area and should ensure that the contract, while within the law, gives the buyer the right to terminate the contract without prejudice or excessive costs.
- Hiring staff from major suppliers (such as consultants) can work in that it is easy to get rid of them – if the supplier

values the relationship it is unlikely to argue about such a request. However, this only works if they can supply such staff in the first place and it does not cause other conflicts of interest.

10.9 Major project risks

In a sense, the risks in a major IT project are a composite of all the other risks listed above. The risk management strategies described above can be applied where appropriate. The two dominant risks in major projects are time and cost overruns. Handling major project risks is a matter of good project management, which can be broken down into:

- proper planning
- clear lines of responsibility
- clear decision-making procedures
- clear lines of communication
- proper controls
- proper procedures.

A detailed description of IT project management is way beyond the scope of this chapter, but the following are some basic do's and don'ts.

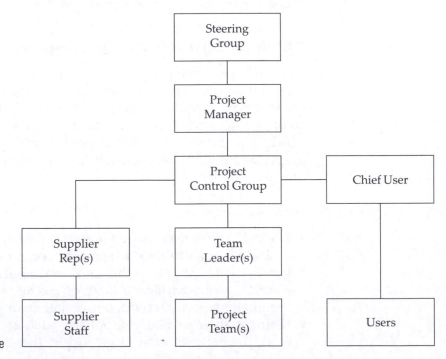

Figure 10.1
Example project management structure

- Implement a proper project management structure. Figure 10.1 gives an overall structure suitable for large IT projects. It can be simplified for smaller projects.

The roles of the various bodies are as follows.

The Steering Group meets periodically. Its role is:

- to review progress
- to make policy decisions where and when necessary
- where necessary, sanction major changes to the project plan
- to approve additional expenditure
- to sign off or accept deliverables at various stages in the project.

The personnel in this group should include:

- the project owner
- the Chief User (or a user representative)
- a representative of financial management
- key user representatives
- other management representative as appropriate
- independent advisers.

The Project Manager attends and reports to the Steering Group. Representatives of suppliers may also be invited to attend when necessary.

The User Group meets as is necessary and is chaired by the Chief User. Its function is to provide:

- input into the project development process
- a focus for user discussion of user issues
- a review group where necessary
- the core group for the acceptance test process.

The Project Control Group meets at least once a fortnight and preferably once a week. It is chaired by the Project Manager. It is made up of:

- the Project Manager
- the Chief User (or a user representative)
- Team Leaders for each sub-component of the project
- suppliers' internal project managers (if the Team Leaders do not fill this role). Typically the account executive or supplier internal project manager attends.

The purpose of the Project Control Group is to manage the project on a day-to-day basis. It sets tasks for the coming week/period and reviews progress at the following meeting.

The Project Control Group, in the person of the Project Manager, can take decisions with regard to short-term timing and resource deployment, but cannot incur significant additional expenditure or approve major changes from the project plan. These must be approved by the Steering Group.

- Use formal checkpoints. These should be at regular intervals. There should be clear deliverables at each point and progress beyond each checkpoint should be dependent on approval and sign-off of the preceding phase.

- Institute a formal reporting mechanism. This should include regular and exception reports. Exception conditions need to be set (for example, one might request an exception report in the event of a delay of over 5 days or a cost overrun of more than £1000).

- Delineate responsibilities clearly. Each member of the project team should be clear on their responsibilities and the limits of their authority.

- For large projects, use a good project management methodology. Examples of such methods are PRINCE 2 and PROMPT. Examples of such methods include the type of project structuring and reporting methods described above, as well as:

  - regular project reporting
  - exception reporting
  - formal project checkpoints
  - formal approval
  - proper project management procedures.

The latter include standard forms and documents which are completed at various points in the project.

The structure and approach outlined above give a powerful control mechanism which helps to keep projects on time and anticipate problems. It will not prevent all project problems. Delays, technical difficulties, etc. will still occur, but such matters will be detected early, giving time to take remedial action before the situation gets out of control.

10.10 Quantifying risk

Risk is measured and expressed using the techniques and terminology of probability. Probabilities and probability distributions can be used to:

- quantify risk
- assess risk
- evaluate the cost of management strategies
- decide on the most cost-effective strategy.

While people routinely use such terms as 'high' or 'low' risk, good decision making demands more precise methods of quantification than this. It is not necessary to be an expert in statistics to use probability-based concepts and techniques. However, familiarity with certain basic ideas is important. The following is a summary of the key concepts with which it is important to be comfortable.

The probability or chance of something happening (called an event) can be like getting a head when tossing a coin, an objective fact. The probability that event A happens is written as:

Probability of A occurring = P(A)

For example:

P(system failure), or

P(delivery will be late)

Probabilities can then be expressed as follows

P(heads) = 1/2 (or 0.5, or 50%)

Although strictly speaking probabilities must lie between zero and one, percentage equivalents are easier to understand and will be used from here on. Probabilities such as the odds of getting a head when tossing a coin are called objective. Objective probabilities are important in many things, not least in games such as bridge, roulette and poker, but objective probabilities are not of much direct relevance in IT risk measurement or management.

Subjective probability on the other hand is based on judgment, opinion, experience or hunch. For example, it might be said that in April:

P(it will rain this day next week) = 25%

This judgment may be based on the gut feel and experience of the person making the statement. It is not a scientific judgment. Subjective judgment is crucial in IT management. Assessment of people in particular is often based largely on subjective impressions. Psychology has established that many non-rational factors can affect all purchasing decisions. How this affects risk in IT purchasing is illustrated in Example 10.1.

Example 10.1: Subjective probability in estimating

All day every day, IT managers must take probability into account, if only subconsciously.

For example, suppose a supplier project manager is asked to give an estimated completion date on the current phase of a complex IT development project. Consciously or unconsciously she will make a judgment on the likelihood of completing the project according to the schedule in front of her and the information on progress to date. This may include assessing the reliability of the programmers' estimates or the subcontractors delivery timetable. On the one hand, she will want to give her client the most accurate answer she can. On the other, she may be reluctant to acknowledge that there may be a delay and may thus tend to be more optimistic than circumstances justify. Equally she does not want to give a date and then miss it if she can at all avoid it. These conflicting motivations will all affect her final answer.

In answering the question, therefore, if she is conservative, she will probably state a date where she thinks that there is less than, say, a 10% chance that the project will be later than that date. If she is more adventurous, she may state a date with a higher risk, say a 30 or 40% chance that it will be later.

In all of the above, unless she is a rare individual, she will not explicitly compute the risk, but that is the process that her mind will be going through.

It may be that our view of the probability of rain in April may be based on something more scientific. It may be based on observation of April days over many years. This type of probability is sometimes called 'statistical'. This type of probability can be important in IT. For example a manufacturer might, after many years of making disk drives, assert that:

P(one of our disk drives will fail in its first 5 years of life) = 0.1%

i.e. there is a one-in-a-thousand chance that, if you buy one of these disks today, it will fail in the first 5 years of operation.

10.10.1 Risk profiles

The above ideas can be developed further. Risk can be expressed as a single probability, for example:

P(the project will be completed on time) = 50%

with the implication that there is a 50% chance it will be later. It can also be expressed as a more informative series of probabilities, for example:

P(project is on time) = 50%

P(project is up to 3 months late) = 25%

P(project is more than 3 months late) = 25%

The latter is often (loosely) called a probability distribution. For it to be a proper distribution, the sum of all the probabilities must (as in the above example) add up to 100%. There are many standard probability distributions. Familiar probability distributions include the Normal and Exponential distributions. These follow a mathematical formula and can be useful in risk management. Subjective probabilities, on the other hand, frequently do not follow a standard distribution.

10.10.2 Interpreting risk

Translating risk into terms that are meaningful to management is not always simple. Consider the example of the disk drive manufacturer used earlier. This was stated as:

P(one of our disk drives will fail in its first 5 years of life) = 0.1%.

This statement is somewhere between a fact and an opinion. As noted, it is based on observation of many disk drives over a long period of time. But while it says something to a potential purchaser about the reliability of the drive, it conveys limited information. For example:

- It could be that these disk drives have a 50% chance of failure in their sixth year of operation.
- The term 'failure' is undefined. It could mean anything from a bad sector, to a total failure where all data would be lost, or a failure in the motor drive where no data would be lost but

the disk would have to go off-line pending repair. If, as is likely, the manufacturer means *any* type of failure, it may be of interest to know what types of failure occur and the likelihood of each type of failure.

It would be convenient if all suppliers would provide such information. Unfortunately, in practice, the standard industry methods of expressing reliability in IT components is to talk about mean time between failures (MTBF). This is the arithmetical average time between device failures (or if you are buying a new machine, the average or expected time until there is a failure or fault).

This terminology is difficult enough to interpret and, because it is a single number, it can also be misleading. All it tells the purchaser is the average time to failure, which implies that some machines will fail earlier and some later. To get a full picture, the user needs to know the distribution of the probability of failure, for example:

Probability it will fail in year 1

Probability it will fail in year 2

.

.

.

Probability it will fail in year 5

and so on.

When considering the risks of machinery failure, the question of time cannot be ignored. The chance of a server failing in an given second is virtually zero. The chance of it failing in a given month is tiny. The chance of a major problem over a five-year period may be appreciable.

10.10.3 The cost of risk

Expressing risks in terms of probabilities can be a bit difficult for managers to interpret or understand, especially when there are many risk factors involved. Probabilities in themselves do not provide a complete metric. Managers need something to which they can relate. The two commonest metrics are, as elsewhere, time and money. As time is nearly always convertible into money, it is therefore useful to express the risk being taken in financial terms.

Risk can be converted to cost by using the concept of expected cost. This is defined as:

Expected cost of the risk = P(problem occurs)

× Cost of that problem.

For example, suppose the probability that a disk drive will fail in a year is 0.02% but that the cost in lost business of such a failure is estimated as £50 000, then the 'cost' or expected value of the risk is:

Expected cost = £50 000 × 0.02% = £10.

If the cost of mirroring the disk was £4500, then clearly the cost of this is not justified by the level of risk exposure. If, on the other hand, the probability of a disk failure in a year was 2.5% and the cost of a failure £100 000 then the position would be:

Expected cost = £100 000 × 2.5% = £2500.

Writing the cost of mirroring the disk off over 3 years, the cost of the mirroring is now justified by the reduction in the expected risk cost. (Strictly speaking, even the mirrored disk will have a chance of failing, however it is likely to be negligible.) Risk management is exactly analogous to insurance: we take a certain loss now rather than risk a much bigger loss in the future.

10.10.4 Risk evaluation

As noted in Example 10.1, subjective risk is rarely stated explicitly. In purchasing decisions, however, it is desirable to quantify risk which, in practice, means putting a cost on it. To do this we need a method of putting a cost on risk management strategies and a way of evaluating those risks. The following is a simple risk management methodology for IT:

1 Identify all potential risks. This will include all of the risks itemized above from whatever source. The scale and scope of risks will vary with the nature of the purchase.
2 Assess each risk for its potential impact on the business or organization. This should include both the operational and financial impact of the failure or problem. These may need to be thought through. Fall-back positions and knock-on effects should be taken into account.

3 Where a risk is trivial or has minimal potential impact, it should be ignored. The approach should be practical. Time should not be wasted on highly unlikely problems that would have minimal practical impact on the organization or its customers.

4 Cost the remaining risks. Each remaining business impact is then costed. This is normally done in financial terms but it can be expressed in other ways (such as time lost or inconvenience to members of the public). This may need the involvement of a number of people including users, management and the Finance Department (to provide the necessary costing expertise).

5 Identify all possible management strategies for each risk. Possible actions are given above in sections 10.3 to 10.9. Not all of these will be appropriate or feasible in any given situation, but many will be.

6 Assess the likely effectiveness of each strategy. Management has to assess how effective a given strategy or action will be. This will normally be expressed as a reduction in the level of risk (or in some cases the elimination of risk completely). Strategies which are likely to be ineffective are removed from further consideration.

7 Cost each strategy. The cost of each remaining strategy is then calculated. Again, this will normally be in financial terms, but may be in other terms such as time.

8 Determine an acceptable level of risk. Management has to decide what level of risk it is willing to accept. To repeat the statement at the outset of this chapter, all IT purchasing beyond the trivial involves some element of risk. Management is about judging the acceptable risk that the business, organization (or it personally) can take.

9 Carry out a cost–benefit analysis. Finally, a cost–benefit analysis should be undertaken to determine whether the overall risk is acceptable and which, if any, risk management strategies should be adopted.

Example 10.2 illustrates this approach.

Example 10.2: A risk evaluation

Company A is about to embark on a major conversion of its systems from a host-based proprietary minicomputer to a distributed system. The budget for the project is £1 500 000 including hardware, re-compilation and testing of software and data conversion. The company has no experience of this type of project. If the project is significantly delayed they will be forced to upgrade their old machine to cope with rapidly growing demand. This is likely to complicate the conversion further and the expenditure will have to be totally written off when the new system is installed.

The risk of the project being late might be reduced by employing a consultancy firm with experience of this type of conversion. This will cost £25 000 a month over the projected twelve-month duration of the project – a total of £300 000.

The risks are then assessed as follows:

Without external help

Risk	Probability	Cost
Project is 1–3 months late	40%	£300 000
Project is 4–6 month late	15%	£1 000 000

Giving:

Expected cost = (40% of £300 000) + (15% of £1 000 000) = £370 000

With external help

Risk	Probability	Cost
Project is 1–3 months late	15%	£300 000
Project is 4–6 month late	0%	£1 000 000

Expected cost = 15% of £300 000 + 0% of £1 000 000 + £300 000*

= £345 000

On this basis, the company should employ the consultants.

*Cost of the consultants.

Actually, the case for employing the consultants in the above example is stronger than the simple numbers suggest. It is probable that the consultants can enhance the project in a number of ways that are not readily quantifiable. Such intangible benefits can be included in a close decision.

10.11 Conclusion: risk and rationality

Humans are not always good judges of risk and, even when the risks are understood, most people (professional gamblers excepted) do not always play the odds logically. Case history 10.8 (also a true story) illustrates this point.

Case history 10.8: Better safe than sorry?

A project manager in a service organization was in charge of developing an executive information system for senior management. This system would gather information from various sources and summarize on screen. Some of this information would come from internal systems, some from outside and some, such as press reports, would be typed in by a number of clerical staff employed for this specific purpose.

The high-powered application server planned was going to cost £30 000. However, the hardware supplier had offered a much more sophisticated machine with mirrored disks and heartbeat-monitored processors at a cost of £65 000. Wondering if this was worth it, she asked a consultant friend of hers over a drink in a bar one evening for his view. Drawing an envelope from his pocket and turning it over he reasoned as follows:

Firstly, the system was not mission-critical. If it failed, there would be some moans from senior managers, but business would continue as it always had before the system was installed.

Secondly, the basic server was quite reliable. The probability of its failing anytime in its first 5 years of operation was estimated to be less than 2%. The consultant assumed that the probability of failure of the more expensive machine was zero.

Thirdly, the total cost of a failure was mostly the overtime that the clerical staff would have to put in catching up. This was estimated at about £20 000 at absolute worst case (a week off the air).

On this basis, the expected cost over 5 years was at most £400.

Despite this, the project manager still spent the extra £35 000 reasoning that the organizational damage and embarrassment to the IT department of such a high profile failure was more important than mere cost!

IT purchasing presents many risks. All can be managed. Some can even be eliminated. Management of most risks is common sense, but it is surprising how often basic errors are made in everything from weak change control to signing contracts with suppliers who shortly afterwards go into liquidation. One key component of risk control in any significant purchase is the contract and this is covered in the next chapter.

Legal aspects of purchasing

11.1 Introduction

It is important for anybody involved in purchasing to understand their basic legal rights and duties. The purpose of this chapter is to give an overview of key issues in this area. That said, in IT, when it comes to legal matters, the first rule is that if a purchase is of significant value and even moderate complexity, get professional legal advice.

The law is a strange animal. At one level there is statute law, that which is written down and decreed by parliament. Then there is case law, natural justice and a host of other concepts sometimes seemingly designed to confuse the layman. On top of all this, if and when a case gets into court, the outcome may come down to the persuasiveness of Counsel on the day or the ability of a judge or jury to grasp the issues involved. In the case of information technology this is a particular problem. The issues involved can be technically complex and as arcane to the judge or jury as the law sometimes seems to computer specialists. The best solution to this problem is, of course, never to end up in a court in the first place, but if you do, while the law provides purchasers with a number of implicit protections (see below), it is never any harm to have a watertight contract on which to base your case.

11.2 Contracts: basic principles

In UK and Irish law, a contract is an agreement between two parties. A contract is normally in writing, but it can be verbal and implicit. By and large the law allows a remarkable degree of freedom to parties drawing up a contract, but there are some rules laid down by the law (national and EU) which place restrictions on what a contract can contain. These boil down to two key points.

1 A contract cannot contain clauses which entitle either party to dodge its obligations if it fails to comply.
2 A contract must be clear and certain.

It is for the latter reason that the English of contracts is often quite different from what a business manager would write. Occasionally, purchasers are quite taken aback when their home-grown draft agreement comes back from their corporate lawyers totally rewritten and with a seemingly scant regard for punctuation.

Whether the parties fully appreciate it or not, all contracts have certain *implicit terms*. These are items which, if not expressly forbidden by a contract, are regarded as being part of the contract, even if they are not spelled out. One example of this is the right of the purchaser to take a copy of software for back-up purposes. Another implied term is that the supplier has the right to sell the product (e.g. it is either the owner or a licenced re-seller of the product). The goods and services sold should comply with their description and should be fit for the purpose for which they are proposed. For services, it is implicit that the supplier has the skills it purports to have and that it will carry out its work properly and carefully. Some of these implied terms can be overruled by inserting specific clauses into a contract, but while the law cannot prevent either party inserting unreasonable and unfair clauses, it can make such clauses unenforceable later on.

11.3 Standard contracts

For most IT purchases, the main exceptions being consultancy, software development and outsourcing (the latter is considered separately below), suppliers will have standard contracts. These are often surprisingly short and cover a number of basics, including:

● terms of payment
● responsibilities of both parties
● liability of the supplier for problems with its product.

As one might expect, such contracts tend to be lopsided. The risks are firmly parked on the purchaser's side. There are often clauses that require the buyer to test the package and having accepted it, the liability of the supplier is limited thereafter. Topics that may be of considerable importance from the purchaser's perspective, such as the system performance, delivery dates and warranties, may be inadequately covered or left open with 'get-out' wording that protects the supplier. Warranties (discussed in more detail below) are often short, sometimes as little as 90 days. Liabilities may be limited in a number of ways including by limiting the obligations of the supplier, by limiting the actions that the supplier is required to take to remedy problems, and by excluding any consequential loss liability.

There are circumstances in which a standard contract is perfectly adequate. Most small hardware and software purchases fall into this category and few people are going to read through the detailed licensing terms on a £200 piece of software. Even for larger hardware purchases and well-established packaged software where there will be no modification, the standard contract is often satisfactory. Lawyers are expensive and should be reserved for those occasions when they are really needed. Unfortunately in IT purchasing, there are many such occasions.

11.4 Negotiated contracts

11.4.1 Pre-contract negotiations

It goes without saying that the purchaser has maximum leverage while the contract is still unsigned. Usually, by the time the contract negotiations start, the purchase decision has been made, at least psychologically. In certain circumstances, there can be a temptation to play hardball (although some suppliers will do this even before they have a contract, see Case history 11.1). Bearing in mind that a contract can be verbal or implied, it does not technically require a signature for a contract to be considered to be in force. For example, a contract might be deemed to come into force when something changes hands (e.g. money or product). For this reason, it is important to be clear when the line between discussion and agreement is crossed. A good way to do this is to ensure that, prior to contract, documents are marked 'draft', 'subject to contract' or 'subject to agreement'.

For major projects, where the investment is likely to be substantial, a pre-contract agreement can be helpful. There are several reasons for this. During negotiations on projects of any size, it is quite common for one or both parties to impart confidential information to the other. The purchaser may give the vendor access to confidential data or business plans. The vendor may make confidential internal information about new products or market strategies available to the purchaser. In such cases a non-disclosure agreement is appropriate.

Another useful document is a statement of intention or letter of intent to proceed, subject to certain conditions. This can be useful to a supplier as it enables it to plan ahead and commit future resources even though it does not yet have a contract (although some suppliers will not commit any resources until a contract is signed). Amongst the reasons for such a statement might be that:

- funding for the project is yet to be put in place
- approval is necessary from some higher authority (such as head office or the finance department)
- the purchaser wants to verify the supplier's financial stability
- a commitment is subject to successful completion of a test run or benchmark.

Another commonly used approach is a 'heads of agreement'. This document sets out in outline form the shape of the eventual contract.

Case history 11.1: Pay first, ask questions afterwards

More from the strange, but true, department.

A university was seeking to buy a library system. It approached a number of suppliers including a vendor widely regarded as one of the market leaders in this area. They invited this company in for a preliminary discussion.

At the meeting the university was impressed with the product and with the reliability and support proposed. They asked for an indicative price, only to be told that the supplier would discuss price only after the contract was signed. The university representatives, thinking they had misheard, asked if the supplier really meant this. Apparently it did.

The university did not buy the package.

11.4.2 Contract content

IT contracts vary with the nature of what is being purchased. Buying a modem card is akin to buying a washing machine: clearly there will be terms of business and the warranty is important, but one is not going to send the paperwork to the corporate lawyers for review. The purchases that matter are those where major systems, usually including hardware, software, custom-building, implementation and support are being acquired. There is a long-term trend in the market for such integrated services to be provided by companies that were formerly hardware suppliers, consultancies and software or services suppliers. Some organizations, particularly those using a best of breed approach, prefer to buy the individual system components and either manage the project themselves or employ a systems integrator to manage it on their behalf.

Major systems projects should always have formal contracts. Ideally there should be one contract with a lead supplier. Other approaches can lead to a legal quagmire if anything material goes wrong. If something does go wrong, suppliers can quickly get into the blame game, leaving the customer floundering.

A contract should contain and/or cover the following.

- Deliverables. The most important part of any contract is a clear and unambiguous statement of what is to be delivered. How to do this is covered in Chapters 6–10. Deliverables are usually attached as a schedule to the contract (see below).
- Deadlines/timetable. A good contract will contain a reasonably detailed timetable setting out what is to be delivered/done at various stages. It is a good idea to avoid having lots of exact 'this must be done by' dates in the contract. There should be a degree of flexibility on both sides. There should also be regular review points with measurable deliverables (design documents, quality plans, test plans, etc.) at each point.
- Duration. A problem with many IT contracts is that there is no clear termination point. This is not just because some IT projects never seem to end, it can simply be that implementation rolls over into support and into another and separate phase (see Case history 11.2). Nonetheless, it is a good idea to have some date when the contract is deemed to be concluded. There should also be a right by both sides to terminate the contract under specified circumstances (see below).
- Purchaser obligations. A contract should state clearly what the purchaser has to provide and/or do. This may include making resources (people, machines, office space) available,

providing test data, giving reasonable access to key managers and so on. One of the greatest sources of problems in projects is supplier complaints about problems with user failure to do their part. The contract should also make explicit the limits on purchaser commitments. As part of this, the purchaser should ensure that its own staff know what they are letting themselves in for and that it puts the resources in place to deliver its part of the deal. Suppliers are not the only parties that over-promise and under-deliver.

- Financial details. This should include all prices, payment terms, payment schedules, details of any discounts and so on. If discounts are being offered, they should be set out in detail, including any trigger points or cut-off levels. Often discounts are offered for bulk buying, being willing to act as a flagship site, and for certain sectors (public, education, charity, etc.). Equally, any penalties or payments for late delivery should be specified. The latter is discussed below under liabilities.

- Escalation procedures. Murphy's Law being what it is, all contracts need procedures to handle problems if and when they arise. Particularly important here is the point at which a problem is escalated to the next level of supplier management attention and effort (see Chapter 2 for more on this subject).

- Arbitration. The contract should specify a procedure for arbitration in the case of a dispute. This is a much better and cheaper option than going to court. Arbitration might be provided by a suitably qualified law firm, a rights commissioner, a professional arbiter or other trusted third party.

- Intellectual property rights. Both sides in an IT contract may have intellectual property rights interests. From the purchaser's perspective, this is most likely to occur in the case of custom software where business processes, algorithms and other forms of knowledge may be incorporated into the software. It is imperative that rights of ownership of such material is clearly stated in the contract. Such knowledge may be part of a purchaser's business competitiveness and the last thing a company wants is the supplier selling the software it has paid to develop to one of its competitors (this has been known to happen). However, there may be circumstances where software developed as part of such a project may be saleable to others, and it makes commercial sense for supplier and purchaser to market it. In this case, the royalties due to the company from such sales can either be spelled out in the contract, or better, be the subject of a separate contract. For any custom software, the paying customer should retain all copyright unless otherwise agreed.

- Confidentiality. Many IT projects involve information which is confidential on one or both sides. The purchaser may have to sign non-disclosure agreements and may wish suppliers to do so as well, including pre-contract (see above).
- Warranties. The term 'warranty' has two meanings, which sometimes causes confusion to the lay reader. The popular meaning of the word warranty is a 'guarantee' period during which a product will be fixed or replaced free of charge should it develop a fault. In a legal sense, a warrant is a statement of fact in a contract (as in 'X warrants that it has the right to sell this software') and if either party breaks such a warrant, then they are in breach of contract and may be liable for damages. It can also be grounds for termination of the contract by the other party. A contract will contain many warranties of this second type. Suppliers will warrant that their hardware and/or software will perform in certain ways. Users will warrant that facilities will be made available to suppliers.
- Indemnities. These allow parties to seek or recover damages without necessarily having to go to court. Typically these will specify recompense in the case of specific failures to perform, usually by the vendor, but sometimes by the purchaser as well. The latter can happen if, for example, a supplier commits resources and then the purchaser cancels or significantly delays the start of a project.
- Limitation of liability. This is one of the most tricky and contentious aspects of contracts. It should be noted up front that the law provides for certain automatic liabilities if the supplier is in breach of contract. This typically covers losses which the purchaser has incurred or which will occur and which were known about at the time the contract was signed. These may be direct (we have paid for this and it doesn't work) or indirect (we have suffered a lot of disruption to the business). The latter in particular is somewhat open-ended. If faced with the question, a court will try to determine what costs might reasonably have been foreseen by the supplier and award damages accordingly. As one lawyer put it, this can result in something of a lottery, depending on how well the judge understands the issues on the day.

For this reason, suppliers will usually insist that there is some upper bound on their liability. In particular they will not cover what is often called consequential loss, i.e. losses which are a direct or indirect (although real) consequence of failure on their part. Some suppliers try to include a clause which limits their liability to returning only what they have been paid to date. When considering supplier liability in a contract, purchasers should consider a number of potential costs:

- The cost of sorting out the problem. If the supplier cannot or will not sort out the problem, it may be necessary to bring somebody else in to do so. This is likely to be expensive and, in the wrong circumstances, extremely so. Fixing the problem could range from a minor debugging exercise to wholesale replacement of hardware, software and personnel.
- Disruption. Rarely is the impact of a major IT project failure confined to those immediately involved. Others are dragged in, senior managers may have to divert their attention to deal with knock-on impacts and so on. This cost may be difficult to quantify, but it is real.
- Loss of opportunity. Failure of a software project may well lead to various other costs such as loss of revenue from sales, cost of savings foregone, loss of a customer, fines for non-compliance with regulations and so on. In severe cases, major business opportunities may be lost. This type of 'consequential loss' is difficult to define (see above) and most suppliers will not open themselves up to such an unquantifiable risk. In some cases, it may be possible for one or both parties to take out insurance. Some firms carry professional indemnity insurance, but this is costly and is passed on to their customers in higher fees and charges.
- Cost of time wasted. Finally, the purchaser may have invested considerable time and effort in the project. If the project fails due to the supplier's incompetence, this expenditure is wasted.

One way of handling this is to use the concept of liquidated damages. This specifies in advance how much the supplier is liable for in the case of things going wrong. As with other clauses, a court can later assess the fairness of this, in particular how foreseeable such costs were at the time the contract was signed.

Two other points are worth bearing in mind. Firstly, the continuing goodwill of suppliers may be important. A confrontational attitude can backfire. It is one thing to intimidate suppliers, but if the worm turns, even if the customer does win in the end, the victory may be a Phyrric one.

Secondly, never forget that purchasers also have liabilities in contracts. If the contract is terminated because of breach by the purchaser, or the purchaser simply terminates it for reasons other than supplier breach, the purchaser may itself be liable for damages. This is usually only for payment for what has been delivered to date, but, as noted above, the supplier too may claim consequential costs.

● Non solicitation. One problem having contractor and/or supplier staff on site is that they are in a good position to lure away the purchaser's staff (and, of course, vice versa, although that is of less concern here). Poaching good people is a common problem. A non-solicitation clause will not prevent somebody defecting to a supplier, but at least it can deter or prevent a supplier actively seeking to recruit a customer's staff.

These are the principal areas that should be covered by a contract. Specific circumstances may necessitate other types of clauses. If the proposed deal is particularly large and complex, it is advisable not just to seek legal advice, but to go to a law firm that specializes in technology contracts.

Case history 11.2: Painting the Forth bridge

The expression 'painting the Forth bridge' is often used to describe IT projects that never seem to end. This is particularly true of protracted custom development projects. Three phenomena occur. Firstly, new requirements emerge as the business develops. Secondly, as users gain an understanding of the technology, they see new possibilities and look for extras. Thirdly, the changes induced by the system lead to new business processes which, in turn, provoke a need for further changes. The following is a typical story.

This was the experience of one moderately sized not-for-profit organization. After many years of running a proprietary minicomputer, it decide to upgrade its systems to a state of the art system. This would be done by a local supplier with which it had a long-term relationship. It did the project by the book, preparing a formal specification and detailed design before committing to the full development. Its preparation paid off. Over an eighteen month period, the system delivered was what was requested, on time and more-or-less on budget.

Unfortunately by this stage, as the Project Manager put it, it had become a case of 'How you gonna keep 'em down on the farm, after they've seen Paree'. Users, heretofore used to a very limited system, suddenly woke up to all sorts of features and the list of requested changes grew and grew. As the organization had stipulated that the contract was fixed price and no changes would be paid for, all but the most urgent of these were simply documented and filed. As a result, when the final product was delivered, the Project Manager had accumulated 159 change and additional feature requests, approximately a full year's additional work by his estimate.

Finally, there may also be general clauses in a contract, for example forbidding either party binding the other as an agent and covering the governing law of the contract, which by default will probably be the country in which the purchaser resides. The latter can, however, be a difficult issue where multiple locations in different countries are involved. If you get into this type of contract, you need professional advice.

11.5 Escrow and related matters

One of the risks when buying software, particularly from smaller suppliers, is that they will go out of business and leave the customer without any immediate means of maintaining the software code. This is clearly the case with customized software, but problems can arise with packaged software too. An escrow agreement is one way of avoiding this problem. Such an agreement works as follows.

- The supplier deposits a copy of the source code and all documentation necessary to support, modify and maintain that code with a trusted third party (usually a solicitor, but there are professional escrow agents).
- The purchaser pays a reasonable fee to cover the cost of this.
- The agreement defines a number of circumstances under which the customer has a right to access or even acquire ownership of the source code. Typical examples of events which can trigger this are:
  - if the supplier goes into receivership
  - if the supplier is taken over – particularly by a competitor of the customer

- if the supplier is in sustained material breach of its liability to support the software
- if the supplier formally discontinues support for the product.

● The customer signs a non-disclosure agreement which in effect says that if the escrow agreement is triggered, the customer may take the software for its use only. It may not sell or disclose details of the software except in as much as it is necessary to have the system supported.

● An arbitration procedure, to be used in the event of a dispute about the terms of the agreement, is defined.

As a general rule, if a purchaser pays for development of custom software, the contract should state that, on payment, the purchaser acquires all rights to the developed code. Suppliers will normally have no continuing ownership rights in such code. However, a number of factors can muddy the waters. Two common problems are embedded code and joint development projects.

● Embedded code is where, in developing a custom solution, the supplier uses some pre-packaged components of its own (these may even be licensed from a third party). This is a particular problem with object-orientated development, the basic premise of which is to avoid re-inventing the wheel. The delivered solution is therefore a mixture of code specially written for the customer and for which the customer has paid, and code owned by the supplier. If a development is going to use such off-the-shelf supplier components, it is imperative to clarify ownership issues up-front. Purchasers should ensure that any licensing issues in relation to such embedded software is covered in the contract. This can be tricky. For example, if the supplier and customer have a disagreement and the customer goes to another supplier for help, the old supplier may withhold source code from the new supplier, making it difficult for the new supplier to provide adequate support. Further complications can arise if the customer decides to re-use some of the software for another application or decides it has a marketable product that it would like to sell to a third party. For all of these reasons, all rights of ownership, access, modification and re-sale should be clearly spelled out and agreed in the contract.

● Joint development. A different set of issues arises where the supplier and the developer agree to share the development cost in some way on the understanding that the resulting

354

product may or can be sold or marketed to third parties later on. There are several variants on this. For example, in building a system, a developer may come up with re-usable modules or objects that it can re-sell elsewhere. Many a software house started life in this way – building a system for a paying customer and later converting that system into a package for sale on the market. In such cases it is again important for both parties to brainstorm their way through the issues and ensure that the contract covers, if not every scenario, then at least the most likely scenarios. This can sometimes be a time-consuming and exasperating process, but it has to be done if later problems are to be avoided.

Some suppliers are not altogether happy about escrow agreements, fearing that they may be triggered too easily and that valuable commercial information may fall into the wrong hands. Purchasers need to be hard-headed about this. If your business depends on a piece of software, the risk of being left without support may simply be too high. A purchaser should always seek an escrow agreement for business-critical software applications, and most particularly when dealing with smaller suppliers. See Case history 11.3.

Case history 11.3: Bailing out

A research institute used a specialized form of financial reporting. For many years they had used a standard financial management package mixed with a lot of adjustments to prepare their accounts and management reports. An external review of this system had recommended that it be replaced with a fully automated system.

This proved to be easier to recommend than to implement. After preparing a statement of requirements and inviting tenders, they only received one realistic tender from a small software company which had a new accounting package designed rather like a Lego kit. It comprised a number of components that could be assembled in different ways. Using this it would (or at least seemed as if it would) be possible to build a system which would exactly meet the organization's needs.

The problem was that the software company was known to be in a weak financial condition and there was a risk that it might go bust. As the organization would be dependent on

---

its programmers and skills, the consultant advising them was understandably concerned about relying on this system. Following the consultant's advice, therefore, the organization requested an escrow agreement. The supplier was initially reluctant to enter into this because it was concerned about its code falling into the hands of a competitor. However, when it became a question of escrow agreement or no deal, they signed up.

Which was just as well because 4 months later the software house did go bust. The escrow clause now gave the Institute the rights to the code (which was held in a solicitor's safe), but still left them with the problem of supporting it. However, they were able to go to another long-established software company who agreed, at a price, to complete the project. It was expensive, but it worked and the Institute is still happily using the software many years later.

11.6 Licences

Software licence agreements come in various forms. A licence may be usable:

- on only one machine at a time
- by only one person at a time
- by a named user or users only
- by a limited number of people at a time
- on specific machines
- by current company employees
- only in certain countries or regions.

It is important to be aware of what licences the company holds and any restrictions in the use of these licences. Many software licences, particularly those for PCs and shrink-wrapped software generally come with a long licence agreement. When the software is loaded for the first time, a pop-up panel asks the user does she accept the licence terms and clicking on the 'Yes' button is deemed to be acceptance of these terms. It is probable that in excess of 99% of users never read these terms before clicking yes, but the IT department needs to be familiar with their more important aspects.

The greatest commercial risk with licences is illegal copying by staff (see Case history 11.4). This may be done in the full knowledge that the law is being broken, but it is often innocent in that the person doing it does not realize that they are breaking the licence agreement.

A lesser risk, for most companies, is that technical users may try to pirate the software. This might be done by recompilation and modification of the software for resale. This is an improbable scenario in most organizations.

A grey area in licensing is shareware. This is software provided over the Internet (or sometimes on other media) where there is no licence, but the author seeks a fee (usually a pretty modest one) for use of the software. There is a temptation not to pay such fees as the author has no way of enforcing payment other than withholding an activation keyword. If the company is using such software (and some of these products are quite useful and respectable), it should be paid for. Many shareware suppliers are one-man bands and will happily do a deal on site licences for what, by the standards of commercial software, is a very low cost.

Case history 11.4: Copy that

A consultant was once asked by a leading household-name multinational firm to advise it on its budgeting process which was 'a bit unwieldy', as the firm's request put it.

On arriving in the company, he found that it was indeed unwieldy, being prepared on 27 separate spreadsheets scattered around the plant, the only communication between which was by innumerable floppy disks. He also discovered that of the 27 spreadsheets, one was legal and the other 26 were illegal copies. His first recommendation was that this situation be 'regularized' as he rather euphemistically put it.

This is by no means an uncommon phenomena.

11.7 Other contract issues

11.7.1 Consultancy

Consultancy projects vary from a couple of days of expert advice on a technical issue up to large IT projects involving hundreds of man-years. In practice, many smaller consultancy assignments are done without drawing up formal contracts and sometimes on just a verbal agreement. Most consultants have terms of business and some will ask potential clients to sign these, but a great deal of consultancy work is based on a proposal (which may be just a letter) by the consultant and its acceptance, sometimes even just verbally, by the client. Trust is placed in the reputation of the supplier. A further problem with consultancy is that the work and terms of reference are flexible. Sometimes the nature of the problem is not clear at the outset, on other occasions a consultancy project can veer off in an unexpected direction. In the latter cases, a written contract can actually be a hindrance.

It should be borne in mind that, as noted at the outset of this chapter, even where there isn't a written contract, once services and money change hands there is an implicit contract which is subject to the general laws of the land. In cases which do end up in court in these circumstances, it can become a case of who said what to whom and, to use an expression quoted above, something of a lottery.

As a point of principle, if there is an established relationship, a good reputation and trust between consultancy supplier and customer, then a written contract may not be necessary. A contract is, of course, always safer, but it comes at a price. The purchaser has to assess this risk.

11.7.2 Termination

An important issue in contracts can be termination of the contract. There may be various circumstances under which one or both parties wish to have the right to terminate. Typically termination occurs because one of the parties is in 'material breach' of its obligations. However, in a similar manner to escrow, there can be other circumstances in which the purchaser might wish to give itself the right to terminate a contract. These could include the supplier running into financial difficulties, the supplier being taken over by another company, particularly a competing company, or the supplier failing to provide adequate support for its products.

11.7.3 Acceptance testing

Where custom software is involved, the contract will contain an acceptance procedure. This is where the buyer formally accepts the delivered product. It normally triggers final payment or a stage payment, and transition from the implementation to the support phase. There are several trade-offs here which a purchaser must consider. In general, the more thorough the acceptance test the better, but acceptance testing is time-consuming and expensive. For its part, the supplier will want to put some time limit on the period allowed for acceptance testing and may wish to have some constraints on what constitutes a sufficiently serious defect to warrant holding up further payment. It is sometimes possible to specify exactly the nature of the tests to be performed, but more often than not this is too tedious or rigid an approach and the purchaser is simply given a period in which to test the system. In the latter case, there should be a provision that if serious problems are encountered, there is automatic extension of the test period – especially if the supplier is slow in fixing the bugs which have been found. Finally, there should be a definition of materiality, i.e. problems which are sufficiently serious to warrant deferral of payment and minor matters which are not.

11.7.4 Outsourcing contracts

Outsourcing is one of the most complicated areas of information technology law. For total outsourcing, i.e. where the entire IT function is handed over to a supplier, the contract can encompass transfer of physical assets, transfer of software and transfer of personnel. Each of these can give rise to separate issues.

- Hardware transfer is the least complicated. If the hardware is owned outright and not subject to any lease or hire purchase agreements, it can be transferred without much problem.
- Software is more complicated. Most software is licensed and the transferability of licences is not something to be taken for granted. It is essential, therefore, that before any software is transferred the licensing arrangements are fully understood and any transfer issues and payments resolved. This can apply to everything from the enterprise resource planning system down to the spreadsheets.
- Staff transfers are the most complex aspect of all. Staff are protected under a number of headings which are designed to prevent workers being exploited or losing out in such a move. The most important regulation here is the Transfer of Undertakings (Protection of Employment) regulations commonly referred to as TUPE. Any purchaser contemplating such a transfer needs good legal (and industrial relations) advice.

11.7.5 Service level agreements

The service level agreement (SLA) is an integral part of any outsourcing contract. A poor SLA can cause all sorts of problems, not least of which is ending up in court. A service level agreement should state both the purchaser's and the supplier's obligations, although the former are normally straightforward (such as permitting access to buildings). In some cases, for example where there may be royalty sharing on jointly developed products, things can get more complicated, but this is beyond the scope of this book. On the other hand, a service level agreement should set out the supplier's obligations in detail and should cover:

- The services to be provided. These may be in the contract, but will be fleshed out here. The degree of detail will vary with the nature and scale of the business.
- The performance requirements. These need to be specified, not just in operational terms (see Chapter 7), but in terms of response time and escalation procedures. Specifying performance requirements is not always easy. It is straightforward enough for hardware, system availability or wide area networks transfer rates, but more difficult for bug-fixing or changes as, by definition, the issues here are much less predictable. As a result, this section of a service level agreement can be quite complex and sophisticated.
- Penalties/reimbursement. The SLA should set out how the customer will be reimbursed for failure of the supplier to meet SLA targets. This may be in the form of rebates on the outsourcing payments. It should also include the right of the purchaser to terminate the agreement if performance is not satisfactory and this problem cannot be rectified within a reasonable time. Remedies, like performance requirements, should be as specific as possible.
- How changes to the SLA will be made. Outsourcing contracts last many years and it is unlikely that the SLA will not need to be changed several times during this period. There should be agreed mechanisms for doing this, including such basics as the agreed pricing structures for changes in volumes or performance level requirements.
- Price control mechanisms. There must be a procedure for approving additional payment beyond those covered by the SLA. If price indexation is not covered in the contract proper, it should be covered in the SLA.

11.8 Conclusion

A great deal of the day-to-day IT purchasing of most organizations does not need explicit attention to the law. The trend towards smaller, less expensive components has eliminated much of the need for elaborate hardware contracts, and the increasing use of packaged software makes the need for negotiated software contracts less frequent than it used to be. However, the large to mega-IT project is going to be a feature of the landscape for the foreseeable future so it pays to know the basics.

In the early years of IT, and even until well into the 1990s, there were relatively few legal firms that knew much about, never mind specialized in, information technology contracts. This has now changed and it is not difficult to find good legal advice in this area. Nonetheless, for getting the contract right on a multi-million pound deal, and in particularly for outsourcing, choosing the right firm is important. Never forget that purchasing IT legal advice is like any other form of IT purchasing. Make sure your supplier has the experience and track record in IT law and contracts that you would expect of your software house in system implementation. As elsewhere in this book, the oldest purchasing advice of all still holds – *caveat emptor*.

Index